Praise for *Sams Teach Yourself Google TV™ App Development in 24 Hours*

"Although the TV has been a networked device for many years only modern platforms, like Google TV, offer developers the ability to create powerful apps. This book is a great practical guide on how to develop your connected TV app."

—Alberto Escarlate, co-founder, Sojo Studios

"Mr. Delessio may have written this book for developers, but it's got great value for interaction designers and product managers needing to understand product creation for interactive TV and multi-screen platforms. If you're responsible for strategizing, requirements or building Google TV, second screen, or device-adaptive applications, you need this knowledge. Though the many code examples are clearly for developers, technical product managers and designers with basic HTML/CSS/Java knowledge can follow along. Interactive television has been a dream for decades. It's actually here now. And this is how to get on board."

—Scott Germaise, Internet entrepreneur and co-founder, About.com, KeepHoldings.com

"Up until this point, I only tested apps for the Google TV; after reading this book, I now have the tools and confidence to start developing my own application."

—Chris Hollis, Google TV Friends

"This book gently steps an Android developer back from the intimate smartphone experience to the big-screen view from the living room couch, and packs plenty of solid, useful information into 24 hours."

—Jonathan Taylor, VP, Mobile Technology, priceline.com

Carmen Delessio

Sams **Teach Yourself**

Google TV™ App
Development

in **24**
Hours

800 East 96th Street, Indianapolis, Indiana, 46240 USA

Sams Teach Yourself Google TV™ App Development in 24 Hours

Copyright © 2013 by Pearson Education

ISBN-13: 978-0-672-33603-4

ISBN-10: 0-672-33603-0

Library of Congress Cataloging-in-Publication data is on file.

First Printing January 2013

Trademarks

Warning and Disclaimer

Bulk Sales

Pearson offers excellent discounts on this book when ordered in quantity for bulk purchases or special sales. For more information, please contact

U.S. Corporate and Government Sales

1-800-382-3419

corpsales@pearsontechgroup.com

For sales outside of the U.S., please contact

International Sales

international@pearsoned.com

Acquisitions Editor
Laura Lewin

Development Editor
Michael Thurston

Managing Editor
Sandra Schroeder

Project Editor
Seth Kerney

Copy Editor
Barbara Hacha

Indexer
Brad Herriman

Proofreader
Jess DeGabriele

Technical Editors
Romin Irani
Ronan Schwarz
Max Tomlinson

Publishing Coordinator
Olivia Basegio

Book Designer
Gary Adair

Composition
Bronkella Publishing

Contents at a Glance

Table of Contents

Preface

A book about Google TV—really?

Yes, really. It seems like we've been waiting for Smart TVs or Interactive TVs for quite a long time. Streaming video and movies on demand has been a concept for many years that has now become reality. Smart TVs with web browsing and apps is the next step and Google TV is there.

With the release of the Android HoneyComb version for Google TV and, more importantly, the creation of an app market in late 2011, Google has created a great ecosystem for television development. The earliest version of Google TV did not provide a way for developers to create and publish apps. That changed with the addition of the Google Play market.

New devices such as the Vizio CoStar and TVs from Sony and Samsung are rolling out with Google TV onboard. Rather than develop their own proprietary systems, TV manufacturers can rely on Google and the Android operating system to provide smart TVs to consumers.

Why Google TV Is Important

Google has used the Android operating system as a common platform across phone manufacturers. Google TV plays the same role for TV manufacturers. There is no common cross-manufacturer platform for TV development. Google TV fills that void.

Google TV provides a new app market.

The iPhone showed that an app marketplace was a key success factor for a new device. The iPad showed that a new form factor with a different size and shape makes a difference for both development of apps and how consumers use them.

Google TV includes both a new market for apps and a new experience for enjoying apps. This is a new opportunity for developers. It is a great time to jump into smart TV development on a Google TV.

Additionally, there really is something new with Google TV: Second-screen apps, in which a phone or a tablet interacts with a TV, providing exciting new opportunities for developers and app designers. Second-screen apps are covered in detail in this book from a conceptual and development perspective. This book also covers the Anymote Library and how to use it with second-screen apps. Your phone and tablet apps will discover, connect to, and control Google TVs.

Who This Book Is For

If you are a web developer who knows HTML, CSS, and JavaScript, this book can help you learn how to optimize your websites and apps for Google TV. There is a jQuery Google TV Library and a Closure JavaScript-based library that can be used with Google TV; both are covered in this book.

If you are a Java programmer with an interest in TV development, this book will cover the basics of Android development so that you can create sophisticated TV apps on Android.

If you are an Android developer and want to learn the fine points of TV development, this book will take you through the details. If you want to take advantage of your Android skills to create second-screen apps, you will be able to rely on this book for both the concepts and implementation details you need.

How This Book Is Organized

This book covers developing web apps, Android apps, and second-screen apps for Google TV.

Hour 1 introduces basic concepts of designing apps for what has come to be called the 10-foot user experience. When building a Google TV app, developers must understand the idea that the user sits 10 feet away from a TV screen.

Hours 2 through 6 cover Google TV development from a web app perspective. Optimizing a site and using Google TV specific libraries are covered.

Hours 7 through 19 are about developing Android apps on Google TV. Android app development building blocks are covered with an emphasis on developing for Google TV. Over the course of Hours 15 through 18, a sophisticated app is developed that displays images from Facebook pages on a TV.

Hour 20 shows how to get information on available TV channels and how to change channels from an app using the Channel Listing provider unique to Google TV.

Hours 21 through 24 focus on second-screen apps. Hour 21 introduces second-screen apps and discusses how they work and how to handle potential design challenges. Hour 22 shows how to download, install, and run a sample app and shows how that app is constructed. In Hour 23, a new second screen app is developed. In Hour 24, the underlying concepts and protocols for communicating with a TV are covered. That knowledge can be used as the basis for other devices or apps to communicate with the TV.

About the Author

Carmen Delessio is an experienced application developer who has worked as a developer, technical architect, and CTO in large and small organizations.

Carmen developed the award-winning "BFF Photo" Android app. The app has more than 300,000 downloads and was the winner of the Sprint App Challenge contest in the Social Networking category.

Carmen began his online development career at Prodigy, where he worked on early Internet applications, shopping apps, and fantasy baseball.

He has written for Mashable, AndroidGuys, and Screenitup.com. Screenitup focuses on second-screen TV apps.

He is a graduate of Manhattanville College and lives in Pound Ridge, New York, with his wife, Amy, and daughter, Natalie.

Dedication

For Amy and Natalie.

Acknowledgments

This book would not exist without the help and guidance of the team at Pearson (Sams Publishing). Thanks to Laura Lewin for constant encouragement, Olivia Basegio for her continued work on the project, and Trina McDonald for staying in contact and suggesting the book. Particular thanks go to Michael Thurston for the insightful comments and suggestions during editing. The thoroughness and clarity that were added make this a much better book.

Thanks, Amy and Natalie, for enjoying Saturday morning ballet classes, birthday parties, and other activities while I was writing.

We Want to Hear from You

As the reader of this book, you are our most important critic and commentator. We value your opinion and want to know what we're doing right, what we could do better, what areas you'd like to see us publish in, and any other words of wisdom you're willing to pass our way.

You can email or write directly to let us know what you did or didn't like about this book—as well as what we can do to make our books stronger.

Please note that we cannot help you with technical problems related to the topic of this book, and that due to the high volume of mail we receive, we might not be able to reply to every message.

When you write, please be sure to include this book's title and author, as well as your name and contact information.

Email: feedback@samspublishing.com

Mail: Reader Feedback
         Sams Publishing
         800 East 96th Street
         Indianapolis, IN 46240 USA

Reader Services

Visit our website and register this book at **www.informit.com/register** for convenient access to any updates, downloads, or errata that might be available for this book.

Developing for Google TV and the 10-Foot User Experience

What You'll Learn in This Hour:

▶ What features are included in the Google TV UI

▶ How a TV is used as a device

▶ What systems operate Google TV

▶ What types of apps are available for Google TV

▶ How to design for the 10-foot user experience

Seeing your app on a big screen is an exciting experience. In the 24 hours covered in this book, you will learn practical hands-on methods to develop web and Android apps for Google TV. In this hour, you'll learn about the basic Google TV user interface and system and how to design apps that take full advantage of the 10-foot user experience.

Google TV UI

When you turn on your Google TV, the Android operating system boots up and the home screen of the TV displays. Figure 1.1 shows the home screen and applications in the menu tray at the bottom of the screen.

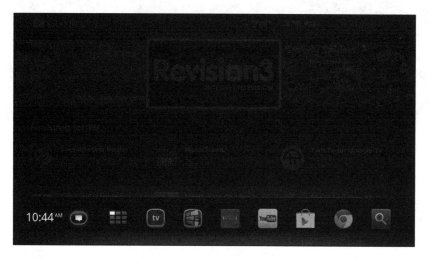

FIGURE 1.1
Google TV screen and menu tray.

The time is displayed. Next to it is a notification indicator. The number indicates that there is one notification message. Selecting the icon will display a notification dialog window and provide the option to clear all messages. Notifications may indicate updates to apps or other app-specific messages.

For navigation between the items on the home screen, every Google TV comes equipped with a remote control. The remote control contains direction keys for up, down, left, and right. Using the direction keys allow the user to highlight an icon, button, or other focusable area of the screen. In the center of the direction keys is a selection key that opens the highlighted item. Together the direction and selection keys are known as the D-Pad. The Google TV remote also has a mouselike device that uses a trackball or trackpad. The mouse device can be used to select and choose items on the screen.

In the menu tray, we see icons for All Apps, Live TV, Overview, Netflix, YouTube, Google Play, Chrome, and Search:

▶ All Apps opens the apps that are available on the device, as shown in Figure 1.2. This includes preinstalled apps that came with the device and apps the user installed from Google Play.

▶ Live TV navigates to the Live TV option set up with Google TV. That may be a cable provider, satellite TV, or another option.

▶ The TV & Movies app is used to search for content on the Google TV device across multiple sources. If a particular movie is available from cable TV and Netflix, both are listed.

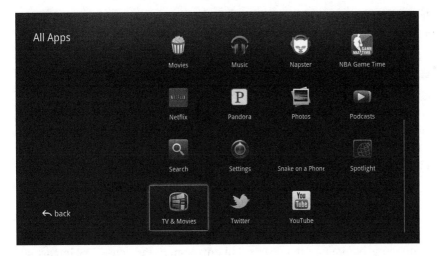

FIGURE 1.2
All Apps reveals all the available apps on the device.

▶ Netflix and YouTube are content apps; we use them to find and view content. Netflix is a subscription service that provides streaming movies and TV shows. YouTube carries user-submitted videos.

▶ Google Play is Google's store for apps, music, and movies. Movie and TV content can be purchased directly. Apps we create for Google TV can be made available for free or for sale on Google Play.

▶ Chrome is a key feature of Google TV. With the Chrome browser, you can use the TV for any Internet task. The Google TV remote contains an alphanumeric keyboard for entering text. You can search the Web, compose emails, or look up your local weather. Chrome is also another access point for free and paid TV and movie content. By using Amazon's Instant Movie site, you can purchase and view a wide selection of movies and TV shows. The Chrome browser supports HTML5 and is a significant development platform for app creation. Hours 2 through 5 will cover developing Chrome web-based apps for Google TV. Your Chrome Bookmarks become another entry point for interaction and content consumption on your Google TV system.

▶ Search opens a Google Quick Search bar for searching web and TV content.

TV as a Device

We are so familiar with TVs that we rarely think of them as devices. We can think of a Google TV as an Android-powered device capable of Internet connectivity and of running the Google

Chrome browser. By considering the capabilities of a Google TV in relation to a desktop computer, tablet, mobile phone, and TV, we can examine the unique aspects of it as a device.

Desktop Computers

Desktop computers have significantly more computing power than a Google TV system. Based on processing speed, initial Google TV processors were in the 1.2 to 1.7GHz range. A MacBook Pro will have a processor speed of 3.2GHz. That does not mean that a Google TV is an underpowered device; it is just not the same as a laptop or desktop computer. It is more than capable of running the Android operating system, Android apps, and the Chrome browser.

Google TV will have a direct ethernet or wireless Internet connection. Like a desktop computer, it is an always-connected device.

After a Google TV system is set up in our home, it is likely to remain in the same spot. Our desktop computers are stationary, but laptops may be used in any room in the house. The impact of the stationary Google TV is really about design, which is covered later in this hour in the discussion of the 10-foot user experience.

Mobile Phones/Tablets

A Google TV is more similar to a mobile phone or Android tablet than any other device. In particular, Google TV runs the Android HoneyComb operating system. An Android tablet will run HoneyComb or a newer version of Android. Because of that, an Android tablet makes a good development device for Google TV work.

It's obvious, but unlike a phone or tablet, a TV is not a mobile device. That leads to some benefits for development. On a mobile device, you may not have a good Internet connection. You can count on a good connection with your Google TV.

Traditional Televisions

A Google TV has channels and a remote control like a traditional TV. That is where the similarity ends, but these features have a significant impact on application development.

For Android apps, channel information can be accessed via a Channel Listing provider. How the Channel Listing provider works and can be used is the topic of Hour 20, "Using the Channel Listing Provider."

Google TVs come equipped with the Anymote protocol for detecting and connecting with remote devices such as Android-based phones or tablets. The communication ability between the TV and a remote device is a unique capability of Google TV. It is the basis for all second screen apps. Second screen apps are covered in Hours 21 to 24.

TV Displays

Computers and mobile phones have displays that are very different from TV displays. Computers use the capability to directly address a pixel on the screen. Each point on the screen is addressable.

TV displays are based on scanlines. TVs scan at 720p, 1080p, or 1080i. That number indicates how many lines a TV can address from the top of the screen to the bottom of the screen. The screen size is determined by the aspect ratio of the TV. Most TVs today use the aspect ratio 16:9. That is 16 pixels wide for every 9 pixels tall. Using the aspect ratio and scan rate, we get a screen size of 1280x720 for 720p systems. For 1080p and 1080i, the screen size is 1920x1080.

Overall, no matter how brilliant the Google TV display might be, it is perceived as being smaller than a computer monitor based on the distance people sit from the screen.

Android abstracts screen sizes and pixel density to provide a set of standard device sizes to developers. A Google TV is considered a large screen rather than an x-large (extra large) screen by Android for display and design purposes.

Figure 1.3 shows the screen size for a phone, tablet, and 42-inch TV.

FIGURE 1.3
Comparing device screen sizes.

Google TV Devices

There are two types of Google TV systems available: a Buddy Box, which can be added to an existing TV to enable it to operate Google TV, and an integrated system in which Google TV is built directly into the TV.

A Buddy Box system may be a box or a Blu-ray player that includes Google TV software. The Buddy Box sits between your current cable or satellite receiver and the TV. When using a Buddy Box, the TV displays the Google TV home screen. You can set up the Google TV remote to control your cable box and other equipment. For development, a Buddy Box and small TV monitor is a great option. Buddy Boxes are available from Sony and Vizio.

With an integrated system, your current cable or satellite receiver is connected directly to the integrated TV. LG and others are creating integrated systems. With an integrated system, the Google TV system is installed directly on the TV.

Google TV systems include Internet connections. You can connect an ethernet connection directly to the TV or Buddy Box or connect wirelessly.

A Buddy Box and an integrated system provide the same interface and overall experience to the user. The difference is in the physical systems.

Google TV Apps

By providing a common platform and a market for apps, Google TV can build an ecosystem in which manufacturers concentrate on hardware and developers concentrate on apps. By bringing an existing web and Android developer community to TV development, Google TV provides a significant advantage over any single manufacturer that intends to provide a developer platform.

There are three types of apps to consider for Google TV: web apps, Android apps, and second screen apps.

Web Apps

You can optimize your website for Google TV or make a unique web experience that targets Google TV. You can use HTML, JavaScript, and CSS to develop web apps for Google TV. JavaScript libraries specific to Google TV help in developing advanced apps.

Web apps are promoted on Google TV via the Spotlight section. The Spotlight features apps in six categories: Games, Lifestyle, Music, News, TV & Movies, and Video. Gallery features web apps submitted by developers.

Because Google TV uses the Chrome web browser, if your web page works well on Chrome, it will likely work well on Google TV. There are steps you can take to fully optimize a site for Google TV, and there are unique aspects of developing a web app for Google TV.

To detect whether your site is being viewed via Google TV, check the user-agent string to see if it contains the values `Large` and `GoogleTV`.

In JavaScript, that is done with the following:

```
var userAgent = navigator.userAgent;
function isGoogleTvBrowser(useragent) {
 return Boolean(useragent.match(/(Large Screen)|GoogleTV/i));
}
```

The Chrome browser supports many features of HTML5, including canvas, SVG, video tags, audio tags, the File API, and the Storage API.

Several JavaScript libraries have been written specifically for Google TV development. A Google TV jQuery UI Library provides navigation and custom controls for Google TV. There is also a Closure Google TV UI Library. They are covered in Hour 4, "HTML5 and jQuery UI Library for Google TV," and Hour 5, "Using the Google TV Closure UI Library," respectively.

To make the video content on your website searchable and more discoverable by users, you can create a Video Sitemap. A Video Sitemap includes metadata for your videos that Google uses to optimize video searches. Video Sitemaps are covered in detail in Hour 6, "Creating a Video Sitemap."

Android Apps

Android Apps have been available on phones since 2009. Since then, thousands of apps have been created and deployed on different-sized phones, on Android tablets, and on Google TV. Google Play makes Android apps available to all Google TV users.

Apps that are optimized and configured for Google TV are easier to find and may be displayed more prominently on Google Play. Android apps are configured using an XML file called a *manifest file*. The manifest file may indicate that an app is available for a specific version or a specific device. There are many settings for the manifest file, including several that are specific to Google TV development. These settings are taken into consideration when apps are shown in the Google Play market. The Android manifest file is the topic of Hour 19, "Mastering the Android Manifest File." Figure 1.4 shows the main screen of Google Play. Apps that are in the Featured for TV section have been set up as TV apps.

FIGURE 1.4
Google Play showing apps featured for TV.

The suite of Android user interface controls and layouts provides for a robust environment for app creation. User interface components for Android include VideoViews for displaying and controlling videos and other common components like TextViews, Buttons, and more.

Android development uses the Java language and common Java libraries are included in the Android Software Development Kit (SDK)

Android App development for Google TV is similar to developing for an Android Tablet. One goal of the Android development system is to make it possible for the same app to run on different screen sizes and resolutions. You can decide to create one app for all screen sizes, or to create separate apps for phones, tablets, and Google TVs.

All second screen apps are built as Android apps.

Second Screen Apps

Second screen apps may be the most unique development opportunity presented by Google TV. Second Screen apps provide interaction between a smartphone or tablet and a TV. When creating a second screen app, you are writing the code for both the TV app and the remote device that interacts with the TV app. The remote device will typically be an iPhone, Android phone, or tablet.

As both a social and interactive experience, second screen apps can be an area for innovation and new ideas. For example, you may use your phone to indicate that a certain move should be made in a game. The decision made on the phone is reflected on the TV.

Apps on the phone that select content for the TV are one type of second screen app. For example, the YouTube remote application lets users browse videos on their smart phones and then play them on their TV. Figure 1.5 shows a phone screen from the YouTube Remote app. The YouTube Remote app uses the fact that the user is logged in on both the TV and the phone apps to communicate between devices.

A second screen app requires two devices. One is the Google TV itself and the other is the device that acts as the remote control.

A Google TV runs two services to facilitate second screen apps. The first service is called *Discovery*. It is the process of the TV and the remote app discovering each other. Think of discovery as being similar to a laptop computer detecting a wireless network. The laptop discovers the network. In this case, the TV is sending out a signal that the remote app discovers.

The second service is called *Pairing*. Pairing refers to making a secure communication connection between the TV and the remote app. It is similar to connecting to a password-protected wireless network.

Both discovery and pairing rely on an underlying communication protocol known as the Anymote protocol.

Figure 1.6 shows the Pairing screen that occurs after discovery.

FIGURE 1.5
YouTube remote app in Google Play.

FIGURE 1.6
Pairing screen on an Android phone.

10-Foot User Experience

The phrase "10-foot user experience" has come to mean the entirety of the TV viewing experience. It encompasses distance from the screen, content, and even social aspects of TV viewing. As Google TV and other intelligent TV systems come to market, it is possible that the use of TVs will change. Currently, TV is primarily an entertainment-centered and passive experience.

Leanback

A TV's primary function is to consume content. It is possible to use your Google TV to compose emails using Gmail and to create documents with Google Docs, but today a Google TV is primarily an entertainment device.

Netflix, YouTube, and LiveTV are all apps for consuming content. The Google TV & Movies app is for finding content. Google Play is a market for content as well as apps. Even the Chrome browser can be used as an app to discover and view content. These apps all provide the opportunity to select and view content.

Watching TV, where the content is a broadcast station or a streaming video, is a passive experience. Current designs for content apps include the ideas that viewers want to lean back and enjoy themselves. This is often referred to as the *lean-back* experience.

The website for YouTube Leanback was designed as a big screen experience that features leanback concepts. YouTube Leanback is available at this URL.

```
http://www.youtube.com/leanback
```

The YouTube Leanback site features minimal navigation, video categories, and full-screen video play. With Leanback it is easy to pick a category and watch many videos in a row.

Figure 1.7 shows the YouTube Leanback interface for a set of featured videos.

TV Is a Social Experience

The 10-foot user experience is a social experience rather than a single-user experience. If we think about the YouTube and Netflix apps, a more rewarding experience is to find and view videos with family or friends rather than by yourself. When developing apps, whether they are for content consumption, games, or something else, it makes sense to consider the experience for everyone in the room, not just the person holding the remote. With second screen apps there are plenty of possibilities to explore in this area.

An example is the web based game called WeDraw. It can be accessed at http://www.wedraw.tv. WeDraw syncs smartphones to a web-based experience that is optimized for TV. Using HTML5, one user is presented with a word to draw with his or her finger. Other users try to guess the word. The TV acts as the common social and visual experience.

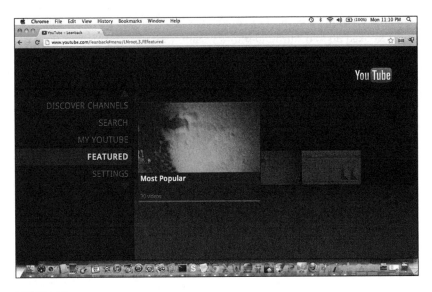

FIGURE 1.7
YouTube Leanback user interface.

Designing for a 10-Foot Environment

Whether a viewer is looking at a small device or a large TV, he or she is usually some distance from the screen. Smartphone users hold their devices close so they can see everything on the small screen. Computer users sit close enough to their monitors to type and interact. TV screens are often 40 inches or more, so users sit farther away from them. The viewing area for TV is often called a 10-foot environment, and this viewing environment needs to be considered when developing a user interface to enrich the 10-foot user experience.

A mobile phone app is a better model for a Google TV app than a desktop computer app. The small screen experience of using a phone is more like that of a person using a remote on a TV than using a keyboard with a computer. Like mobile apps, TV apps should not be cluttered and should provide clear choices for users. There should be enough space between the elements in a TV app to foster clear navigation.

When developing for the 10-foot experience, understand that the primary means of navigation will be the D-Pad. Users will click directional keys to select content. If the mouse is used in your app, ensure that the clickable area is large and that there is visual feedback that an item is click-able. Highlighting the item typically does that.

The 10-foot user experience factors in all of the TV's capabilities, including audio. A TV will often have speakers or be hooked up to a surround-sound system, which is much louder than what is found on a smartphone or computer. A best practice is to give users the ability to easily mute or reduce the sound of the app. For Android apps, there is a feature called AudioFocus that indicates when an app has control of the audio and when the app loses control. For example, if you are playing background music for a game and the user switches to TV, the game has lost AudioFocus. These scenarios are covered in more detail in Hour 20.

Summary

In this hour, we covered the Google TV User Interface and Google TV systems. We also discussed the types of apps that can be created for Google TV: Web, Android, and second screen. With that understanding of Google TV, we examined the 10-foot user experience and what it means to design for the social and entertainment experience that is Google TV.

Q&A

Q. What are the two types of Google TV systems?

A. Google TV can be purchased as a Buddy System or an integrated TV. A Buddy System is a separate box that hooks to a TV and supplies the Google TV System. With an integrated system, the Google TV operating system is built directly into the TV.

Q. What languages or technologies can be used when developing for Google TV?

A. For web apps, JavaScript, HTML, and CSS are used. For Android apps, Java is used.

Q. What is the difference between Discovery and Pairing for second screen apps?

A. Discovery and Pairing are both services that run on Google TV. Discovery is the process of a remote app on a phone discovering the TV. Pairing is the process of securely connecting to the TV. This is similar to finding and connecting to a wireless network.

Q. Have any libraries been created specifically for Google TV web development?

A. Yes, the Google TV jQuery UI Library and Closure Google TV Libraries are both JavaScript libraries for Google TV.

Workshop

Quiz

1. When would you use the Anymote protocol?
2. What is meant by leanback?
3. Which of the following are not characteristics of Google TV?

    a. Anymote protocol

    b. Large screens

    c. Extremely powerful processors

Answers

1. The Anymote protocol is used in second screen apps. It is used to communicate between a remote control and TV.

2. TV viewing is a passive experience for content consumption. That is referred to as leanback.

3. The correct answer is c. Google TVs are powerful enough to run a Chrome browser and Android apps, but they are not as powerful as desktop computers.

Exercises

1. If you have a Google TV system, try a number of different apps and consider the design features of the 10-foot user experience.

2. If you do not yet have a Google TV system, try both the YouTube Remote and WeDraw apps in a Chrome browser.

HOUR 2
Optimizing Web Pages for Google TV

What You'll Learn in This Hour:

▶ How content is displayed on TV screens

▶ How videos are played on Google TV

▶ How to properly display text and fonts on Google TV

▶ How to navigate Google TV

Now that you've learned about some of the key aspects of developing for Google TV, let's apply that to creating web pages that are optimized for viewing on the Chrome browser found on Google TVs. In this hour, we'll develop and optimize web pages that display images and videos. Starting with basic examples, we'll cover screen resolution, zooming, playing videos, and navigation.

Displaying Content on TV Screens

An HDTV will show photos and videos in full size and in stunning color. Looking at content on a TV instead of a computer screen or a tablet is truly a different experience. Web pages created for Google TV should take advantage of the whole screen for displaying content, and make navigation simple to understand and easy to use via a remote control.

TVs are optimized for viewing, but are underpowered compared to computers and even tablets. The CPU power and memory available for a TV are typically much less than for a computer. A Google TV runs Android Apps and the Chrome browser and performs well, but the main function of a TV is to show broadcast TV and movies.

Autozoom

You may turn on your Google TV, start the Google Chrome browser app, navigate to your site, and discover that your site looks pretty good on Google TV. That's great. This is largely because the Chrome browser on Google TV uses a feature called *autozoom* to automatically display websites optimally for a device.

Autozoom will factor in screen resolution and the HTML on your current site to determine an optimal viewing experience. Autozoom was created so that all sites display reasonably well in the browser. However, by optimizing an HTML page specifically for the TV screen, it is not too hard to do a better job than autozoom.

NOTE

Autozoom Doesn't Mean Zooming

Autozoom does not refer to zooming in and out on the screen. It means getting the best fit for the page being displayed.

Understanding Screen Resolution and Overscan

When we buy TVs, we see references to 720p or 1080i/p. These numbers refer to the screen resolution of the TV based on the number of pixels. A 1080p device is 1080 pixels high and 1920 pixels wide; that is, 1,920x1,080 pixels. A 720p device has a screen resolution of 1,280x720 pixels.

The actual display area of a TV may be smaller than the screen resolution. The display area of the TV shows the content. The total theoretical screen resolution may be reduced by up to 5%. Television broadcasts use the margins of the TV screen to support extra information such as closed captioning and to adjust for the picture edges. This is known as *overscan* and must be factored into page design.

Displaying an Image on the Full Screen

Photos and images will pop out when viewed on a TV. Again, it will seem like a new experience. To show a full screen image, we must consider screen resolution and overscanning. We'll go through several examples to show how this can be done.

The simplest way to display an image on a page is with a direct URL to the image. In that case, the browser does the work of displaying the image and accounting for overscan. The following URL is a direct reference to an image on the web:

https://s3.amazonaws.com/bffmedia.examples/delessio_family_pool.jpg

Though that may be sufficient for a personal site with a list of images, it is unlikely that it will be something that will be commonly used. When viewed on Google TV, this URL shows a large photo. There is a scrollbar. To see the bottom of the image you must scroll down. The original image size in this case is 1,600 pixels wide by 1,199 pixels high.

A web page showing the same image would be structured as an HTML document and would use the IMG HTML tag as shown in Listing 2.1.

LISTING 2.1 HTML to Display a Single Image

```
1:  <!DOCTYPE html>
2:  <html>
3:  <body>
4:  <img src="https://s3.amazonaws.com/bffmedia.examples/delessio_family_pool.jpg"
5:            alt="family photo"  />
6:  <body>
7:  </html>
```

This will display the same as linking directly to an image, but it gives us the HTML structure we need to start modifying how the page looks. The direct link to the image is now used as the source for the HTML image tag. The HTML image tag includes "family photo" as the alternate text to be displayed if the image is not available.

By adding width and height to the image tag, we can begin to customize the display. We will add `height` to the image tag and let the `width` scale automatically:

```
<img src="https://s3.amazonaws.com/bffmedia.examples/delessio_family_pool.jpg"
alt="family photo" height="720" />
```

By adding `height`, it may seem that we have adjusted the image to display nicely for 720p screens, but there are several issues to consider. One is autozoom and the other is overscan. With autozoom on, this image displays precisely as if width and height were not specified. To turn autozoom off, we'll add another tag, shown in Listing 2.2, to the head section of our HTML document.

LISTING 2.2 HTML to Display a Single Image with Autozoom Off

```
1:  <!DOCTYPE html>
2:  <html>
3:  <head>
4:  <meta name="gtv-autozoom" content="off" />
5:  </head>
6:  <body>
7:  <img src="https://s3.amazonaws.com/bffmedia.examples/delessio_family_pool.jpg"
8:            alt="family photo" height="720"  />
8:  <body>
9:  </html>
```

By using the Google TV specific tag `gtv-autozoom` we have turned autozoom off in Listing 2.2. Now when viewed on a 1080p screen, the photo takes up about 70% of the screen height and 50% of the screen width. On a 720p screen, the photo fills the display from top to bottom, but depending on your TV, there will likely be a scrollbar. That is due to overscan.

To handle overscan, the recommended dimensions for a 720p screen are 1152 pixels wide by 648 pixels high, as shown in Figure 2.1. The recommended dimensions for a 1080p screen are 1728 by 972.

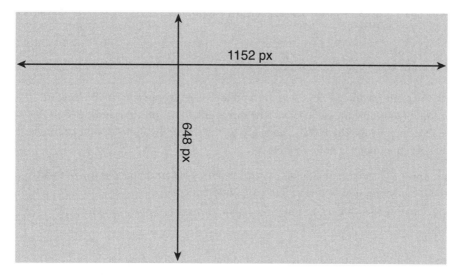

1152 px

648 px

FIGURE 2.1
Recommended dimensions for 720p TV screen.

By using the recommended dimensions and some JavaScript to detect screen size, we will show an image that displays well for both a 720p and 1080p TV screen. In Listing 2.3, the alert command is used to display the precise screen size in a window. We use that screen size to determine how to set the image height. If the screen size returned is greater than 720, we set height to 972, which is the recommended height for a 1080p screen. Otherwise, the height is set to 648, the recommended height for 720p screens. Note that width is not specified. We set the height, and width is set by the browser.

LISTING 2.3   Adjusting Image Height for 720p or 1080p

```
1:  <!DOCTYPE html>
2:  <html>
3:  <head>
4:  <meta name="gtv-autozoom" content="off" />
5:  </head>
6:  <body>
7:  <SCRIPT language="JavaScript">
8:      <!--
9:      alert(screen.height);
10:      if ( (screen.height>=720))
```

```
11:     {
12:         document.write(
13:     '<img src="https://s3.amazonaws.com/bffmedia.examples/delessio_family_pool.
jpg"
14:     height="972" alt="screenshot" />');
15:     }
16:     else
17:     {
18:         document.write(
19:     '<img src="https://s3.amazonaws.com/bffmedia.examples/delessio_family_pool.
jpg"
20:     height="648" alt="screenshot" />');
21:     }
22:     //-->
23:     </SCRIPT>
24:     </body>
25:     </html>
```

So far we have accounted for screen size by turning autozoom off. Another strategy, particularly for existing HTML pages, is to adjust autozoom using JavaScript code. This strategy should be used when autozoom does not display an existing page well and overzooms the content.

The JavaScript to do this considers screen size and the size of the display area in the browser window. For height, we can read these values using screen.height and window.innerHeight, respectively.

The proper zoom ratio can be determined by taking the window dimensions as a percentage of the full screen. This approach reduces the amount of zooming.

In Listing 2.4, the zoom ratio is determined in the init() function. The page's onLoad function calls init() to change the zoom ratio. A JavaScript alert displays the ratio (see Figure 2.2).

LISTING 2.4   Adjusting the Autozoom Ratio

```
1:  <!DOCTYPE html>
2:  <html>
3:  <head>
4:  <script language="JavaScript">
5:  function init() {
6:      var w = screen.width;
7:      var h = screen.height;
8:
8:      var bw = window.innerWidth;
10:     var bh = window.innerHeight;
11:
12:     var wRatio = bw/w;
13:     var hRatio = bh/h;
```

```
14:    var ratio = (wRatio + hRatio) / 2;
15:
16:    document.getElementsByTagName('body')[0].style.zoom = ratio;
17:    alert(ratio);
18: }
19: window.onload=init;
20: </script>
21: </head>
22: <body  >
23: <img  src="https://s3.amazonaws.com/bffmedia.examples/delessio_family_pool.jpg"
24: height="648"  alt="screenshot"  />
25: </body>
26: </html>
```

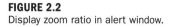

FIGURE 2.2
Display zoom ratio in alert window.

Playing Video

Many Google TV web apps will take advantage of a television's ability to display videos. Google provides several HTML templates for displaying multiple videos, selecting videos, and playing videos. Before we get to that, we will look at the HTML5 video tag and recommendations for playing video on web pages that are optimized for Google TV.

HTML5 Video Tag

The HTML5 video tag shown in Listing 2.5 is very similar to the image tag that we have been using in our examples. In the tag, we refer to the source of the video and can specify the width and height. The attribute `controls` indicates that the default controls for playing a video should be used.

LISTING 2.5   HTML Video Tag

```
1:   <video controls="controls" >
2:     <source src= "http://www.bffmedia.com/trailer_1080p.ogg" type="video/mp4" />
3:   </video>
```

Video Recommendations for Google TV

Because TV is a casual experience that is less interactive than using a PC or a tablet, one recommendation is that videos begin to play automatically. A second recommendation is to play videos at full screen size. We can use what we have learned about screen resolution to change the height of our video. The `autoplay` attribute takes care of automatically starting the video. In Listing 2.6, `autoplay` is set in line 16.

LISTING 2.6   Adjusting Video Height for 720p or 1080p

```
1:   <!DOCTYPE html>
2:   <html>
3:   <head>
4:   <meta name="gtv-autozoom" content="off" />
5:   </head>
6:   <body>
7:   <SCRIPT language="JavaScript">
8:     <!--
9:     alert(screen.height);
10:    if ( (screen.height>=720))
11:    {
12:    document.write('<video controls="controls"
13:          autoplay="autoplay" height=972 >
14:          <source src= "http:// http://www.bffmedia.com/trailer_1080p.ogg"
15:   type="video/mp4" /></video>');
16:    }
17:    else
18:    {
19:    document.write(
20:        '<video controls="controls" autoplay="autoplay" height=648 >
21:        <source src= "http://www.bffmedia.com/trailer_1080p.ogg"
22:        type="video/mp4" /></video>');16:     </video>');
23:    }
```

```
24:  //-->
25:  </SCRIPT>
26:  </body>
27:  </html>
```

Displaying Text and Color

TVs are designed to show movement and bright colors well. When putting text on the screen, an optimal design will account for the size and readability of the text. TV screens show colors differently than computer monitors do. Certain colors look sharper with higher contrast, and some may distort the expected display.

Best Practices for Text and Color Display

Google has provided some specific design guidelines for Google TV for handling both text and color (see Figure 2.3).

The following are things you should do when displaying text and color on a TV:

▶ Break text into small chunks that can be read at a glance.

▶ Keep line length at about 5-7 words per line.

▶ Use light text on a dark background.

▶ Use text size of 21pt on 720p and 28pt on 1080p.

▶ Use #F1F1F1 or 240/240/240 (RGB) for solid colors (a near-white color).

▶ Test your websites' low quality displays.

The following are things you should not do when displaying text and color on a TV:

▶ Have line length shorter than 3 words or longer than 12 words.

▶ Use text smaller than 18pt on 720p and 24pt on 1080p.

▶ Use pure white (#FFFFFF).

▶ Use bright whites, oranges, or reds.

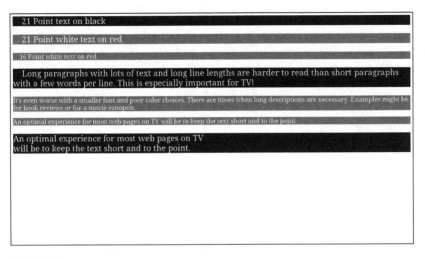

FIGURE 2.3
Displaying text for Google TV.

In Listing 2.7, the text color, size, and background color are specified. This shows the text "21 Point text on black" with four leading spaces.

LISTING 2.7   **Text Size and Color**

```
1:   <p style=font-size:21;color:F1F1F1;background:black;">
2:       21 Point text on black
3:   </p>
```

Fonts

Google TV supports the `Droid Sans` and `Droid Sans Serif` font families. There are several ways to take advantage of other fonts. We can use the CSS3 to define a font or to use Google Font APIs.

TIP

Google Web Fonts

Google provides hundreds of open source fonts that you can use in your web pages. See http://www.google.com/webfonts.

A true type font with extension `.ttf` can be used to define a specific font for use on a Google TV web page. The true type font is used to define the `font-face` and the `font-face` is used in the style sheet. At a high level, we can use fonts that are not supported natively on the device by importing a true type font.

In Listing 2.8, the TrueType font `bonsai.ttf` is used as the source to define a `font-face`.

LISTING 2.8   Defining a Font-Face

```
1:  @font-face
2:  {
3:      font-family: Moonstar;
4:      src: url("http://gtvdemos.appspot.com/static/fonts/bonsai.ttf");
5:  }
```

In Listing 2.9, in lines 4 and 5 make a font from an external stylesheet available for our use. In lines 7-11, the font-family tangerine is used to define a new style called `font-demo-google`. That font is used in line 23, demonstrating how to incorporate a Google Font into the page. Listing 2.9 uses both a CSS3 font-face and a Google web font to display text. Lines 12-20 define a font-face and style that is used on line 23.

LISTING 2.9   Adding Unique Fonts

```
1:  <!DOCTYPE html>
2:  <html>
3:  <body >
4:  <link rel="stylesheet" type="text/css"
5:      href="http://fonts.googleapis.com/css?family=Tangerine">
6:  <style>
7:  .font-demo-google {
8:    font-family: 'Tangerine', serif;
9:    font-size: 36px;
10:     text-shadow: 4px 4px 4px #aaa;
11: }
12: @font-face
13: {
14:     font-family: Moonstar;
15:     src: url("http://gtvdemos.appspot.com/static/fonts/bonsai.ttf");
16: }
17: .font-demo-css {
18:     font-family: Moonstar, sans-serif;
19:     font-size: 36px;
20: }
21: </style>
22: <p class="font-demo-css">Font test using CSS3's @font-face</p>
```

```
23:    <p class="font-demo-google">Font test using Google's Font API</p>
24:    </body>
25:    </html>
```

Lines 6 and 16 define font styles that are subsequently used in lines 21 and 22 to display text with the desired font. Results are shown in Figure 2.4.

FIGURE 2.4
Font test using CSS3's @font-face.

Navigating the Big Screen

Actions required to navigate on your web page should be very clear and simple. That is generally the case with all web pages, but some additional considerations exist with Google TV. People are generally less actively engaged when watching a TV. The viewer will be using a remote control and not a mouse. Navigation should work well using directional keys and avoid requiring clicking. For existing sites, this may not be reasonable to implement, but it is a good goal.

Making Navigation Obvious

It is usually clear on web pages when buttons and links are used for navigation, but there are times when navigation using images, Flash, and complicated menus is not obvious. Guidelines for navigation on a TV can be summarized as "make it obvious!" Some ways to make navigation obvious follow:

- ▶ Make selections big and easy to see. Use extra padding to make selections easy targets.

- ▶ Highlight selections. It should be obvious that something is selected. Use a hover state for this.

- ▶ Limit scrolling. Scrolling on the TV with a remote is a less natural motion than scrolling on a computer with a mouse or up and down on a tablet.

▶ Take advantage of the width of the TV screen. Use left-hand navigation controls and avoid top navigation.

▶ Avoid interfaces that use a small target—like an X to close a window.

One simple way to do this is to define hover states for links and buttons, as shown in Listing 2.10.

LISTING 2.10   Hovering on Links and Buttons

```
1:  <style type="text/css">
2:  a:hover {font-size:24; font-weight:bold; color: red;}
3:  button:hover {font-size:24; font-weight:bold; color: red;}
4:  </style>
5:  <a href="#">Hover Link</a>
6:  <button>Simple</button>
```

Supporting Remote Control Navigation

The user of our web page is likely sitting on a couch—and holding a remote control. The D-Pad or 4-way directional arrows on the remote should work as a primary tool for navigation. The remote may be held in one hand or may be a keyboard that sits on the user's lap. In either case, ideally the user will be able to navigate through the site using the D-Pad.

In addition to the directional keys, we can detect an Enter/Select key on the remote. We can also detect all the media keys such as Play, Pause, Previous, and Next. These keys should be supported when handling music or video.

Listing 2.11 takes our video tag example and adds a Play/Pause button. Clicking the button will pause and restart the video. The remote control key for play and pause is supported. Google maps remote keys to values that we can access in JavaScript. We detect the remote control key presses in JavaScript by checking for the onKeyDown event on the page.

Listing 2.11 includes play and pause remote keys by looking for a keycode with the value 179.

LISTING 2.11   Supporting Play and Pause on a Remote

```
1:  <!DOCTYPE html>
2:  <html>
3:  <body>
4:  <button onclick="playPause()">Play/Pause</button>
5:  <br />
6:  <video id="video1" controls="controls" autoplay="autoplay" height=648 >
7:    <source src= "http://www.w3schools.com/html5/movie.mp4" type="video/mp4" />
8:  </video>
```

```
9:   <script type="text/javascript">
10:  var myVideo=document.getElementById("video1");
11:  function playPause()
12:  {
13:    myVideo.play();
14:    myVideo.pause();
15:  }
16:  window.onload = function() {
17:        document.onkeydown=function(e){
18:          if (!e) e=window.event;
19:          switch(e.keyCode) {
20:            case 179:
21:              playPause();
22:              break;
23:          }
24:        }
25:      }
26:  </script>
27:  </body>
28:  </html>
```

Keys and keycodes for navigation are listed next. These values apply to all Google TVs.

- ▶ Left Arrow: 37
- ▶ Right Arrow: 39
- ▶ Up: 38
- ▶ Down: 40
- ▶ Enter/Select: 13
- ▶ Stop: 178
- ▶ Play/Pause: 179
- ▶ Skip Forward: 176
- ▶ Skip Backward: 177
- ▶ Rewind: 227
- ▶ Fast Forward: 228

▼ TRY IT YOURSELF

Checking Your Own Pages on Google TV

If you have an existing website, check it on an actual Google TV device. First-generation devices like the Logitech Revue are inexpensive and provide a good option for checking your content. This is particularly important if you expect your site to be helpful when web browsing on a TV.

1. Open the list of applications on the Google TV.

2. Select the Google Chrome browser.

3. Navigate to your web page.

4. Check the display and navigation.

5. Navigate through your site using the remote control.

When using the D-Pad, you should be able to select all focusable elements. The arrangement of items on the screen should make a grid that works well with both left and right and up and down keys.

Summary

In this hour, we used a simple image tag on an HTML page to explore the ins and outs of how a TV displays web content. Common screen resolutions were examined and autozoom and overscan were explained. We explored the HTML5 video tag and were able to control the video from the device's remote control. Design considerations regarding text display and navigation were covered.

Q&A

Q. **The most common screen resolutions for TVs are 720p and 1080p. If I don't modify my website, will it look okay on these screens?**

A. Yes, because autozoom is built in, your site should look okay, but it may not look perfect.

Q. **What can I do if my website does not look "pixel perfect" on Google TV?**

A. There are several options. You can design for one screen resolution (1080p) and let autozoom handle other resolutions. You can design separate optimal experiences for 720p and 1080p. Or you can control autozoom programmatically using JavaScript.

Q. **Why should I design pages for screen heights less than 720 pixels for 720p screens?**

A. Because of overscan. The recommended dimensions for 720p screens are 1152x648.

Q. **What can I assume about remote controls for Google TVs?**

A. Assume that there are four directional keys and an Enter/Select key. This is known as the D-Pad. You can assume common media controls such as play/pause, stop, rewind, and fast-forward. You will design for these controls, but it is likely there will be a point-and-click mechanism, too.

Workshop

Quiz

1. TVs display videos well. Is optimal TV display achieved by using fast CPUs like computers?

2. Which of the following is not recommended for playing videos?

    a. Displaying in full screen

    b. Allowing the user to start and stop video using the remote control

    c. Making the user responsible for starting the video when the page is displayed

3. Which of the following is not recommended for displaying text?

   a. Using short paragraphs

   b. Using white (#FFFFFF) for backgrounds

   c. Using text size of 21pt on 720p and 28pt on 1080p

4. What two methods can be used to create custom fonts for Google TV?

5. Is this statement true or false? Numeric codes for remote control keys vary by manufacturer, but they can be looked up in a table.

Answers

1. The correct answer is No. TVs are underpowered compared to computers and even tablets.

2. The correct answer is c. The autoplay attribute should be used to start videos immediately.

3. The correct answer is b. Use (F1F1F1), which is a near-white color.

4. CSS3 Fonts and Google Web Fonts can be used.

5. The correct answer is False. The remote keys are standard.

Exercises

1. Modify Listing 2.11 to handle the Stop keypress on the remote in the same way as the Play/Pause button.

2. Modify Listing 2.11 to size the screen appropriately for 720p and 1080p screens.

3. Combine an image, a video, and the video controls into a single page that factors in good navigational design.

Using Google's Video Templates

What You'll Learn in This Hour:

▶ What features the templates provide
▶ How the templates are structured
▶ How to download and view the templates
▶ How to update the templates with your own videos

Using the HTML5 video tag is a foundation for creating compelling web pages for Google TV. Google helps us take that to the next level by providing two complete HTML5 video templates. In this hour, we'll examine these templates in detail and use them as a basis for showing our own videos. The hour begins with a description of the video templates and then provides instructions on how to download and use the templates.

NOTE

Previewing Pages in the Google Chrome Browser

Checking out your pages in the Google Chrome browser is a good way to test and get a feel for how they will play on Google TV.

Google Video Templates

Google provides two video templates. Template 1 is designed for sites that contain many videos, and it includes a video selection page and a video play page. Template 2 is designed for sites with fewer videos and provides all the navigation on a single page. All videos can be accessed from a single page. There are many similarities between the templates, and we'll explore those.

Template 1—Handling Many Videos on Separate Pages

One of the main differences between Template 1 and Template 2 is the navigational structure. As you can see in Figure 3.1, Template 1 uses an intro page with left-side navigation for the categories. Videos within the category are shown on the right. Selected videos play on a separate page. Template 1 can be viewed online at this URL:

```
http://gtv-resources.googlecode.com/svn/trunk/templates/html-01/index.html
```

FIGURE 3.1
Template 1: category and video page.

Template 2—Handling Fewer Videos on a Single Page

Template 2 shows all videos and navigation on a single page, as shown in Figure 3.2. A video begins playing immediately when the page opens. Category navigation and video selection is supported as in Template 1, but all navigation occurs on the page that displays the video. Template 2 can be viewed at

```
http://gtv-resources.googlecode.com/svn/trunk/templates/html-02/index.html
```

FIGURE 3.2
Template 2: single page for video play and navigation.

Common Video Features

There are differences in appearance, but both templates support the following features when playing videos:

- ▶ Custom buttons for video controls such as Play and Pause
- ▶ Custom progress bar for video time and remaining time
- ▶ Full-screen video
- ▶ Navigation that fades out as video begins
- ▶ Rollovers to redisplay navigation
- ▶ Button overlays

Examining the Template Structure

Both templates are made up of JavaScript, CSS, HTML, and image files. A common directory structure is used for both templates. Under the root directory are three subdirectories for JavaScript, CSS, and images. HMTL files are placed in the root directory. Figure 3.3 shows the directory structure for Template 2.

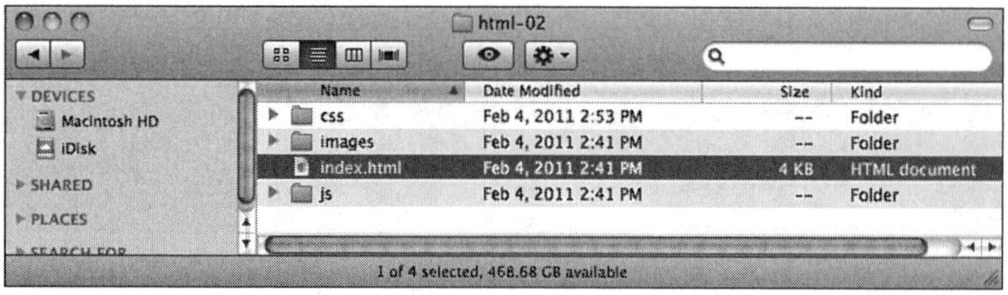

FIGURE 3.3
Directory structure for Template 2.

Table 3.1 and Table 3.2 list the files used in the templates. Common filenames are used across templates.

Template 1 includes two HTML pages. The index.html page handles navigation and the fullscreen.html page shows the video. There is a corresponding JavaScript file for each HTML page. Each template includes its own style sheet. The only file that is identical in both templates is the dataprovider.js file, which defines the video content for the templates.

TABLE 3.1   Template 1 Files

HTML	JavaScript	CSS
index.html	index.js	styles.css
fullscreen.html	fullscreen.js	
	dataprovider.js	

Figure 3.4 shows the relationships between the HTML pages, the JavaScript, and the styles.css file. Index.js receives data from dataprovider.js and dynamically creates the page. The Google TV jQuery UI Library is used in index.js.

TABLE 3.2   Template 2 Files

HTML	JavaScript	CSS
index.html	index.js	styles.css
	dataprovider.js	

Figure 3.5 shows the corresponding diagram for Template 2. In Template 2, index.js reads the results of data provider.js and creates the page to display. In Template 2, all functionality takes place on a single page.

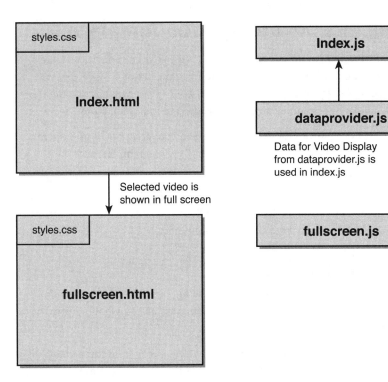

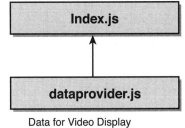

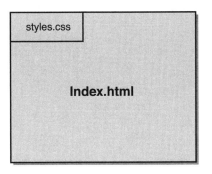

FIGURE 3.4
Template 1 HTML and JavaScript diagram.

FIGURE 3.5
Template 2 HTML and JavaScript diagram.

Understanding the JavaScript for Template 2

When you look in the JavaScript directory for Template 2, you will see a lot more than `index.js` and `dataprovider.js`. For example, the directory contains `gtvcore.js`, `keycontrol.js`, and `sidenav.js`. These files are part of the Google TV UI Library. We will be covering that library in detail in Hour 4. The goal is to understand what is used to make Template 2 work.

For now, it makes sense to consider the Google TV UI Library as a core component of the templates. In this hour, we'll do that and focus on the other elements of the templates.

For setting up the page and loading data, Template 1 works just like Template 2. The difference is that Template 1 displays videos on a separate page. That makes Template 2 a good model for understanding how video data is used in both Template 1 and Template 2. The same JavaScript file for providing data, `dataprovider.js`, is used in both templates.

Setting Up the Page: Index.js

`Index.js` initializes the functionality and controls of the page for Template 2. It is loaded using the web page `index.html`. The HTML5 video display, video progress bar, navigation, and the fade out are all handled in `index.js`.

The functions defined in `index.js` are shown in Listing 3.1. (Don't worry if all these details do not make sense yet. Our current goal is to understand the structure of the templates.)

LISTING 3.1 Index.js Starting the Template Page

```
1:   **
2:   * Starts the template page.
3:   */
4:   gtv.jq.TemplatePage.prototype.start = function() {
5:     var templatePage = this;
6:     templatePage.keyController = new gtv.jq.KeyController();
7:     templatePage.preloadImages();
8:     templatePage.doPageZoom();1:
9:     templatePage.instanciateData();
10:    templatePage.makeTooltip();
11:    templatePage.makeProgressBar();
12:    templatePage.makeVideoControl();
13:    templatePage.makeTabs();
14:    templatePage.startFadeTimeput();
15     $(document.body).css('visibility', '');
16:    templatePage.keyController.start(null,
17:                          false,
18:                          gtv.jq.VideoControl.fullScreenLayer);
19:   };
20:   var templatePage = new gtv.jq.TemplatePage();
21:   templatePage.start();
```

Loading the Data: Dataprovider.js

`Dataprovider.js` provides all video data to the template page. The data includes the video category, video source, video title, and video description.

In the example for Template 2, the values for categories and video are hard-coded. The video data is returned in random order to demonstrate the functionality of the template pages.

The following JavaScript will create a new DataProvider using the jQuery Library:

```
Var x= new gtv.jq.DataProvider();
```

A `DataProvider` has a `getData()` function for returning data.

The best way to think of this functionally is that `index.js` displays the page and `datapro-vider.js` provides data for the page. To explain this, we'll create an example.

Listing 3.2 shows how `index.js` instantiates and uses the data provider.

LISTING 3.2   Index.js Reading from Data Provider

```
1:   /**
2:    * Instanciates data from the data provider.
3:    */
4:     var templatePage = this;
5:     templatePage.dataProvider = new gtv.jq.DataProvider();
6:     templatePage.data = templatePage.dataProvider.getData();
7:   };
```

To really understand what `dataprovider.js` gives us, we can write a short JavaScript program to display the data returned. That is done in Listing 3.3. Though we can get a good sense for understanding the data required to run the template by studying `dataprovider.js`, the data required can be explicitly listed with the code in Listing 3.3. We create a file called `Data.html` to create a data provider and to show the data returned.

LISTING 3.3   Data.html to Dump Data from Dataprovider.js

```
1:   /**
2:    * Instanciates data from the data provider.
3:    */
4:     var templatePage = this;
5:     templatePage.dataProvider = new gtv.jq.DataProvider();
6:     templatePage.data = templatePage.dataProvider.getData();
7:   };
```

Lines 1 to 3 import the necessary JavaScript files for the project. We use the `dataprovider.js` file that is included with the templates.

This works great, but the output is an unhelpful string of data that looks like the following:

```
{"categories":[{"name":"Dev Events","videos":[{"thumb":"images/thumbs/thumb13.jpg
...
```

Fortunately, we can use some tools to make this readable and helpful. By taking the result of `data.html` and putting it into the site `http://jsbeautifier.org/`, we get readable and helpful results.

Figure 3.6 shows the data returned by `dataprovider.js` in a readable format.

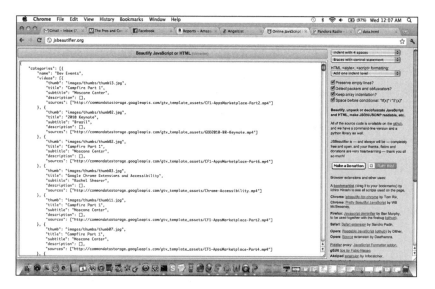

FIGURE 3.6
Structured data displayed via `jsbeautifier.org`.

It is clear now that we get a `JSON` object named `categories`. The `categories` object contains an array of name objects and video objects. Each video object contains a `thumbnail`, `title`, `subtitle`, `description` and `sources` field. The `sources` field contains the URL of the video.

Using Templates to Show Your Own Videos

A goal of working with Google's templates is to use them with your own videos. By understanding the output of `dataprovider.js`, we are in a good position to create our own simplified version to demonstrate how we would do this with our own data.

To keep things simple, we will modify the existing `dataprovider.js` file. It is a good idea to make a copy of the original!

As we examine the contents of Figure 3.6, we can simplify our task by making a data provider with two categories and two videos each. Rather than randomly assigning videos, we'll specifically define the videos and descriptions to use. One set of videos is from the Google Template files and the other set is from the movie *Big Buck*. *Big Buck* is an open source movie that can be found at http://www.bigbuckbunny.org. It is a project of the Blender Foundation at www.blender.org. The video object for the *Big Buck* videos is defined in Listing 3.4.

LISTING 3.4 Creating Video Objects

```
1:   gtv.jq.DataProvider.prototype.getData = function() {
2:     var buck_videos = [
3:       {
4:          sources:
5:          ['http://bffmedia.com/trailer_400p.ogg'],
6:          title: 'Big Buck 400p Video Trailer',
7:          thumb: 'http://www.bffmedia.com/buck1.png;,
8:          description: ['Common Creative Project Movie'],
9:          subtitle: ' Smaller Version'
10:        },
11:        {
12:          sources:['http://bffmedia.com/trailer_1080p.ogg'],
13:          title: 'Big Buck 1080p Video Trailer',
14:          thumb: 'http://www.bffmedia.com/buck2.png',
15:          description: ['Common Creative Project Movie'],
16:          subtitle: 'Big Buck is a Rabbit'
17:        }
18:    ];
```

In Listing 3.4, we directly create video objects with the expected names for the fields. This creates a variable called buck_videos. A variable called event_videos is also created. Notice that the description field is populated. We'll see how that is used on the page.

Now that we've created variables containing all video data, we create a single variable to return to the page. Listing 3.5 takes the video objects and assembles them into a variable called data with two categories.

LISTING 3.5 Creating a Data Object with Categories and Videos

```
1:   var data = {
2:       categories: [
3:       {
4:        name: 'Dev Events',
5:        videos: event_videos
6:       },
7:       {
8:        name: 'Big Buck',
```

```
9:        videos: buck_videos
10:      }
11:      ]
12:    };
13:    return data;
```

That data is put together and returned to the page. We expect to see two categories with two videos each, as shown in Figure 3.7.

FIGURE 3.7
Simplified app with two categories and two videos.

Note how the data corresponds to the page display. The title, subtitle, and description provided
are used on this page. We added the description, "Big Buck is a Rabbit."

▼ TRY IT YOURSELF

Showing Your Own Videos on Google TV

Using the `dataprovider.js` and Listings 3.4 and 3.5 as models, create a page with a list of
your own videos. You will need to do the following:

1. Download and install Template 2 as described.

2. Create a list of videos URLs and related information.

3. Create a new `dataprovider.js` file with information about your videos.

Retrieving Videos Using AJAX

We have successfully modified the Google TV template to display the videos we have selected. We did this by modifying the `dataprovider.js` JavaScript file. This provides an easy way to list our own video files.

There are several other ways to serve videos using `dataprovider.js`. For services that offer a JavaScript API, we could call JavaScript, receive a list of videos, and modify that list to match the required format. Another is to use the Facebook JavaScript SDK to retrieve a list of your own videos.

It is also common to have a server-side program that feeds data to the client. That is, `dataprovider.js` will make an AJAX call to retrieve the data from the server. The server is responsible for formatting the data properly.

The Google TV Library is built using the jQuery JavaScript Library. Calling AJAX using jQuery is straightforward.

To use jQuery to retrieve data from the server, use the command:

```
jQuery.getJSON()
```

To fully implement an Ajax solution, your server would provide JSON content in the JSON format that is expected by `dataprovider.js`.

Summary

In this hour, we examined a Google TV optimized HTML template in detail. By understanding the data source of the videos, we were able to change the list of videos displayed and to add our own descriptions. These templates serve as a basis for creating our own HTML pages that are optimized for Google TV. The design of the templates display advanced features like custom buttons, overlays for navigation, and navigational controls that fade in and fade out.

Q&A

Q. **Google provides optimized HTML templates to encourage Google TV development. Does Google require that these templates be used or restrict how they are used?**

A. Google does not require any specific templates to be used, but it does include a Terms of Service agreement for use of the templates.

Q. **Is modifying the JavaScript** `dataprovider.js` **file the only way to change the list of videos displayed?**

A. Modifying this file is one way to change the list of videos, but the `dataprovider.js` file can use AJAX to get a list of videos from a server. In that case, the server controls the video list.

Q. **In the two optimized templates, what is the only common JavaScript file?**

A. The two templates display the same list of videos in different ways. The data for the templates is the same, so the `dataprovider.js` file is the same for both.

Workshop

Quiz

1. Optimized HTML templates use HTML, JavaScript, and what else?

2. Which of the following is not a feature of the templates?

    a. Playing videos in full screen

    b. Swiping from video to video

    c. Navigational controls that fade out

3. What is the main difference between the two templates?

Answers

1. The templates use Cascading Style Sheets (CSS).

2. The correct answer is b. There is no capability to mouse or swipe between videos. There is a Next button.

3. The difference between the two templates is in the navigation. Template 1 lists categories on one page and displays videos on a second page. Template 2 does this all in one page.

Exercises

1. If you are very familiar with Facebook or other another JavaScript API that provides a list of videos, use that API to populate the optimized template for Google TV.

2. If you are familiar with server-side coding in PHP or another language, use AJAX and server code to populate the template.

3. Find the specific URLs of some online videos and modify `dataprovider.js` to play these videos with titles and descriptions that you provide.

HTML5 and jQuery UI Library for Google TV

What You'll Learn in This Hour:

▶ What features are included in the video tag
▶ How to control the video
▶ How to add styles to video controls
▶ How to use jQuery Google TV Library Controls

In Hour 3, "Using Google's Video Templates," we examined the optimized HTML5 templates provided by Google. In this hour, we'll dive deeper into the advanced use of the HTML5 <video> tag and cover the jQuery Google TV UI Library. The library creates controls, handles complex navigation, and provides a structure for creating complex web pages optimized for TV.

Video Properties and Controls

We'll take an incremental approach to adding features to standard HTML5 video control. The first step is to understand the properties that are available us.

In Hour 2, "Optimizing Web Pages for Google TV," we created a simple HTML5 video tag. We used JavaScript to implement Play and Pause, and we supported the used of the remote control by mapping the Play and Pause keys to a function in our app.

There are other functions we can perform using a video tag. We can set the volume of a video, mute it, set the speed of video play, and get and set the current time of the video.

At the end of Hour 2, we created a simple video control with a single button for playing and pausing a video. As we examine the optimized HTML5 templates, we see a more advanced and appealing user interface and additional buttons for fast-forward and rewind. The HTML5 video control is the foundation in both cases.

The HTML5 video tag is an instance of an HTML5MediaElement. HTML5MediaElement interface has properties and methods specific to handling media:

▶ **Poster**—Poster is used to display an image while the video downloads or until the user chooses Play.

▶ **Loop**—When loop is true, the video will repeat.

▶ **Muted**—A video can be muted or unmuted.

▶ **Volume**—Volume represents the audio volume and can have a value of 0.0 for silence to 1.0 for loudest.

▶ **CurrentTime**—CurrentTime represents the current position of the video. Resetting CurrentTime to a new value moves the video to the indicated location. For example, given a video tag called myVideo, myVideo.currentTime+=10; will skip 10 seconds forward from the current location. CurrentTime can also be used to skip back in the video or to jump to a specific location.

▶ **PlaybackRate**—PlaybackRate represents how fast a video will be played. The normal playback rate will be multiplied by this value, so a PlaybackRate of 1.0 indicates normal speed and a PlaybackRate of 2.0 indicates double speed. This can be used for implementing fast-forward and slow motion.

▶ **Controls**—When present and set to true, the control property indicates that the video controls will be provided by the browser. This will typically include pause, progress bar, and volume controls.

Adding Video Controls

Listing 4.1 defines a video tag with attributes for autoplay and poster set. As shown in Figure 4.1, a series of buttons are defined to act on the video by using JavaScript and setting the HTML5MediaElement properties. The JavaScript variable, myVideo, is associated with the video tag. The onClick events of the buttons call JavaScript functions or directly manipulate the myVideo variable.

The functions mute and playPause each check the current state of the video and switch to the alternate state. That is, if the video is paused, it begins playing. If the video is muted, it is unmuted. All other buttons directly act on the video.

LISTING 4.1 Interacting with Video

```
1:   <!DOCTYPE html>
2:   <html>
3:   <body>
4:   <button onclick="playPause()">Play/Pause</button>
5:   <button onclick="myVideo.currentTime+=10">Skip Ahead</button>
6:   <button onclick="myVideo.currentTime-=10">Skip Back</button>
8:   <button onclick="myVideo.currentTime=50">Jump to</button>
8:   <br>
9:   <button onclick="myVideo.playbackRate++">Speed up</button>
10:  <button onclick="myVideo.playbackRate--">Slow Down--</button>
11:  <button onclick="myVideo.volume+=1">Volume up</button>
12:  <button onclick="myVideo.volume-=1">Volume Down</button>
13:  <button onclick="mute()">Mute On/Off</button>
14:  <video id="video1" controls="controls" autoplay="autoplay"
15:      poster="http://www.bffmedia.com/poster.png" height="648"
16:      src="http://www.bffmedia.com/trailer_1080p.ogg" > />
17:  </video>
18:  <script type="text/javascript">
19:  var myVideo=document.getElementById("video1");
20:  function playPause()
21:  {
22:  if (myVideo.paused)
23:    myVideo.play();
24:  else
25:    myVideo.pause();
26:  }
27:
28:  function mute()
29:  {
30:   if (myVideo.muted)
31:     myVideo.muted = false;
32:   else
33:     myVideo.muted=true;
34:  }
35:  window.onload = function() {
36:      document.onkeydown=function(e){
37:      if (!e) e=window.event;
38:      switch(e.keyCode) {
39:        case 179:
40:          playPause();
41:          break;
42:      }
43:    }
44:  }
45:  </script>
46:  </body>
47:  </html>
```

FIGURE 4.1
Video tag with basic controls.

Implementing Fast Forward and Rewind

By increasing the value of `playBackrate`, we can make the video play faster. That is a good approach for implementing fast-forward.

Implementing rewind will take a bit more work. The idea is to set the value of `currentTime` for the video back when rewind is selected. Remember that `currentTime` represents the current position of the video. If 10 seconds of the video have played, the `currentTime` will be 10.

For our purpose, we will rewind 1/10th of a second when the rewind function is called. We'll call rewind multiple times. When the video gets to the beginning, we will make it pause. While rewinding, we can hit the Play/Pause button to stop rewinding. The code for rewind is shown in Listing 4.2.

LISTING 4.2   Implementing Rewind

```
1:    /**
2:    var timer;
3:
4:    function playPause()
5:    {
6:        clearTimeout(timer);
7:        myVideo.playbackRate=1.0;
8:        if (myVideo.paused)
```

```
9:          myVideo.play();
10:        else
11:          myVideo.pause();
12:    }
13:
14:    function rewind(){
15:        myVideo.currentTime-=1
16:        if (myVideo.currentTime>0){
17:                clearTimeout(timer);
18:                timer = setTimeout("rewind()", 100);
19:        }else{
20:                clearTimeout(timer);
21:                myVideo.pause();
22:        }
23:    }
```

The key to implementing rewind is to call the rewind function repeatedly. In Listing 4.2 on line 18, the JavaScript function `setTimeOut` is used to call the function `rewind` 100 milliseconds from the current time. Because we are decreasing the `currentTime` of the video by 1 second on line 15, this has the effect of rewinding the video 10 seconds for every second that passes.

If the video is completely rewound or the user presses Play or Pause, the `timer` created on line 18 is cleared by calling `clearTimeout`. Because rewind calls itself recursively at a regular interval, we have implemented a repeating call that moves the video back by 1 second. This implementation also allows other events to fire.

Adding Our Own Progress Bar

HTML5 introduces a new visual element called `range` that shows a range of values. Users have the ability to move a slider from left to right to set the value. This might commonly be called a slider, a progress bar, or a seek bar. We will use this control to display the progress of our video and to give the user the ability to jump to certain points in the video by moving the slider.

Up until this point, our video tag declaration has included the controls attribute:

```
<video id="video1" controls="controls" ...
```

By including controls, we are indicating that the browser should provide a progress bar and a volume control. In this section, we will omit the `controls` attribute and create our own simple progress bar by creating a `range` element in the HTML as follows:

```
<input type="range" step="any" id="progressbar">
```

In Listing 4.3, we create a variable called `progressBar` in line 3 to refer to the `progressbar` element created in the HTML. Listing 4.3 ties the progress bar to the video duration.

LISTING 4.3 Progress Bar

```
1:    var setup=false;
2:
3:    var progressBar = document.getElementById('progressbar');
4:    function initProgress() {
5:       if (!setup){
6:          progressBar.min = 0;
7:          progressBar.max = myVideo.duration;
8:          setup=true;
9:       }
10:
11:   progressBar.onchange = resetProgress;
12:   function resetProgress() {
13:      myVideo.currentTime = progressBar.value;
14:   }
15:
16:   function updateProgress() {
17:       progressBar.value = myVideo.currentTime;
18:   }
19:
20:   myVideo.addEventListener('durationchange', initProgress);
21:   myVideo.addEventListener('timeupdate', updateProgress);
```

To set the maximum value for the progress bar, we need to know how long the video is. We can get that by looking at the duration of the video. The problem is that we do not immediately have the video duration. The video must be downloaded before the duration is available to use. We get around this by setting an event listener that checks when the duration changes. See line 20 of Listing 4.3. When that happens, we call function initProgress to set the values.

Similarly, we use an event listener called timeupdate to get the time changes in the video and update the progress bar. The last piece of business is reading the seekbar status and moving to the proper point in the video. The video is updated in the resetProgress function. The resetProgress function is called when the progress bar changes.

Adding Some Style

We have created a functional video player page. It includes a progress bar and play, pause, fast-forward, rewind, and volume controls. The page uses a video tag, buttons, and a range element to accomplish this. We have become accustomed to seeing more than basic form buttons on web pages. We can create a simple style sheet and apply it to these buttons for an improved visual design. The buttons will have color and a border and will change color when the user hovers over them with the mouse. This is shown in Listing 4.4.

LISTING 4.4 Stylesheet for Buttons: video-styles.css

```
1:    body {
2:        background: #f1f1f1;
3:        overflow: hidden;
4:    }
5:
6:    .video-button {
7:        width: 92px;
8:        height: 37px;
9:        margin: 0 6px;
10:       border: 2px solid #454545;
11:       border-radius: 5px 5px / 5px 5px;
12:   }
13:
14:   .video-button:hover {
15:       color: #FFF;
16:       background: #900;
17:   }
18:
19:   .video-seek {
20:       width: 860px;
21:       height: 37px;
21:   }
```

The stylesheet defines a look for `video-button` and for `video-button:hover`. Buttons will appear as gray with black text, as shown in Figure 4.2, but when the button is hovered over with the mouse, the font color turns white and the background is maroon. The button width, height, and shape are set. The range element is styled with the `video-seek` style to give it the proper length and height.

Listing 4.5 shows how the controls are defined on the page and use the classes defined in the stylesheet.

LISTING 4.5 Applying the Style

```
1:    <div>
2:        <button class="video-button" onclick="playPause()">Play Pause</button>
3:        <button class="video-button" onclick="myVideo.currentTime+=10">
4:    Skip Ahead</button>
5:        <button class="video-button" onclick="myVideo.currentTime-=10">Skip Back</
button>
6:        <button class="video-button" onclick="myVideo.playbackRate++">
7:    Fast Forward</button>
8:        <button class="video-button" onclick="rewind()">   Rewind  <<   </
button>
9:        <button class="video-button" onclick="myVideo.volume+=1">Volume +</button>
```

```
10:        <button class="video-button" onclick="myVideo.volume-=1">Volume -</button>
11:        <button class="video-button" onclick="mute()">Mute</button>
12:    </div>
13:    <div>
14:        <input class="video-seek" type="range" step="any" id="progressbar">
15:    </div>
```

FIGURE 4.2
Video tag with simple styles applied.

Using the jQuery GTV UI Library

CAUTION

Beta Library

The jQuery GoogleTV Library is a beta release. Always check the latest project info and source code for updates.

For many websites, HTML5 will provide all the functionality required for a good experience with video and GoogleTV. For sophisticated user interfaces and for developers who already use the jQuery Javascript Library, the Google TV JQuery UI Library is a good choice. The goal of the library is to facilitate the creation of web interfaces for the 10-foot living room experience.

Running a jQuery GTV Web App

The code for the library includes JavaScript, HTML, and CSS files. To get the library and example code, go to http://code.google.com/p/gtv-ui-lib/.

This page contains the library project. It includes API reference links, examples, and the actual jQuery GTV Library. Look for a section on the Google TV jQuery UI Library and navigate to source and examples. To get the most up-to-date library, choose the source tab and download the source and example code. The page includes instructions on using the subversion source control system to get the code. You may also download a zip file of the library.

The download will include the Google TV jQuery Library, the Clojure Library, and several demos and examples. To see the library in action, find the folder on your computer where the code was installed. Choose the `gtv-jquery-demo` folder and open the `index.html` file in a Chrome browser. Though this file is optimized for Google TV, it will work in any Chrome browser.

The example displays a help screen that includes navigation hints on using the app. The app itself includes a table of user interface controls that can be created using the library.

Each control can be highlighted and selected to show an example of a function within the library. Figure 4.3 shows that initial screen.

The controls included in the library are listed next. The library also includes two pages for showing photos and videos. Those are the BuilderPhotoPage and BuilderVideoPage.

- ▶ `RowControl`—Shows a scrolling, horizontal list of items on the page.

- ▶ `SideNavControl`—Shows a menu presenting a list of choices in a horizontal or vertical orientation. Can be statically displayed, can pop-out from a side, or fade in.

- ▶ `SlidingControl`—Shows a paging display of rows of items. Pages of items slide in from the right/left as the user navigates.

- ▶ `PhotoControl`—A photo slideshow display with Play, Pause, Next, and Back buttons. Media keys on the remote control are supported.

- ▶ `VideoControl`—A video playback control with Play, Pause, Next and Back buttons. Supports media keys.

- ▶ `RollerControl`—Shows a multirow "roller" that vertically animates scrolling rows into focus as the user navigates.

- ▶ `RotatorControl`—Shows a single row that rotates in each item from a list into view as the user navigates up/down.

- ▶ `StackControl`—Provides a central display for a single items and "stacks" items to the left and right, rotating in each item as the user navigates left/right through the stack.

- ▶ `BuilderPhotoPage`—Constructs a page with a photo slideshow and a scrolling thumbnail display, given a URL to a JSON-compatible feed of photos.

- ▶ `BuilderVideoPage`—Constructs a page with a YouTube video player and a scrolling thumbnail display, given a URL to a YouTube feed.

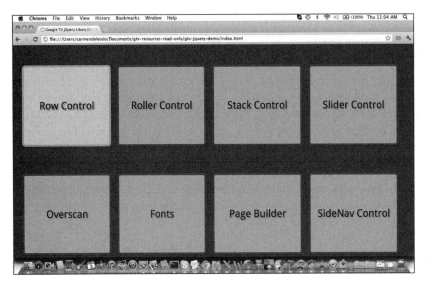

FIGURE 4.3
jQuery GTV UI Demo page.

We'll look at the code for constructing a RowControl with the goal of understanding how controls are created and displayed. Figure 4.4 shows the RowControl from the demo app that we downloaded. We will create a simpler version to illustrate the functionality.

FIGURE 4.4
RowControl jQuery GTV UI demo.

Creating and Showing a RowControl

When any jQuery Google TV control is created, it takes a set of parameters called CreationParams. CreationParms are a JSON object containing the required definition for the control. When a control is displayed, it takes a similar set of parameters called showParams. We'll examine these parameters for a RowControl. That will illustrate the general pattern for using these controls.

Table 4.1 lists the parameters used in CreationParams and their definitions.

ContainerId is the place on the HTML page where the control will be placed. This will typically be a <div> element. We can declare a default keyController to create a control.

A KeyController is part of the Google TV UI Library and defines navigation on the page.

We must create a styles object to tell the controller how to display.

The styles object contains CSS styles associated with each part of the control. We'll examine the specific styles in more detail.

TABLE 4.1 Parameters for CreationParams

Parameter	Type	Required	Definition
containerId	String	Yes	Container where control will be place
keyController	KeyController	Yes	KeyController for this control
styles	Object	Yes	CSS Styles associated with the item in this control
layerNames	String	No	Layer to add control to
choiceCallback	Function	No	Callback function if item is selected

In addition to defining the CreationParams for a control, we must define the ShowParams. Table 4.2 lists the definitions for those parameters.

TABLE 4.2 Parameters for ShowParams

Parameter	Type	Required	Definition
topParent	jQuery.Element	Yes	Parent element on the page that holds the control
contents	gtv.jq.ControlContents	Yes	Contents of the control—for example, a list of images

The `contents` parameter for `ShowParams` can take one of three types. It is always a list of items to be displayed on the control. Whether the `RowControl` displays images, buttons, or something else, the `contents` parameter contains the list of things to be displayed.

The contents parameter may contain an array of `Items`, `CaptionItems`, or a `ContentsArray`. `Items` means any HTML elements like buttons. `CaptionItems` include a caption to be displayed under the item. A `ContentsArray` is an array of `ControlContents`. `ControlContents` provides a way to populate controls that have multiple rows.

Creating a RowControl

A `RowControl` displays items from left to right across the screen. To keep it simple, we will populate the row control with form buttons. For a `RowControl`, we specify styles for the entire row, the item, and the `<div>` that contains the item. We also define a style for what happens when we hover on the item. By choosing different background colors, we can see which style is associated with each element on the page. Listing 4.6 shows the styles defined to be used with the `RowControl`.

LISTING 4.6 Styles for Row Control

```
1:    <link rel="stylesheet" href="../source/css/controls.css" />
2:
3:    <style>
4:    .scroll-row-style {
5:      overflow: hidden;
6:      width: 100%;
7:      background-color: red;
8:       padding: 10px;
9:      position: relative;
10:   }
11:   .scroll-div-style {
12:     margin: 5px;
13:      padding: 10px;
14:     background-color: green;
15:   }
16:   .scroll-items-div-style {
17:   }
18:   .scroll-item-style {
19:     background-color: blue;
20:     border-radius: 10px;
21:     color: #ddd;
22:     padding: 10px;
23:     font-size: 20pt;
24:     border: #58b solid 6px;
```

```
25:   }
26:   .item-hover {
27:     border: yellow solid 6px !important;
28:   }
29:   .scrolling-page {
30:     position: absolute;
31:     width: 95%;
32:   }
33:   </style>
```

To make the distinctions clear, we used red for the row, green from the scroll-div, blue for the item and yellow for hovering. See Figure 4.5.

The JavaScript in Listing 4.7 follows the pattern in the example code of using a makePage function to assemble the page. A keycontroller is created and used with the new control. A container for the control is defined and the CreateParam and ShowParam data is defined as previously described.

LISTING 4.7   JavaScript for Row Control

```
1:  <script type="text/javascript"
2:    src=
3:    "http://ajax.googleapis.com/ajax/libs/jquery/1.4.2/jquery.min.js">
4:  </script>
5:  <script type="text/javascript" src="../source/js/scrollrow.js"></script>
6:  <script type="text/javascript" src="../source/js/gtvcore.js"></script>
7:  <script type="text/javascript">
8:  function makePage(topParent) {
9:    var keyController = new gtv.jq.KeyController();
10:    keyController.start();
11:    var container = $('<div></div>').addClass('scrolling-page');
12:    topParent.append(container);
13:    var numItems = 10;
14:    var itemArray = new Array(numItems);
15:    for (var i = 0; i < numItems; i++) {
16:      itemArray[i] ='<button> button ' + (i+1) +'</button>';
17:
18:    }
19:    var styles = {
20:    row: 'scroll-row-style',
21:    itemsDiv: 'scroll-items-div-style',
22:    itemDiv: 'scroll-div-style',
23:    item: 'scroll-item-style',
24:    hover: 'item-hover'
```

```
25:    };
26:
27:        var createParams = {
28:          containerId: 'row-container',
29:          styles: styles,
30:          keyController: keyController
31:        };
32:        rowControl = new gtv.jq.RowControl(createParams);
33:        var controlParams = {
34:          topParent: container,
35:          contents: {
36:            items: itemArray
37:          }
38:        };
39:        rowControl.showControl(controlParams);
40:
41:        rowControl.enableNavigation();
42:    };
43:    $(document).ready(function() {
44:        makePage($("body"));
45:    });
46:    </script>
```

The important logic in this example populates a list of button items. Ten buttons are defined and put into the variable `itemArray`. Then `itemArray` is used as the items parameter for the variable `controlParams`. The variable `controlParams` is used to call `showControl`:

```
rowControl.showControl(controlParams);
```

Other controls are created similarly. The relationship between the stylesheets used and the definition of the control is important. By starting with the examples from this book or from the Google TV code site, you can experiment with various attributes and combinations. Working through the styles content parameters is very helpful.

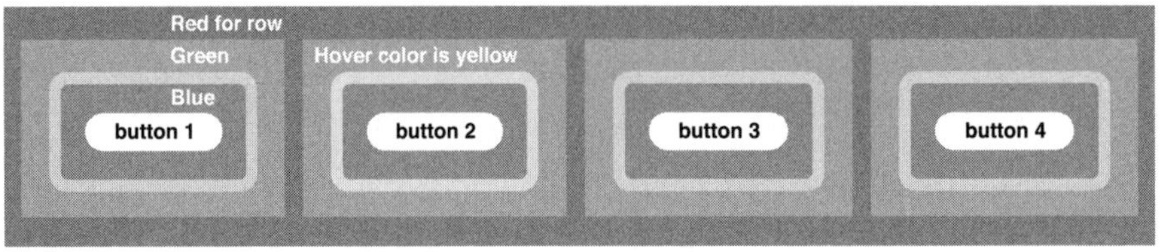

FIGURE 4.5
Row control with red, green, and blue styles.

Summary

In this hour, we examined the HTML5 video tag in detail. To implement our own video controls, we worked with both JavaScript and styles. By doing so, we understood the events and properties associated with the video tag. We examined a `RowControl` from the jQuery GTV UI Library in detail to show how the library creates and uses controls.

Q&A

Q. An attribute of a video tag is the `playBackRate`. The `playBackRate` makes a video go faster and slower. Can it be used to implement rewind?

A. Unfortunately, no. It would be nice to set the `playBackRate` to a negative number to implement rewind.

Q. When we implement a progress bar for a video, what values do we need to know?

A. A progress bar requires a minimum and maximum value. Because we are tracking the time of the video, we need the duration of the video. Each video has a duration property, but it may not be immediately available.

Q. How is `currentTime` used as a video attribute?

A. For a video, `currentTime` represents the current position of the video. If 10 seconds of the video have played, then `currentTime` will be 10. There is a related event called `time-update` that fires whenever the `currentTime` of the video changes. We used it to update the progress bar.

Q. When creating a jQuery GTV UI control, what kinds of parameters are passed?

A. There are `CreateParams` for creating the control and `ControlParams` for showing the video.

Workshop

Quiz

1. Does the video tag support Google TV's remote control?
2. Which of the following is not an attribute of a video tag?
   a. width
   b. autozoom
   c. autoplay
3. What is the alternative to implementing my own progress bar?
4. What language is the jQuery GTV UI Library written in?

Answers

1. The video tag does not directly support the remote control. Remote control support is implemented in JavaScript.

2. The correct answer is b. Autozoom is an attribute of Google TV, not the video tag.

3. The controls attribute in the video tag tells the browser to use native controls for the video. The native control will include a progress bar.

4. JavaScript.

Exercises

1. The code in the hour supports remote control keys for play and pause. Enhance the video code from this hour to support remote control keys for fast-forward, rewind, mute, and volume.

2. Create a set of videos and add Next Video and Previous Video buttons to this code to load in new videos.

HOUR 5
Using the Google TV Closure UI Library

What You'll Learn in This Hour:

▶ What is Closure

▶ How to use Closure in an HTML page

▶ What Google TV components are available for Closure

Hour 4, "HTML5 and jQuery UI Library for Google TV," focused on the jQuery Google TV UI Library. That library used jQuery to provide a set of user interface components that are optimized for Google TV. Closure is another library that uses JavaScript to support Google TV. If you are not already using jQuery, Closure is a very good alternative. In this hour, we'll consider the design considerations that went into Closure, create a simple HTML page using Closure, and dive into the TV components that are supported by Closure.

Using Closure for Google TV Web Apps

The Closure Library is a cross-browser JavaScript Library. It is used in many Google products including Gmail, Maps, Reader, and Google+. The Closure Library works with a set of Closure tools, including a Closure Compiler for optimizing JavaScript and a set of Closure templates. The Closure Library provides low-level utilities like DOM manipulation, AJAX, data structure, UI components, and more.

The Google TV Closure UI Library uses core elements of the Closure Library, but it is *not* the same as the Closure Library. That may be confusing, but we will review the reasons for this and the differences between the two libraries.

The Google TV Closure UI Library does not use Closure Components because the model for focus on PCs is different from TVs, and a different model is required. A browser running on a PC focuses on elements based on tabbing between them. TVs use the D-Pad for changing focus and can move in four directions. That difference is the main reason the Google TV Closure UI Library does not use Closure components directly.

The remainder of this hour focuses on Google TV Closure UI Library. For brevity, we'll refer to the Google TV Closure UI Library as "the library" throughout the rest of the hour.

The library does not provide a standard look, but it is highly flexible and can be used creatively for TV UI designs. One goal of the library is to make it very clear which element on the TV screen has focus. This is important in a TV UI where focus may not always be obvious with standard HTML and CSS.

Figure 5.1 shows a demo web page with some of the UI elements available in the library. It can be viewed at http://tvuidemos.appspot.com.

FIGURE 5.1
Demo web page using the library's UI elements.

The project for the library can be found in the same place as the jQuery Library:

http://code.google.com/p/gtv-ui-lib/

To retrieve the Google TV Closure UI Library code and examples, use this subversion command or download the Closure zip files from the project site:

```
svn checkout http://gtv-ui-lib.googlecode.com/svn/trunk/closure gtv-ui-lib
```

Figure 5.2 shows the folder structure for the Closure portion of the project.

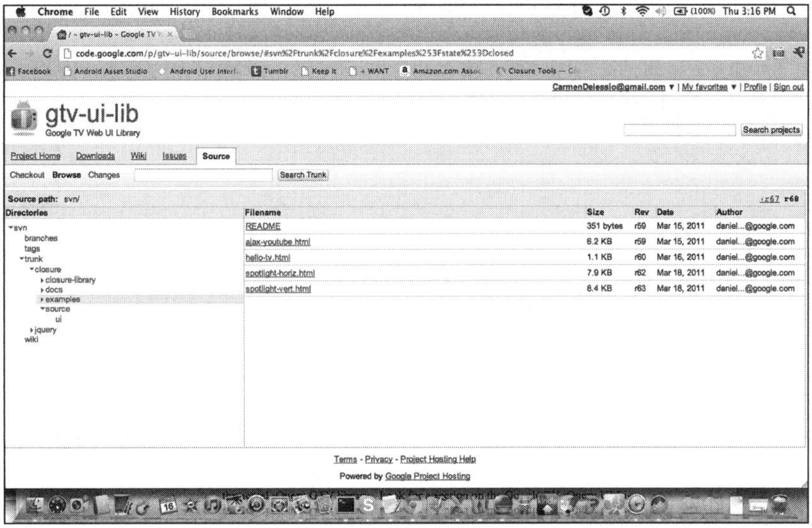

FIGURE 5.2
Google TV Closure UI Library folders.

Using the Library to Create an HTML Page

The downloaded library includes a file called `hello-tv.html` in the examples folder. It is a very simple page that says "Hello World." Initially, the word *Hello* is highlighted. By using arrow keys on a PC or D-Pad keys on a TV, the highlighted word is switched back and forth.

You can see it here:

http://gtv-ui-lib.googlecode.com/svn/trunk/closure/examples/hello-tv.html

Examining the source for this HTML page provides a way to understand the dependencies of using the Closure Library and how component focus works.

Creating a Dependency File

The core library for Closure is a JavaScript file called `base.js`. When building an HTML page with Closure, the `base.js` file must be included. Another file called `deps.js` must also be included. This is the dependency file and it lists the JavaScript files to be added to the project. There is a default `deps.js` file. Other JavaScript files may be added.

To create an HTML page that uses the Google TV UI Library, the JavaScript files for the library must be listed in the `deps.js` file. Closure provides a command line script for creating `deps.js` files. Note that the `hello-tv.html` file in the examples directory includes a working `deps.js` file that has the references to the library. That `deps.js` file can be used directly. The process of creating a new `deps.js` file is covered, but not required for the examples.

This command will create a `tv-deps.js` file:

```
gtv-ui-lib/closure-library/closure/bin/build/depswriter.py \
  --root_with_prefix="gtv-ui-lib/source ../../../../gtv-ui-lib/source" \
  --output_file=tv-deps.js
```

This runs `depswriter.py`. It is a Python script that reads the source directory and creates the `tv-deps.js` file. The script can be run directly on a Mac. Python may need to be installed on a Windows machine to run the script.

To install Python on Windows, download the proper Windows version from http://www.python.org/download/releases/. The Windows downloads are installation files and include clear installation procedures.

To run a Python script on Windows, note that the program name is python and the parameter name is the name of the script. This is the format for running a script called `pytest.py`.

```
python pytest.py
```

The script to run to create the `deps.js` file is `depswriter.py`. The parameters for the script are `root_with_prefix`, which contains the source files to include, and `output`, which contains the file to create.

The `tv-deps.js` file contains references to other JavaScript files and makes them available to Closure. This line makes the `button.js` file available:

```
goog.addDependency('../../../../gtv-ui-lib/source/ui/button.js', ['tv.ui.Button'],
['tv.ui',
'tv.ui.Component']);
```

The HTML

The source for `hello-tv.html` is shown in Listing 5.1. We can consider the source code for the `hello-tv.html` as being divided into four sections:

▶ Declarations—JavaScript declaring all include files and required files.

▶ Styles—HTML defining any CSS styles.

▶ Components—HTML defining the components for the page.

▶ Actions—JavaScript calling the library to act on the components.

LISTING 5.1   Hello-tv.html File Using Google TV Closure UI Library

```
1:  <!DOCTYPE html>
2:  <html>
3:    <head>
4:      <!-- Custom paths to Closure Library and GTV Closure UI Library files -->
5:      <script src='../closure-library/closure/goog/base.js'></script>
6:      <script src='../source/deps.js'></script>
7:      <!-- End custom script includes -->
8:      <script type='text/javascript'>
9:        goog.require('tv.ui');
10:       goog.require('tv.ui.Component');
11:       goog.require('tv.ui.Container');
12:       goog.require('tv.ui.Document');
13:     </script>
14:     <style type='text/css'>
15:       .tv-component.tv-component-focused {
16:         color: #fff;
17:         background-color: #000;
18:       }
19:     </style>
20:   </head>
21:   <body>
22:     <div class='tv-container-horizontal'>
23:       <span class='tv-component' id='hello'>Hello</span>
24:       <span class='tv-component' id='world'>World</span>
25:     </div>
26:     <script type='text/javascript'>
27:       tv.ui.decorate(document.body);
28:       var elementToFocus = goog.dom.getElement('hello');
29:       var componentToFocus = tv.ui.getComponentByElement(elementToFocus);
30:       tv.ui.Document.getInstance().setFocusedComponent(componentToFocus);
31:     </script>
32:   </body>
33: </html>
```

The following list identifies specific lines in the code where the library is included, where styles are defined, and where components are created:

▶ Lines 5 and 6 of Listing 5.1 include the base library and the dependency file in this page. The JavaScript functions in those files are now available for use.

▶ Lines 8 to13 show the required functions from the library.

▶ Lines 14 to 19 define the style for a focused element.

▶ Lines 26 to 31 define two components and indicate what to do when an element has focus.

The page shows the words "Hello World" with `Hello` highlighted. When moving between the words, the highlight is on the focused word. Highlight is defined in the stylesheet named `.tv-component.tv-component-focused`. The two words are defined, are assigned the class `tv-component`, and live in a container of the class `tv-container-horizontal`.

Line 30 indicates how focus should be handled with the function `setFocusedComponent`.

Intuitively, we may understand that the `setFocusedComponent` function will use the style `.tv-component.tv-component-focused`, but we can make the connection directly by looking at the source code.

The JavaScript file `document.js` contains the `setFocusedComponent` function. That function calls the `dispatchFocus_` function of `component.js`. Stepping through `component.js` we find the function `onFocus`, which is shown in Listing 5.2.

LISTING 5.2   The onFocus Function

```
1:   /**
2:    * Handles focus event.
3:    * @param {goog.events.Event} event Focus event.
4:    * @protected
5:    */
6:   tv.ui.Component.prototype.onFocus = function(event) {
7:     // Add focused class to element.
8:     goog.dom.classes.add(this.element_, tv.ui.Component.Class.FOCUSED);
9:     event.stopPropagation();
10:  };
```

Line 8 adds the class `tv.ui.Component.Class.FOCUSED` to the current element. That class is defined as `'tv-component-focused'`. That makes the connection between the style and the setOnFocused function from Listing 5.1.

Buttons, Lightboxes, and Other Components

Listings 5.1 and 5.2 defined two TV components that displayed differently depending on focus. The Google TV Closure UI Library defines components as classes. Listing 5.1 defined a component of class `'tv-component'`. Using styles, components are displayed in different ways. The classes supported in Closure are the following:

▶ Button—`tv-button`. A component that can fire an action.

▶ Component—`tv.ui.component`. A Component that can be focused.

- Link—tv-link. A better-looking link for Google TV.

- Container—tv.ui.Container. A generic Container for content.

- Grid—tv.ui.grid. A grid of information.

- Lightbox—tv.ui.Lightbox. An interface that shows multiple images with one image in focus.

- TabContainer—tv-tab-container. A tabbed interface for showing related content.

Buttons

We will create an example for each class supported in the library. To show how basic actions on a page are handled, we'll start with Buttons.

The goal is to create a simple example that uses Buttons and Closure. When a button is clicked, a message will be displayed. We will need to display the buttons and handle the associated action. The file button-demo.html should be created in the same folder as hello-tv.html. It will use the same base.js and deps.js files.

Listings 5.3–5.7 break button-demo.html down into includes, styles, components, and actions.

LISTING 5.3   Button Includes

```
1:   <!DOCTYPE html>
2:   <html>
3:     <head>
4:       <script src='../closure-library/closure/goog/base.js'></script>
5:       <script src='../source/deps.js'></script>
6:       <script type='text/javascript'>
7:         goog.require('tv.ui');
8:         goog.require('tv.ui.Component');
9:         goog.require('tv.ui.Container');
10:        goog.require('tv.ui.Document');
11:        goog.require('tv.ui.Button');
12:        goog.require('tv.ui.DecorateHandler');
13:      </script>
```

Styles are defined for Button display in normal state and hover state. Styles are also defined for body and for action-output. We will use a div with the style action-output to write a message when a button is pressed. That style is defined in lines 29 to 38 in Listing 5.4.

LISTING 5.4 Button Styles

```
1:  <style>
2:    .button-demos {
3:      margin: 20px auto;
4:      width: 430px;
5:    }
6:    .button-demo {
7:      border: 1px solid white;
8:      display: inline-block;
9:      padding: 1px;
10:     margin: 3px;
11:   }
12:   .button-demo-inner {
13:     color: white;
14:     padding: 2px 6px;
15:     text-decoration: none;
16:   }
17:   .button-demo:hover,
18:   .button-demo.tv-component-focused {
19:     outline: none;
20:     -webkit-box-shadow: 0 0 30px #6391de, 0 0 15px #f2f2f2, 0 0 5px #FFF;
21:   }
22:   .button-demo, .button-demo-inner {
23:     border-radius: 5px;
24:     cursor: pointer;
25:     display: inline-block;
26:     -moz-border-radius: 5px;
27:     -webkit-border-radius: 5px;
28:   }
29:   #button-action-output {
30:     color: red;
31:     font-weight: bold;
32:     margin: 10px auto;
33:     padding: 20px;
34:     text-align: center;
35:     text-shadow: none;
36:     width: 400px;
37:     -webkit-border-radius: 5px;
38:   }
39:   body {
40:     background-color: #000;
41:     background-repeat: no-repeat;
42:     color: #FCFCFC;
43:     font-family: "Droid Sans TV", "Droid Sans", Verdana, sans-serif;
44:     font-size: 18px;
```

```
45:     margin: 0;
46:     overflow: hidden;
47:     padding: 0;
48:     text-shadow: rgba(0, 0, 0, 0.75) 0 -1px 1px;
49:   }
50:   </style>
```

The class `tv-button` defines a Button component. In this case, we put two buttons within a horizontal TV container. The container and buttons are shown in Listing 5.5.

LISTING 5.5 Button Components

```
1:   </head>
2:     <body >
3:       <div class="tv-container-horizontal button-demos">
4:         <div class="tv-button button-demo">
5:           <div class="button-demo-inner">
6:           Button One
7:           </div>
8:         </div>
9:         <div class="tv-button button-demo">
10:          <div class="button-demo-inner">
11:             Button Two
12:          </div>
13:         </div>
14:        <div   id="button-action-output"></div>
```

Listing 5.6 ties the action of clicking a Button to displaying the result onscreen. The function `updateText` in line 3 gets the div named `button-action-output` and updates the `innerHTML` with the passed parameter named `text`.

The variable `decorateHandler` is defined in line 2. It is used to associate the buttons with an action through the use of the function `addClassHandler`. A listener is set up for click events on the buttons. When this happens, the `updateText` function is called.

The function `postponeRender` is used to decorate the document body. The `postponeRender` function runs after the Buttons have been defined and takes into account the `addClassHander` functionality. Running the same JavaScript without the function `postposeRender`, like we did in Listing 5.1 for `hello-tv.html`, will style the buttons correctly, but will not result in any action when they are clicked. Figure 5.3 shows how the page will display.

LISTING 5.6 Button Actions

```
1:  <script type="text/javascript">
2:          var decorateHandler = new tv.ui.DecorateHandler();
3:          function updateText(text) {
4:            var actionOutputEl = goog.dom.getElement('button-action-output');
5:            actionOutputEl.innerHTML = text;
6:          };
7:          decorateHandler.addClassHandler('button-demo', function(button) {
8:            goog.events.listen(button, tv.ui.Button.EventType.ACTION, function(e) {
9:              updateText('You clicked ' + e.target.getElement().innerText);
10:           });
11:         });
12:         tv.ui.postponeRender(function() {
13:           tv.ui.decorate(document.body, decorateHandler.getHandler());
14:         });
15:     </script>
16:   </body>
17: </html
```

FIGURE 5.3
Button example.

Components

A Component is the basic element of the library that we saw in the `hello-tv.html` example. Components can be set to display differently when they receive focus by setting different styles.

Listing 5.7 shows the Style definitions for four components. Listing 5.8 shows how those components are defined in the body of the HTML page. The code in these listings does not show the JavaScript includes or function calls. To render the components, a `tv.ui.DecorateHandler` must be used and the `postponeRender` function must be called, as it is in Listing 5.6.

LISTING 5.7   Defining Component Styles

```
 1:   .component-demo {
 2:      border: 1px solid white;
 3:      padding: 5px;
 4:      margin: 20px;
 5:      -webkit-border-radius: 5px;
 6:   }
 7:   .different-size {
 8:      height: 50px;
 9:      width: 200px;
10:      margin: 0 auto;
11:   }
12:   .component-demo.tv-component-focused {
13:      background-color: rgba(255, 255, 255, 0.3);
14:   }
15:   .different-highlight.tv-component-focused {
16:      background: none;
17:      -webkit-box-shadow: 0 0 20px #6391de, 0 0 7px #f2f2f2, 0 0 2px #FFF;
18:   }
19:   .different-zoom {
20:      margin: 0 auto;
21:      text-align: center;
22:      width: 200px;
23:   }
24:   .different-zoom.tv-component-focused {
25:      zoom: 2;
26:      -webkit-transition: all 1s ease;
27:   }
```

The styles are used in Listing 5.8 on the HTML page. Figure 5.4 shows the resulting page.

LISTING 5.8   Using Component Styles

```
1:   <div class="tv-container-vertical">
2:   <div class="tv-component component-demo">
3:   <p>Use any HTML here, like text or an image:</p>
4:    <img src="http://www.google.com/tv/static/images/logo_146x38.png"/>
5:   </div>
6:   <div class="tv-component component-demo different-size">Different sizes.</div>
7:   <div class="tv-component component-demo different-highlight">And different
8:   highlight.
9:   </div>
10:  <div class="tv-component component-demo different-highlight different-zoom">
11:    Zoom it
12:  </div>
13:  </div>
```

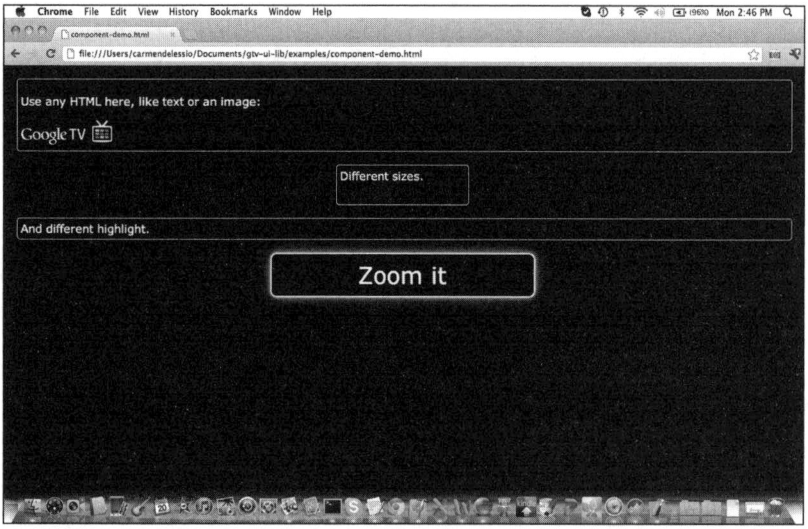

FIGURE 5.4
Component example.

Containers

We have used Containers in all our examples so far. Containers exist to hold other components, and they influence how those components are laid out. We have used horizontal and vertical containers as holders for other components. Containers can help with page layout and organization.

The button example in Listing 5.5 used a horizontal container on line 3:

```
<div class="tv-container-horizontal button-demos">
```

The component example used a vertical container on line 1 of Listing 5.8:

```
<div class="tv-container-vertical">
```

Links

Traditional links have default behaviors that may not be optimal for Google TV. With a traditional link, the destination of the link is shown in the browser when the link is rolled over. The color of the link changes to the browser default setting for focused links. For those reasons, and to provide the capability of adding styles to links, the library includes a `tv-link` class. This `div` provides a link to Google:

```
<div class="tv-link" href="http://www.google.com">Google</div>
```

Grids

Grids display content in a series of rows and columns.

The style for each row and for each item in the grid is defined. In the case of Listing 5.9, there is a `photo-grid-row` and a `photo` style. The styles in Listing 5.9 and components in Listing 5.10 are combined to show a grid with four photos on the page.

LISTING 5.9   Grid Styles

```
1:   tv-grid {
2:     height: 580px;
3:   }
4:   .photo-grid {
5:     overflow: hidden;
6:     margin: 10px;
7:   }
8:   .photo-grid .photo-grid-row {
9:     display: block;
10:    white-space: nowrap;
11:  }
12:  .photo-grid .photo {
13:    border: 1px solid #626262;
14:    cursor: pointer;
15:    display: inline-block;
16:    height: 133px;
17:    margin: 7px;
18:    overflow: hidden;
19:    width: 200px;
```

```
20:    box-shadow: 0 0 10px #000;
21:    vertical-align: top;
22:    -webkit-box-shadow: 0 0 10px #000;
23: }
24: .photo-grid .photo:hover,
25: .photo-grid .photo.tv-component-focused {
26:    -webkit-box-shadow: 0 0 30px #6391de, 0 0 15px #f2f2f2, 0 0 5px #FFF;
27: }
28: .photo img {
29:    width: 200px;
30: }
31: .photo.portrait img {
32:    margin-top: -60px;
33: }
```

As you can see in Figure 5.5, we use two unique photos and repeat them to show the grid of four images.

FIGURE 5.5
Grid example.

LISTING 5.10 Grid Components

```
 1:  <div class="tv-grid photo-grid tv-container-vertical">
 2:      <div class="tv-container-horizontal photo-grid-row">
 3:        <div class="tv-button photo portrait">
 4:  <img src="http://www.bffmedia.com/bffphotopic.png"></div>
 5:        <div class="tv-button photo landscape">
 6:  <img src="http://www.bffmedia.com/delessio_family_pool_1080.jpg"></div>
 7:      </div>
 8:      <div class="tv-container-horizontal photo-grid-row">
 9:        <div class="tv-button photo landscape">
10:  <img src="http://www.bffmedia.com/delessio_family_pool_1080.jpg"></div>
11:        <div class="tv-button photo portrait">
12:  <img src="http://www.bffmedia.com/bffphotopic.png"></div>
13:      </div>
14:  </div>
```

Lightboxes

A Lightbox shows a series of photos that "pop" into focus. This is done with a combination of CSS stylesheets and JavaScript. There is a required set of classes that is included in a file named `lightbox.css`. That file can be found in the downloaded classes for the library. It is included in the file using:

```
<link rel="stylesheet" href="lightbox.css" type="text/css"/>
```

The reference to the Lightbox tv component is required:

```
goog.require('tv.ui.Lightbox');
```

By adding additional styles for scrolling and a smooth transition, the effect of the photos sliding into view is achieved. Listing 5.11 shows the Lightbox Style definition and Listing 5.12 uses those definitions on the page.

LISTING 5.11 Lightbox Style Components

```
 1:  .tv-lightbox-background {
 2:    opacity: 0.9;
 3:  }
 4:  .tv-lightbox .tv-container-start-scroll,
 5:  .tv-lightbox .tv-component img {
 6:    -webkit-transition: all 1s ease;
 7:  }
 8:  .tv-lightbox .tv-component.tv-container-selected-child img {
 9:    -webkit-transform: scale(1);
10:  }
```

The JavaScript for the Lightbox demo defines an array of photos. The photos are Strings that correspond to URLs of photos. A call to the `Lightbox.show` function takes the array and a starting index as parameters. It displays the photos.

LISTING 5.12 **Showing the Lightbox Using JavaScript**

```
1:   <script type="text/javascript">
2:        var decorateHandler = new tv.ui.DecorateHandler();
1:        var photos = [
3:          'http://www.bffmedia.com/bffphotoalbums.png',
4:          'http://www.bffmedia.com/bffphotopic.png',
5:          'http://www.bffmedia.com/bffphotoaviary1.png',
6:          'http://www.bffmedia.com/bffphotoaviary2.png'
7:        ];
8:        tv.ui.Lightbox.show(photos, 0 );
9:        tv.ui.postponeRender(function() {
10:           tv.ui.decorate(document.body, decorateHandler.getHandler());
11:        });
12:   </script>
```

Figure 5.6 shows a Lightbox example. The photo on the left fades out as the one on the right is displayed.

FIGURE 5.6
Lightbox example.

TabContainers

A TabContainer shows a top row of tabs and their associated content. By clicking the tab, the content for that tab is shown, and the tab itself is highlighted. A TabContainer is an easy and convenient way to show related content.

Listings 5.13 and 5.14 show the HTML code that defines tabs and the related tab content.

In Listing 5.13, tabs are defined to display Info, Image, and Video. Line 2 includes the class tv-tab-container-bar.

LISTING 5.13 TabContainer HTML for Tabs

```
1:  <div class="tv-tab-container tv-container-vertical">
2:    <div class="tv-tab-container-bar tv-container-horizontal demo-tab-bar">
3:      <div class="demo-tab tv-component">Info</div>
4:      <div class="demo-tab tv-component">Image</div>
5:      <div class="demo-tab tv-component">Video</div>
6:  </div>
```

Listing 5.14 contains the associated content. For example, line 3 of Listing 5.14 creates a div with the style tab-demo-content. That div contains the content associated with the Info tab.

LISTING 5.14 TabContainer HTML for Tab Content

```
1:    <div class="tv-tab-container-content tv-tab-container-focus-attractor
2:  tv-container-horizontal demo-tab-content-container">
3:      <div class="tab-demo-content tv-component">Some info about Google TV</div>
4:      <div class="tab-demo-content tv-component">
5:  <img src = "https://developers.google.com/tv/images/remote-logo.png"></div>
6:      <div class="tab-demo-content tv-component">Some video</div>
7:  </div>
8:  </div>
```

Listing 5.15 shows the StyleSheets for the TabContainer, and Figure 5.7 shows the resulting page.

The style sheets for the TabContainer include the size and color of both the tabs and content areas.

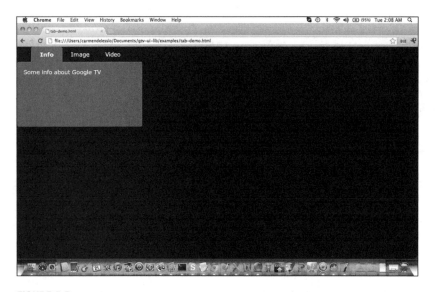

FIGURE 5.7
TabContainer example.

LISTING 5.15   TabContainer Styles

```
 1:    .demo-tab-bar {
 2:    height: 46px;
 3:    text-align: center;
 4:    white-space: nowrap;
 5:    width: 400px;
 6:    }
 7:    .demo-tab {
 8:      display: inline-block;
 9:      line-height: 46px;
10:      text-align: center;
11:      width: 100px;
12:      vertical-align: bottom;
13:      -webkit-border-top-left-radius: 5px;
14:      -webkit-border-top-right-radius: 5px;
15:    }
16:    .demo-tab.tv-container-selected-child {
17:      background-color: #4c6ea7;
18:      font-weight: bold;
19:    }
20:    .demo-tab-content-container {
21:      background: #4c6ea7;
22:      height: 200px;
23:      position: relative;
24:      width: 400px;
```

```
25:    -webkit-border-radius: 5px;
26:  }
27:  .tab-demo-content {
28:    opacity: 0;
29:    padding: 20px;
30:    position: absolute;
31:  }
32:  .tab-demo-content.tv-container-selected-child {
33:    opacity: 1;
34:  }
```

The `TabContainer` component can be extended to implement more complex menu systems. Menu functionality relies on more complex stylesheets being implemented.

Closure supports making AJAX calls with a function called `goog.net.Jsonp`. Complex apps relying on retrieving remote data, parsing it, and displaying it will use `goog.net.Jsonp` and other underlying Closure Library functions.

TRY IT YOURSELF ▼

Adding Your Own Style

The examples in this hour rely on defined styles that are easy to change. Changing styles result in different displays on the resulting HTML pages. Changing colors and sizes on the Grid or Lightbox example will change the display. You can add new photos to the Grid or Lightbox and add a new tab and content area to a TabContainer. Start by adding a new tab and content to a TabContainer.

1. Download and verify the Google TV Closure UI Library. You can do that by opening one of the sample files in a browser.

2. Add a new tab, using Listing 5.13 as a model. You are adding a new `div`.

3. Similarly, add new content for the tab, using Listing 5.14 as a model.

Summary

In this hour, we installed and used the Google TV Closure UI Library. The library makes it easy to focus on and highlight components in a TV web user interface. Basic components include Button and Links. Sophisticated components include Grids, Lightboxes, and TabContainers. The Google TV Closure UI Library uses JavaScript, Closure, and stylesheets to create and use these components. The UI components in the library were specifically created for Google TV. Sophisticated and interactive user interfaces can be created from the components.

Q&A

Q. What is the purpose of `base.js`?

A. The JavaScript file named `base.js` contains the core library for Closure. This file is included on any page that will use the Google TV Closure UI Library. A file called `deps.js` is also included. The `deps.js` file contains references to other required files for the library.

Q. How are Lightboxes and Grids similar?

A. Both Lightbox and Grid components are used to organize and display other content. Both are excellent for displaying photos. TabContainers also organize and display content.

Q. Is the Closure Google TV UI Library the same as the Google Closure Library?

A. No, but the Google TV UI Library is built on Closure. Closure components are optimized for viewing in a browser on a computer, and the model for focusing on components is different between a TV and a computer. The Google TV Closure UI Library does not dictate a look and feel. The look is customized using stylesheets.

Workshop

Quiz

1. What is the purpose of the `deps.js` file?

2. In the JavaScript for a Lightbox, what is being passed to the `show` function?

```
tv.ui.Lightbox.show(photos, 0 );
```

3. What does the function `postponeRender` do?

Answers

1. The `deps.js` file includes references to the Google TV Closure UI Library files. The `deps.js` file is included in any page we created using the library.

2. An array of photo URLs and a starting index is passed.

3. The function `postponeRender` will be called after the page has displayed. Calling decorate in this function will account for dynamic elements like `addClassHandlers`.

Exercises

1. Open the `hello-tv.html` file in a browser. That will assure that you have properly downloaded and installed the library.

2. Create a new `TabContainer` with titles One, Two, and Three and associated content 1,2,3. For a bigger challenge, put a Lightbox or Grid in the content area for a TabContainer.

HOUR 6
Creating a Video Sitemap

What You'll Learn in This Hour:

▶ How the search feature works for movies and TV shows on Google TV
▶ How to include sitemaps using Google Webmaster tools
▶ What elements are available in a Video Sitemap
▶ How to utilize tags in a Video Sitemap

Videos included in websites can be made more discoverable by Google Search through the use of a Video Sitemap. This is particularly important for Google TV. In Google TV, the Quick Search bar and the TV & Movies app both return video results. In this hour, we will consider how these apps work and how a Video Sitemap is used to surface videos on Google TV.

Searching on Google TV

The navigation bar on Google TV includes a search option. Entering the title of a movie or TV show into the search field reveals several apps that direct the viewer to the video or information about the video. For example, a search for "Moneyball" in the search app provides the results shown in Figure 6.1.

The first option takes the user to the TV & Movies app. In that app, the user finds additional information about the movie and has the option to rent it. All the items in Figure 6.1 are search results based on the entered term. The results are broken out by app. In addition to the TV & Movies app, the user can view all results, see web results from Google.com, view the results on Wikipedia in the Chrome browser, or view the results on YouTube.

Google has processes to discover and index videos that make these search results possible. These indexing and searching processes are a core function of Google technology. When you post a YouTube video or add content to your site, it is found and indexed by Google and will show up in normal search results. That is, these videos will show up when you use the google.com site in a web browser and when you use the Quick Search bar app on phones and TVs.

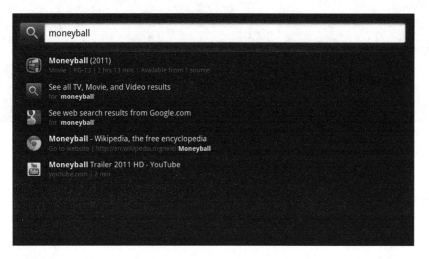

FIGURE 6.1
Search results from the Google TV navigation bar.

Google TV must handle online content and broadcast content. Google can programmatically search and index online content. Additional curation is done to include indexed video data and broadcast data in the TV & Movies app. Adding additional metadata to videos via a Video Sitemap facilitates this process.

Sitemaps and Google Webmaster Tools

Search engines crawl websites, which means they follow links from one site to another to locate relevant data and create a search index. A sitemap facilitates the indexing of a site to help search engines crawl the site more effectively and intelligently. The sitemap consists of an XML document that provides all the URLs and metadata for the site. It is basically a list of all the pages on a site. The sitemaps protocol is defined at http://www.sitemaps.org. Listing 6.1 shows a simple sitemap with a single URL.

LISTING 6.1   Basic Web Sitemap for a Single URL

```
1:   <?xml version="1.0" encoding="UTF-8"?>
2:   <urlset xmlns="http://www.sitemaps.org/schemas/sitemap/0.9">
3:      <url>
4:         <loc>http://www.bffmedia.com/</loc>
5:         <lastmod>2012-01-01</lastmod>
6:         <changefreq>monthly</changefreq>
7:         <priority>0.8</priority>
8:      </url>
9:   </urlset>
```

The <loc>, <lastmod>, and <changefreq> elements are for the URL location, last modified data, and change frequency, respectively. Their values are self-explanatory. The element <priority> indicates the relative value you put on the pages. It may range from 0.0 to 1.0. The default priority is 0.5.

Google Webmaster Tools is a site that provides many features for webmasters to monitor site health and to optimize site performance. It includes the capability to submit sitemaps to Google. Google Webmaster Tools is accessed using a Google account. The URL for Google Webmasters Tools is http://www.google.com/webmasters/tools/. After a sitemap is created, it should be submitted to Google via this Webmaster Tools site. Figure 6.2 shows the Sitemaps section of Google Webmasters Tools.

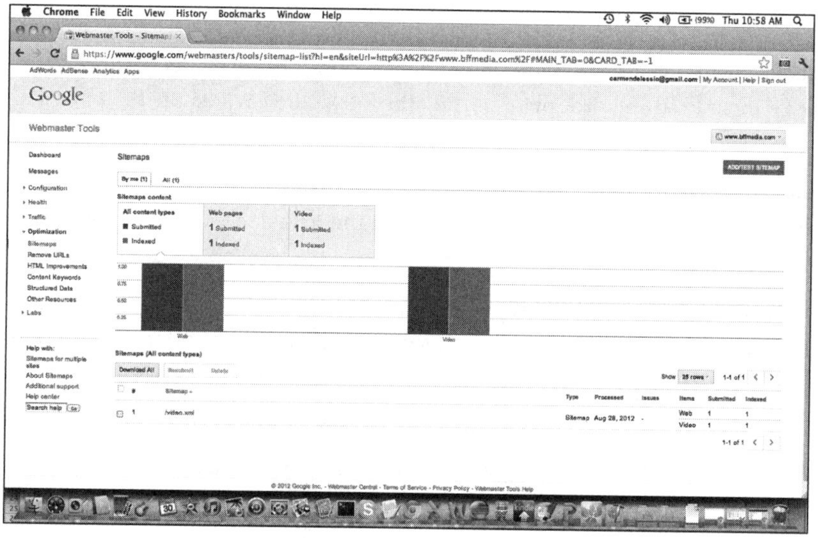

FIGURE 6.2
Sitemap section of Google Webmaster Tools.

Adding Details to Video Sitemaps

Listing 6.1 showed a web sitemap that includes a single URL. A Video Sitemap is a specialized sitemap that includes additional metadata for videos. We will examine the elements of a Video Sitemap and then identify the elements that are particularly important for Google TV.

In the same way that a sitemap lists the URLs for a site, a Video Sitemap lists the videos that are available. Videos listed are indexed by Google and shown in Google.com and Google TV search results. That has the potential to drive more traffic to your site. In addition, the details in a Video Sitemap provide hints for better display of the content. For example, when using a Video Sitemap, you get to choose the thumbnail displayed in the search results.

Each video in the Video Sitemap must include the following:

▶ Title—`<video:title>`

▶ Description—`<video:description>`

▶ Page URL where video plays—`<loc>`

▶ Thumbnail URL—`<video:thumbnail_loc>`

▶ Video file location and/or the player URL—`<video:content_loc>` or `<video:player_loc>`

These are the required elements. There are many optional elements. The elements that are important to Google TV include `video_id`, `price`, and others that are covered further in this hour.

The video file location can be set up to handle embedded videos like those from YouTube or other video sites. The element `<video:content_loc>` will contain the actual video file to play. The element `<video:player_loc>` will contain the player and URL information for a *specific* video.

This is a link to a video on YouTube: http://www.youtube.com/watch?v=NGc7gW-jcVA. It plays a video on the YouTube site. It is possible to identify the specific video file we would need to add to a site map

By choosing `Share` and then `Embed` on YouTube, the following embed code is shown:

```
<iframe width="420" height="315" src="http://www.youtube.com/embed/NGc7gW-
jcVA" frameborder="0" allowfullscreen></iframe>
```

YouTube produces an `iframe` that can be embedded in any HTML page. The Video Sitemap can use the `src` field as the content location for the video. Listing 6.2 shows a complete Video Sitemap for a YouTube video.

In Listing 6.2, the following values are used for the required video sitemap elements:

▶ Title—Line 9–Kindle Fire Demo

▶ Description—Line 10–BFFPhoto App on Kindle Fire

▶ Page URL where video plays—Line 4—http://www.bffmedia.com

▶ Thumbnail URL—Line 7—http://i3.ytimg.com/vi/NGc7gW-jcVA/1.jpg

▶ Video file location and/or the player URL—Line 12—http://www.youtube.com/embed/NGc7gW-jcVA

LISTING 6.2   Video Sitemap with Required Elements

```
1:   <urlset xmlns="http://www.sitemaps.org/schemas/sitemap/0.9"
2:           xmlns:video="http://www.google.com/schemas/sitemap-video/1.1">
3:     <url>
4:       <loc>http://www.bffmedia.com</loc>
5:       <video:video>
6:         <video:thumbnail_loc>
7:         http://i3.ytimg.com/vi/NGc7gW-jcVA/1.jpg
8:         </video:thumbnail_loc>
9:         <video:title>Kindle Fire Demo</video:title>
10:         <video:description>BFFPhoto App on Kindle Fire</video:description>
11:         <video:content_loc>
12:             http://www.youtube.com/embed/NGc7gW-jcVA
13:         </video:content_loc>
14:     </video:video>
15:       </url>
16:   </urlset>
```

Tags That Provide Additional Info on Google TV

The Video Sitemap protocol uses various tags that Google TV takes advantage of to provide additional information to users searching for content. Among them are tags that indicate a video's ID, price, and restrictions, and other tags that locate specific episodes and live video.

Video ID

A goal of Google TV is to show content when and where it is available. A movie may be available on Netflix, Amazon Instant Videos, Google Play, and via broadcast on HBO. To assure that all these sites refer to precisely the same movie, the video ID attribute is used. The video ID attribute is highly recommended for use in Video Sitemaps and for Google TV.

The video ID attribute content comes from one of three independent sources: TMS (Tribune Media Service), Rovi, and Freebase. Tribune Media Service and Rovi are commercial providers of TV and movie data. Freebase is an open database.

This tag is particularly important if you are working with broadcast network or cable content. It is also important if you are creating an original web series. It is unlikely that an individual will be using TMS or Rovi. If these are services your company uses, you should take advantage of that when creating your Video Sitemaps.

More than one video ID attribute may be used in a Video Sitemap. If your content is listed in TMS or Rovi, you can use both those IDs. It is possible to add new content to Freebase at http://www.freebase.com. That might be appropriate for a new web series, for example.

When using video ID, a `type` is specified. The `type` will indicate the ID provider and whether the ID refers to a `series` or a `program`. Types include `tms:series`, `tms:program`, `rovi:series`, `rovi:program`, and `freebase`.

These are examples of `<video:id>` tags that use Tribune Media Service codes. The first is for a program and the second is for a series.

```
<video:id type="tms:program">EP000000060001</video:id>
<video:id type="tms:series">00000006</video:id>
```

Price

When we searched for "Moneyball," a number of options were returned, including a search result that read, "Available from one source." Choosing that option would lead us to details about the movie on the TV & Movies app. The app includes a button to rent the movie. If the Rent button is selected, the user is given the option to rent from Amazon Videos. Figure 6.3 shows this.

Two attributes are used to provide this information in the Video Sitemap. The attributes are `price` and `requires_subscription`. Additional data is provided in the `price` attribute. The `price` attribute will specify a `currency` and a `resolution` so we can know what the video price is in U.S. dollars and that the video will play in HD. The `type` value for `price` is either `purchase` or `rent`.

The attribute `requires_subscription` has a value of `yes` or `no`, depending on whether a subscription is required to watch the video. A subscription may be required, regardless of whether a video is free. Listing 6.3 shows these variations.

LISTING 6.3 Price and Subscription Options

```
1:    <video:price currency="USD" type="rent" resolution="hd">5.99</video:price>
2:    <video:price currency="USD" type="rent" resolution="sd">3.99</video:price>
3:    <video:price currency="USD" type="purchase" resolution="hd">11.99</video:price>
4:    <video:price currency="USD" type="purchase" resolution="sd">8.99</video:price>
5:    <video: requires_subscription>no</video:price>
```

FIGURE 6.3
Rent a video user interface on Google TV.

Restrictions

Restrictions in a Video Sitemap prevent the video from showing up in search results. Restrictions can be placed on countries and platforms. A video is either allowed or denied. For countries, the two-letter ISO codes are used. The platforms that can be specified are tv, web, and mobile.

You may decide that a particular video that is optimized for computer or TV viewing is not well suited for playing on a mobile device. That would be one reason to restrict the content. If you have created language-specific versions of a video, you may want to restrict content by country.

To restrict results, the values allow and deny are used on the relationship field. The following snippet allows the video to show up in results in Great Britain, the United States, and Canada. The video is restricted from showing up in results on mobile devices.

```
<video:restriction relationship="allow"> GB US CA</video:restriction>
<video:platform relationship="deny">mobile</video:platform>
```

Episodes

Episode tags generally refer to TV content. We all know some people who can name specific episodes of *Star Trek*, *The Big Bang Theory*, or other shows, and who would benefit from searching by episode name. Episodic content can apply to a web series, too.

Episode tags have three required attributes:

▸ `video:tvshow`—Information about a single episode.

▸ `video:show_title`—The title of the TV show (not the episode title).

▸ `video:video_type`—The type of video. The allowed values for type are `full`, `preview`, `clip`, `interview`, `news`, and `other`.

Optional attributes are the following:

▸ Episode Title `<video:episode_title>`—The title of the episode.

▸ Season Number `<video:season_number>`—The season number for shows with multiple seasons.

▸ Episode Number `<video:episode_number>`—The episode number in a season. For multiple season shows, each season begins at episode 1.

▸ Premiere Date `<video:premier_date>`—The date the video was first broadcast, in YYYY-MM-DD format.

For example, "The Trouble with Tribbles" is the title of episode 15 in season 2 of *Star Trek*. The broadcast date for "The Trouble with Tribbles" was 1967-12-29.

Listing 6.4 shows what this looks like in a Video Sitemap.

LISTING 6.4   Indicating Episodes in a Video Sitemap

```
1:  < <video:tvshow>
2:          <video:show_title>Star Trek</video:show_title>
3:          <video:episode_title>The Trouble with Tribbles</video:episode_title>
4:          <video:season_number>2</video:season_number>
5:          <video:episode_number>15</video:episode_number>
6:          <video:premier_date>: 1967-12-29 </premier_date>
7:  </video:tvshow>
```

Live Streaming

Live content can be indicated in the Video Sitemap. To indicate live content, three attributes must be included. The attributes indicate that the content is live and provides a start and end date. The specific attribute names are `live`, `publication_date`, and `expiration_date`.

Including this sitemap data has two advantages when live streaming shows up in search results. If the content will begin in less than eight hours, the Google search results will include a countdown timer. It will be updated until the event is live, and it reads something like this: "Live video will start in 2 hours and 30 minutes." For events that are already live, the search results will include the word "Watch" before the result.

The following example shows the live tags and dates with time included:

```
<video:live>yes</video:live>
<video:publication_date>2011-04-29T05:00:00-04:00</video:publication_date>
<video:expiration_date>2011-04-29T23:00:00-04:00</video:expiration_date>
```

The date and time is in the format YYYY-MM-DDThh:mm:ss+TZD. TZD stands for Time Zone Designator. TZD can be expressed as the number of hours the local time is different from UTC (Coordinated Universal Time). For practical use, UTC is equivalent to Greenwich Mean Time (GMT). For example, UTC-5:00 is 5 hours earlier than UTC and corresponds to Eastern Time in the United States.

Other Attributes

Other video attributes help with searching and provide more info about the video:

▶ Tag <video:tag>—Up to 32 short descriptive tags may be included. These should be words or short phrases to help in searching.

▶ Family Friendly <video:family_friendly>—Has a value of yes or no. If the value is no, this content will not show up in search results when safe searching is set.

▶ Rating <video:rating>—The rating for the video from 0.0 to 5.0.

▶ Number of views <video:view_count>—The number of times the video has been seen.

▶ Duration <video:duration>—The length of the video in seconds, from 0 to 28,800 seconds (8 hours).

TRY IT YOURSELF ▼

Start Using Google Webmaster Tools

If you are not already using Google Webmaster tools, give it a try. It will provide an opportunity to submit a Sitemap and a Video Sitemap.

1. Create a simple sitemap with just a single URL for your site.

2. Then add a video sitemap for any video that appears on your site.

Summary

In this hour, we covered the reasons to create a Sitemap and Video Sitemap. We examined how Google TV takes advantage of the attributes in a Video Sitemap to provide a more robust user experience. Using a Video Sitemap makes it more likely that your videos will show up in Google Search results and provides advantages in how those results are displayed.

Q&A

Q. Will restricting a video to a country in a Video Sitemap prevent the video from being played in that country?

A. No, Video Sitemaps control how content is presented in search results. The important concept is that Video Sitemaps define what is searchable. They do not prevent content from being played.

Q. What is a good example of how a Video Sitemap can be used to specify the content that is displayed in search results?

A. If a thumbnail is specified in a Video Sitemap, that thumbnail will be used in search results. Overall, Video Sitemaps help to assure that video content is included in search results and provide control over how the search results are displayed.

Q. What does TMS stand for?

A. TMS stands for Tribune Media Service. It is one source of video IDs that can be used in Video Sitemaps. The purpose of video IDs is to identify identical content across multiple platforms, even when the title or other identifying information is not identical. Whether a show is on broadcast TV, available for rent, or available on the Web, a video ID assures that the same video will be identified in the same way in search results.

Workshop

Quiz

1. What are two advantages of using a Video Sitemap for live content?

2. What app uses price and rental information on Google TV?

3. What restrictions may be placed on a video within a Video Sitemap?

Answers

1. Using a Video Sitemap for live content will provide a countdown to the event in search results for the 8 hours leading up to the event. When the event is live, the search results will indicate that.

2. The TV & Movies app uses this information to present options for viewing or purchasing.

3. Restrictions can be by country or by platform. Countries are identified by 2-digit ISO codes and platforms are tv, web, and mobile.

Exercises

1. Create a video sitemap example that contains one video.

2. Create a sitemap that contains live content that starts on a day that is 7 days in the future. Set the start time to 4 p.m. your local time and the end time to 5 p.m.

HOUR 7
Android and Google TV

What You'll Learn in This Hour:

▸ What is Android
▸ How to work in the development environment
▸ How to test your apps
▸ How to set up an Android project in Eclipse

Android is the operating system for Google TV. When we run web apps on the Chrome browser, the browser is running on the Android operating system. Android was created as a smartphone operating system and was intended to support many types and sizes of phones. With Android 3.0, known as Honeycomb, Android provided support for tablets. Honeycomb is the basis for Google TV. After Honeycomb, the Android 4.0 release is known as Ice Cream Sandwich (ICS). JellyBean follows Ice Cream Sandwich and was released as version 4.1.2 in July 2012. Version 4.2 is also known as JellyBean, and was released in November 2012.

In this hour, we'll cover the development of Android as a TV platform. We'll cover the operating systems Honeycomb, Ice Cream Sandwich, and JellyBean. This hour includes an introduction to the Android development environment and instructions on how to debug on a live Google TV device.

Android, the Google TV Operating System

In October 2008, the HTC Dream or G1 phone was released with the 1.0 version of the Android operating system. The phone was available to T-Mobile customers in the United States and via other providers in Europe.

At the time the G1 was released, the Android Software Development Kit (SDK) had been available to developers for a year, but there were few applications available in the early days. In March 2009, there were approximately 2,300 applications in the Android market. By late 2010, the number of Android apps was over 100,000; currently more than 500,000 apps are available.

Android began as an independent company in 2003 and was purchased by Google in 2005. The Android operating system is based on Linux, and the development environment uses the Java language.

The History of Android

Android was developed to run on different hardware and to support multiple screen sizes. The goal was to support phones with slide-out keyboards as well as phones with larger screens and no keyboards. When building a user interface for an Android app, methods to support multiple screen sizes and densities were included from the start. Density refers to the number of pixels in a physical area on the screen. We can think of density as dots per inch (DPI). With an operating system capable of supporting multiple hardware devices and screen sizes, Android supports tablets and eventually Google TV.

Android operating system releases are known by their dessert-based code names. Android 1.5, released on the G1 in 2009, was known as Cupcake. Donut, Éclair, Froyo, and Gingerbread followed Cupcake. Each release contained improvements and new features that targeted phones.

Google TV devices were released based on Android 2.1, the Éclair release. In May 2011, Google announced that Google TV devices were being upgraded to Honeycomb 3.1 and would be able to access the Android market. Current Google TV versions are running Android 3.2. The 3.1 release and support for the Google Android Market made developing for Google TV a more significant opportunity. It was the first time that an independent developer could create an app and make it available for a Google TV device.

The Android Ecosystem

The iPhone provides several lessons for Google TV developers. Apple provides both the hardware and software for the iPhone. The software is specific to the device, and the development environment is tied to the software. That controlled environment makes it relatively easy for iOS developers to create pixel-perfect apps. Apple creates the hardware and the software, and it works with phone carriers to provide the network.

The Android development environment requires phone developers to create apps for different devices and manufacturers. That can be more of a challenge for developers, but it also drives the growth of Android as a platform. Multiple phone manufacturers and carriers use Android and support many smartphones running Android. That has led to Android surpassing iOS as the leading smartphone operating system.

Smart TVs are likely to follow a similar path. Google TV runs on Logitech, Sony, Vizio, and other devices. By providing a common platform, Google TV allows manufacturers to focus on hardware and not on software. Vizio produced TVs with its own software and has now moved to Google TV. Samsung created its own smart TV software, but is now moving to Google TV. It is expected that Apple will release Apple TV as a product with tightly integrated hardware and software. With Google TV as a common platform across manufacturers, it should end up with a good share of the smart TV market.

A second lesson of the iPhone is that robust app markets help make devices successful. The Android market became available with the Android 3.1 release on Google TV and is now known as Google Play. Users can buy apps, videos, and music on Google Play. A market that provides a way for developers to get their apps to users is a key to creating a platform. Apps can be provided for free and sold on Google Play.

Understanding the Development Environment

The cornerstone of Android development is the Android SDK. Though it is possible to use the command line or any IDE you are familiar with, it is safe to say that most Android development is done on Eclipse.

Java is the development language for Android. Google created its own version of Java for Android known as Dalvik, and was recently sued by Oracle for patent and copyright violations over this. Google prevailed, so it appears that this will not be an issue in the future.

There is an add-on for Google TV development that requires running a Linux machine, but most Google TV development can be done running an emulator on a Windows or Macintosh computer. Testing on a live device is a great option, particularly with the availability of inexpensive Google TV devices. In this hour, we'll cover these options.

The Android SDK

Developing on Android starts with downloading and installing the Android SDK. Current information is available by following the download links and specific instructions on http://developer. android.com/. There are installation and environment setup instructions for both Windows and Macintosh machines.

Downloading and installing the SDK is the first step in the process. You will not be able to develop an application with the SDK only because the SDK is not the entire development environment. It includes the core SDK tools to set up the rest of the environment.

After you have the SDK, you will need to download at least one platform and the latest platform tools. That is done via the SDK itself. On Windows, run the SDK `Manager.exe` file in the Android folder. On Mac or Linux, open a terminal window and navigate to the tools directory in the Android SDK and then execute `android sdk`. The SDK Manager opens and shows the recommended packages to install. Figure 7.1 shows the SDK Manager.

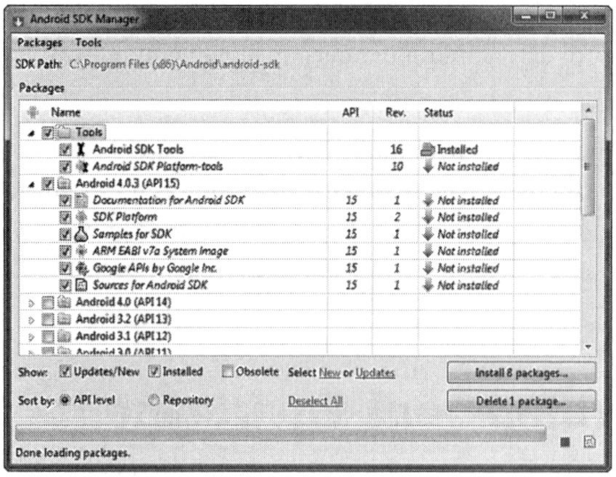

FIGURE 7.1
The SDK Manager.

NOTE

Path Environment Variable

Include the SDK /tools and /platform-tools in your PATH variable for easy access to them.

Android Tools and Platform are required. All other packages are recommended. Samples can be helpful for finding example code. System images are helpful for using different environments in the Android Emulator.

Eclipse Plug-in (ADT)

Eclipse is an advanced integrated development environment (IDE). Android includes a plug-in for Eclipse known as the Android Development Tools, or ADT. The plug-in extends Eclipse to make it easy to develop Android apps. The ADT helps to quickly set up Android projects, work on an Android UI, and export a final project.

If you do not have Eclipse installed, you need to download and install it. There are several versions. Eclipse Classic is recommended, but the Java EE and other versions will work. To download, follow the instructions at http://www.eclipse.org/downloads/.

The ADT is installed after Eclipse has been downloaded and installed. To install the ADT, open Eclipse and choose Help, and then Install New Software from the menu. This is shown in Figure 7.2. Choose Add and enter the information for the ADT plug-in. The name is ADT Plugin and the URL for the repository is https://dl-ssl.google.com/android/eclipse/. This is shown in Figure 7.3. Choose OK and choose to download the developer tools. If issues occur with the download, change https to http in the repository. Installation will complete and you will be asked to restart Eclipse.

At this point, the SDK and ADT are installed, but not set up. To set up the ADT, choose Preferences from the menu in Eclipse. Choose Android and specify the SDK location. The SDK location is the folder where the SDK is installed. It is typically something like `android-sdk-mac_x86` or `android-sdk-windows`. That will complete the setup of the ADT.

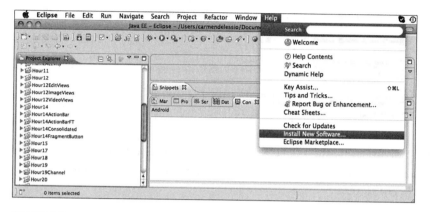

FIGURE 7.2
Installing the ADT in Eclipse.

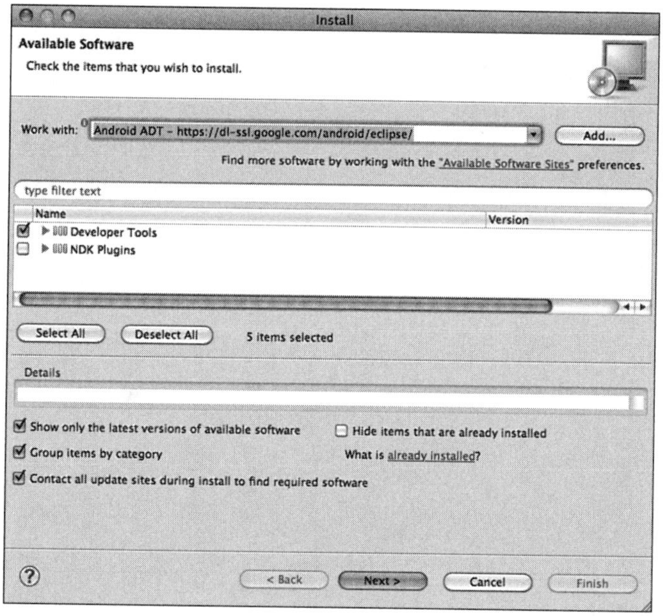

FIGURE 7.3
Setting up the ADT.

Testing Your Apps

There are several ways to test an Android app for Google TV. One is to create an Android Virtual Device (AVD) and another is to test directly on a Google TV. Those methods are covered in detail. The third method is with the use of a Google TV add-on, but the add-on is supported only on Linux. For those developing on Linux, see the Android developer site for the latest info on the Google TV add-on.

Using the Android Emulator

When you run the Android Emulator, you are running an AVD. The emulator will start directly from Eclipse if we choose to run the app and an emulator is available.

In this section, we'll use Eclipse to create an AVD that runs Android 3.1 and that has a screen resolution of 720p. That is the same Android version and screen size as a Google TV device. It is not a perfect replica, but it will run most of the examples in this book. The exceptions are those that do things like change channels.

In Eclipse, choose Window and then AVD Manager. If there are any virtual devices, they will be listed in the AVD Manager window. Choose New to create a new device. Figure 7.4 shows an AVD definition.

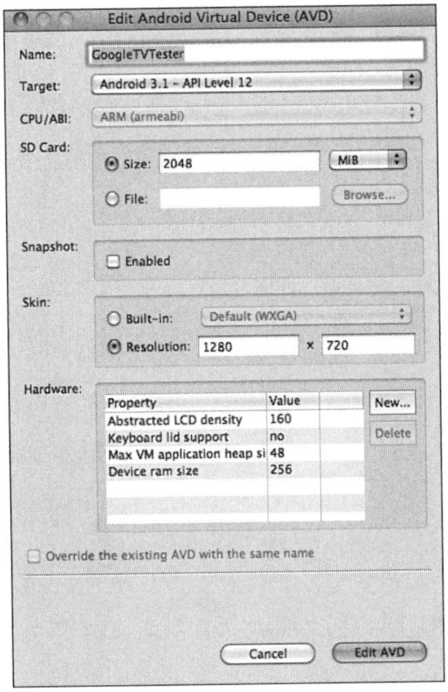

FIGURE 7.4
Creating an AVD.

The name of the AVD can be anything you want. In this case it is `GoogleTVTester`. The Target should be Android 3.1 – API Level 12. The resolution was set to 1280x720, which is the same as 720p.

For apps that require an SD card, the size of the SD card is needed. For other apps this is optional. Here it is set to 2048. In Hours 14 to 18, the examples download images from Facebook and write them to the SD card, so this is required for those examples. In general, the larger the file size, the slower the emulator performance. It is fine to not specify an SD card unless needed.

The AVD Manager includes a button to start an AVD. Doing so will start an emulator using the specified AVD. Eclipse will try to use a running device or emulator to run an app. If no target device is available, you are given the choice to select one or start an existing AVD.

Working Directly on a Device

Using a Google TV device directly for development requires minimal setup. Devices are available from Sony, Logitech, Vizio, and others. Refurbished and new Google TV devices can be found for $99 USD. A Google TV box can be hooked up to an existing TV.

Your Google TV device is wirelessly connected, and that provides a way to set up wireless debugging. Modifying and debugging an app on the TV in your living room is one of the first indications that developing apps for Google TV really is a new and different experience.

To run and debug apps directly on a Google TV over wireless, you will need the IP address of your development computer and the IP address of your Google TV device. After you have the IP addresses, a few changes are required to the settings on the TV. We will go over this step by step.

To get the IP address on a Mac, go to a terminal window and type **ifconfig**. You will see a number of things. Look for an IP address something like inet 192.168.1.102, and note the address. On Windows, go to Accessories, Command Prompt and type **ipconfig**. Note the IP address.

Next we will find the IP address on Google TV. First, start the Settings app. Choose Network, as shown in Figure 7.5. Next choose Status. The menu choice reads, View Detailed Network Status. The first listing in the detailed status is the IP address. Note the address; it will be something like 192.168.1.101.

Staying in the Settings app, we need to set up the Google TV device for debugging. Choose Applications. On that window, check the Unknown Sources check box, as shown in Figure 7.6. Choose Development. Set Remote Debugging to true by checking the check box, as shown in Figure 7.7. In the Debugger IP Address, set the IP address to that of your development machine. In this case, that was 192.168.1.102.

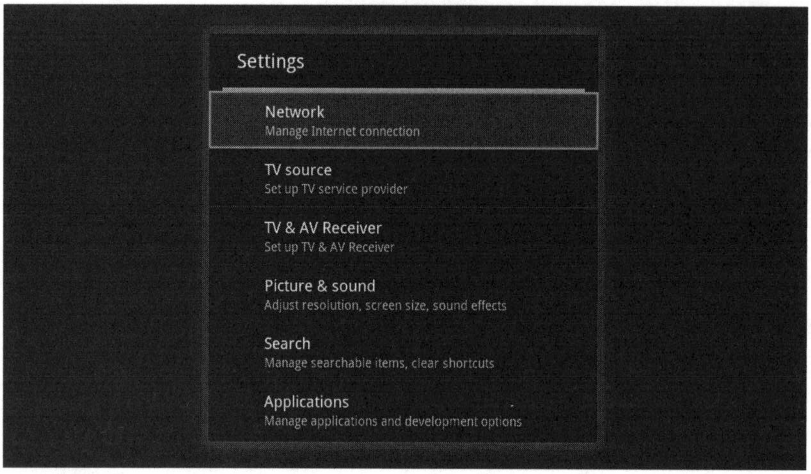

FIGURE 7.5
The Settings app.

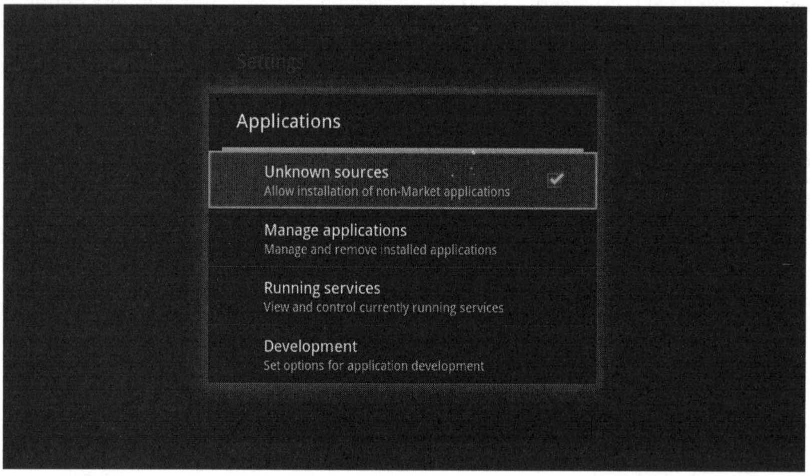

FIGURE 7.6
Set Unknown Sources.

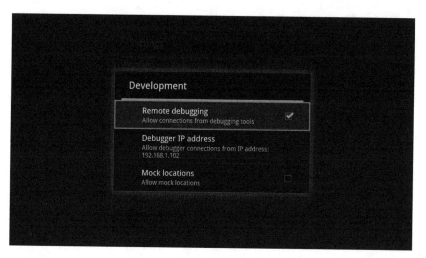

FIGURE 7.7
Set Remote Debugging and Debugger IP Address.

Now it is possible to debug directly on the device. In a terminal window on a Mac or on command-line on Windows, we can start a debugger with the following command:

```
adb connect 192.168.1.101
```

That tells the debugger to connect to the IP address of the Google TV device that we determined was 192.168.1.101. The response should say:

```
connected to 192.168.1.101:5555
```

Another command we can use at this point from a terminal window is DDMS. DDMS stands for Dalvik Debug Monitor Server. It can be run from the command line or within Eclipse. By running DDMS from the command line and choosing Device, Screen Capture from the menu, we can capture screenshots of the running Google TV system. Figure 7.8 shows DDMS with menu selection for screen capture.

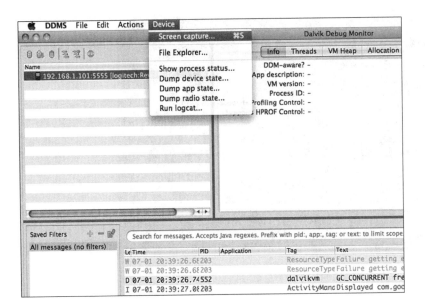

FIGURE 7.8
DDMS for screen capture.

Setting Up an Android Project in Eclipse

We'll use Eclipse to set up, run, and debug our project. We'll use the GoogleTVTest AVD that we created in this hour to see a simple app in action. When we create a new Android project in Eclipse, a full app is generated. We will examine the components of that app to understand how projects are set up.

Creating a New Project

To create a new project in Eclipse, use the menu and choose New, Other, Android project. Depending on your version of Eclipse and operating system, there may be slight differences, but the correct choice should be obvious.

You will be asked to create a new project in the workspace. For this example, use Hour7 as the project name, as shown in Figure 7.9, and choose Next.

Choose a build target of Android 3.1 or later, as shown in Figure 7.10. Build targets are the platform versions installed in the SDK. If you choose a version later than 3.1, you will need to set your minimum SDK version appropriately for Google TV. That is covered in Hour 19, "Mastering the Android Manifest File," when the Android Manifest file is discussed. The minimum SDK should be set to 12 in that case.

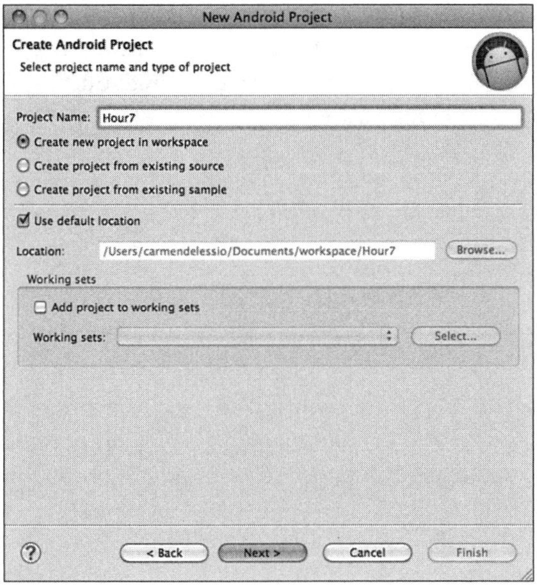

FIGURE 7.9
Create a new Android project.

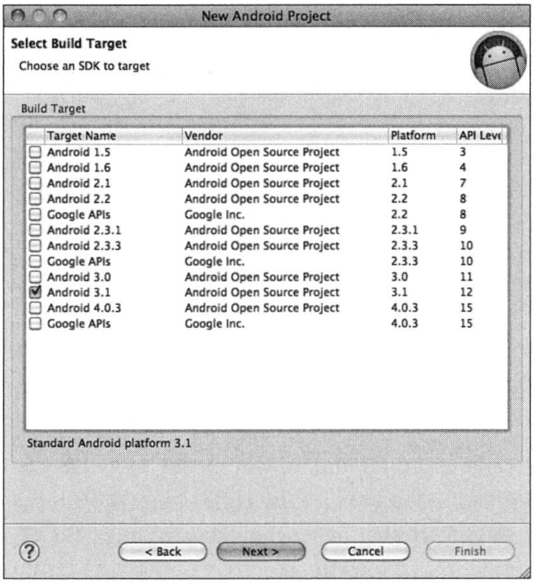

FIGURE 7.10
Choose a build target of Android 3.1 or later.

You will now be asked to set the application name and package name, as shown in Figure 7.11. The package name is very important. It is what will uniquely identify your app to the Android system and on the Android market. Typically, you would use a reverse domain name structure using a domain name that you own. In this case, com.bffmedia.hour7.

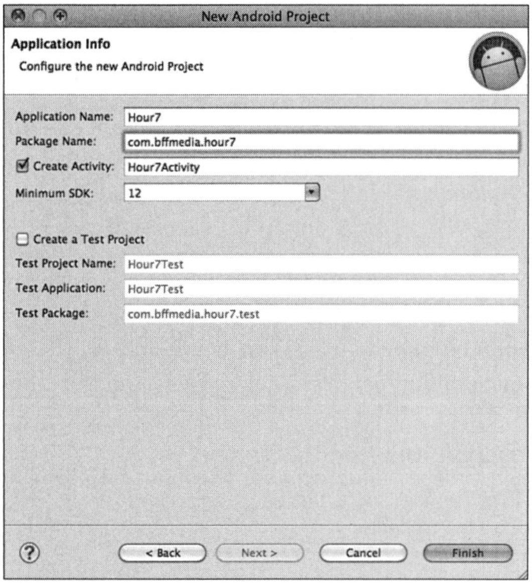

FIGURE 7.11
Set the Package Name.

At this point, the Android project Hour7 is created. In Figure 7.11 we specified that an Activity called Hour7Activity should be included.

Project Structure

Our first goal is to examine precisely what is generated when we request to create a new Android project in Eclipse. The folder structure in Figure 7.12 is seen when we expand the Hour7 project in Eclipse.

Every element of Figure 7.12 is required for an Android project, but we will modify only a few as developers. When we set up the project, we requested that an Activity called Hour7Activity be created. We can see that the Hour7Activity.java file was created and exists in the Hour7 src folder using the package name com.bffmedia.hour7. Clicking the Hour7Activity.java file will make it available for editing in Eclipse.

FIGURE 7.12
Project structure shown in Eclipse.

The folders for the project are as follows:

▶ **Layouts in /res/layout**—A `main.xml` file is created under /res/layout. That is a layout file that describes the user interface of the app.

▶ **Images in /res/drawable folders**—These folders hold images with different densities, such has high density, medium density, and low density.

▶ **Constants in /res/values folders**—A `strings.xml` file allows us to create string constants to use in the app or in the user interface.

▶ **Android Manifest file Android.xml**—It is very important and tells both the Android system and the Android market about the app. It is covered as a separate topic in Hour 19.

Functionally, not very much happens in the Hour7 Application. Listing 7.1 shows the entire `Hour17Activity.java` file and Listing 7.2 shows the `main.xml` file. The skeleton app displays the layout defined in `main.xml`.

An `Activity` is usually the full-screen view of a user interface. A full-screen `activity` is by far the most common use, but technically, activities can also be used as floating windows or embedded within other activities. Users interact with the activity that is running. An app can have one or more activities. It is useful to think of an activity as the full-screen view where the user interacts with the app.

LISTING 7.1   Hour7Activity.java

```
1: package com.bffmedia.hour7;
2: import android.app.Activity;
3: import android.os.Bundle;
4: public class Hour7Activity extends Activity {
5:     /** Called when the activity is first created. */
6:     @Override
7:     public void onCreate(Bundle savedInstanceState) {
8:         super.onCreate(savedInstanceState);
9:         setContentView(R.layout.main);
10:    }
11:}
```

Listing 7.1 defines an Activity called Hour7Activity. Lines 6 to10 override the onCreate method. Line 9 sets the view to be R.layout.main. That corresponds to the main.xml file that was generated by Eclipse when we created our app. When an Android project is compiled, a folder called "gen" is created. The "gen" folder is shown in Figure 7.12. The gen folder contains a file called R.java. That file should not be modified directly; it defines constants based on the /res/layout and other folders in the project. In line 9 of Listing 7.1, R.layout.main refers to the definition in the R.java file. In general, the R.java is not something that is of concern to an Android developer, but it is important to make the connection to the project that Eclipse creates.

Listing 7.2 shows the main.xml file that defines the user interface for the Activity. It consists of a TextView embedded in a LinearLayout. We'll learn more about those in Hours 8 to11. In Eclipse, we can view and edit a layout file directly or graphically. Figure 7.13 shows the graphical view of Main.xml in Eclipse.

LISTING 7.2   Main.xml

```
1: <?xml version="1.0" encoding="utf-8"?>
2: <LinearLayout xmlns:android="http://schemas.android.com/apk/res/android"
3:     android:layout_width="fill_parent"
4:     android:layout_height="fill_parent"
5:     android:orientation="vertical" >
6:     <TextView
7:         android:layout_width="fill_parent"
8:         android:layout_height="wrap_content"
9:         android:text="@string/hello" />
10:</LinearLayout>
```

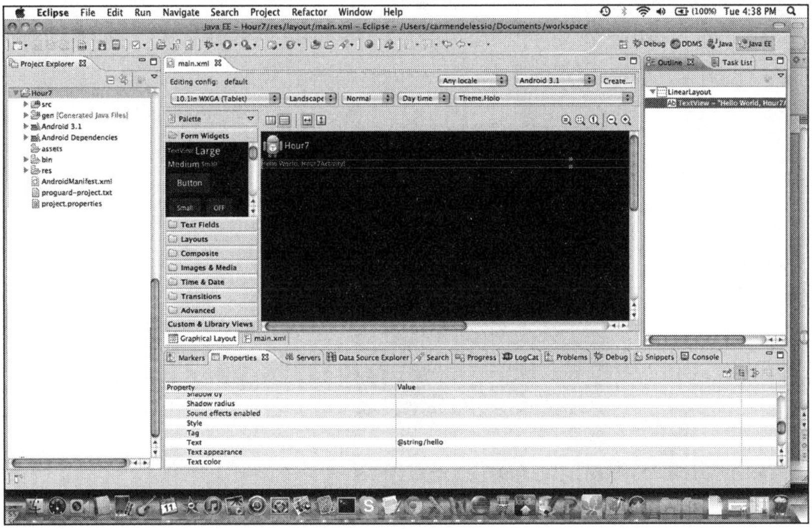

FIGURE 7.13
The `Main.xml` layout shown in Eclipse.

The `main.xml` layout includes a reference to `@string/hello`. That is a value defined in the `strings.xml` file. `Strings.xml` is shown in Listing 7.3.

LISTING 7.3 Strings.xml

```
1: strings.xml
2: <?xml version="1.0" encoding="utf-8"?>
3: <resources>
4:     <string name="hello">Hello World, Hour7Activity!</string>
5:     <string name="app_name">Hour7</string>
6: </resources>
```

Running the App

We'll run this app unmodified. That will show us the steps to run the app and allow us to view it in the emulator. After that, we will modify the code to log the events associated with the Activity life cycle. To run the app, highlight the project and choose Run As and Android Application, as shown in Figure 7.14.

Because we have an AVD defined, it will be used as the target for loading and running the app. We can choose the option Run Configurations seen in the right-most menu in Figure 7.14 to set specific options for running the app.

Figure 7.15 shows some of the options. Choosing Manual is helpful if you are testing on both a device and an emulator. It lets you pick the target at runtime. For an app that will run on a phone, you may want to do most of the debugging on the phone and occasionally test on different AVDs.

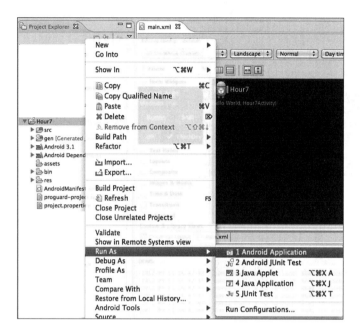

FIGURE 7.14
Run the app.

FIGURE 7.15
Run configurations.

In our case, the app begins to run in the emulator. You should see the process of a booting Android device, which may take a few minutes. You may have to unlock the screen to see the apps that are available. Figure 7.16 shows the Hour17app is available in the emulator. Figure 7.17 shows the app itself.

FIGURE 7.16
Emulator running.

FIGURE 7.17
Hour7 app in the emulator.

Summary

In this hour, we covered the background of Android as a smartphone operating system. Details on how to become a Google Play registered publisher were provided, and the general development environment for Android and options for debugging were covered.

Q&A

Q. What are the components of the Google TV development environment?

A. The development language is Java. The target operating system is Android. Typically, the Eclipse IDE is used with the ADT. The Android SDK and platform tools are required

Q. What folders are used in an Eclipse Android project?

A. There are folders for source code, XML layouts, and images required for the project.

Q. How are Google TV apps tested?

A. A Google TV app can be tested directly on a device or by using an AVD. The Android emulator runs AVDs.

Workshop

Quiz

1. After the Android SDK in installed, what two other things must be installed to begin Android development?

2. What does AVD stand for?

3. How is the IP address of your development machine relevant to debugging using a Google TV device?

Answers

1. At least one Android platform and platform tools are required.

2. AVD stands for Android Virtual Device. AVDs can be defined with different characteristics. The Android emulator uses AVDs to run apps.

3. The IP address of the development machine is entered in the Settings application of the Google TV device as the Debugger IP address.

Exercises

1. Download Eclipse and the Android SDK and create your own AVD.

2. Set up an Android Project in Eclipse and run the app in the Emulator using the AVD you created.

Using Android Layouts for Your Google TV App

What You'll Learn in This Hour:

▶ What are layouts and how are they used
▶ The relationship between code and layouts
▶ The effects of changing layout properties
▶ How to use padding and margins in your UI

In this hour, you will learn how widgets are added to the screen with layouts. Layouts are part of the presentation layer in Android and are used in phones, tablets, and on Google TV. The job of the layout is to position widgets, like Buttons or TextFields, at the proper position on the screen. The same layout can be used on a phone or on Google TV, but there are ways to optimize the viewing experience for each device.

A number of layouts are available. They include a LinearLayout, FrameLayout, and RelativeLayout. We'll cover the principles of handling layouts using a LinearLayout. Then we'll apply what we've learned to the other types of layouts.

Layout Basics with LinearLayout

A LinearLayout positions widgets in either a column or a row. The LinearLayout's orientation property determines the direction. If the orientation is vertical, the widgets will be stacked in a column. If the orientation is horizontal, the widgets will be placed in a row. Although there are many common attributes across layouts, the difference between different types of layouts is the order and rules they use for drawing widgets on the screen.

What Precisely Is a Layout?

Before we create a sample LinearLayout, let's look at the definition.

One definition of layout is that it is an XML file that defines the attributes of the layout and the widgets used.

If you look at the Android documentation on LinearLayout, you will see that LinearLayout is an extension of a `ViewGroup` class. The `ViewGroup` class is defined as a view that can contain other views. A View in Android is the most basic component for building a user interface. Every Button, TextField, or Layout is a type of view. A ViewGroup is a container for other views referred to as child views. A LinearLayout is a specific type of ViewGroup that defines how each child view is drawn on the screen.

It is worthwhile to have an idea of the class hierarchy of a layout. It helps us define a layout as a container for user interface elements that has specific rules applied when new elements are added. That is the same as saying that a layout is a ViewGroup with rules to define how child views are added.

Practically, we define a layout as an XML file that is used in our Android apps to display elements on the screen.

XML Layout

We have the choice to work directly with XML or to use the tools supplied in Eclipse to work with the widgets in a visual way. The Eclipse environment has a visual interface for adding widgets and changing widget properties without directly touching the XML. As you use the tools, you may find yourself switching between visually editing the layouts and editing the XML directly.

Listing 8.1 defines a LinearLayout in XML. The layout includes a `TextField` and a `Button`.

LISTING 8.1 LinearLayout in XML

```
 1:    <?xml version="1.0" encoding="utf-8"?>
 2:    <LinearLayout xmlns:android="http://schemas.android.com/apk/res/android"
 3:        android:orientation="vertical"
 4:        android:layout_width="fill_parent"
 5:        android:layout_height="fill_parent">
 6:        <TextView android:layout_width="fill_parent"
 7:            android:layout_height="wrap_content"
 8:            android:text="Hello Google TV"
 9:            android:id="@+id/greeting"/>
10:        <Button android:text="Button"
11:            android:id="@+id/button1"
12:            android:layout_width="wrap_content"
13:            android:layout_height="wrap_content" />
14:    </LinearLayout>
```

Lines 2 through 5 in Listing 8.1 define a `LinearLayout` with a vertical orientation and width and height set to `fill_parent`. Typically, when `fill_parent` is used this way, the result is that we are filling the entire screen of the Activity. It is possible to have layouts within layouts, and in that case, `fill_parent` will fill the size of the outer layout. Also, a TextView is defined in line 6 and a Button in line 10. Note that both of these widgets are defined within the LinearLayout.

Android projects follow a specific directory structure. We defined an XML file and must place it in the proper location within the project. The resources directory is called `res/`. The `res/` directory contains a subdirectory called `layout/` and that is where our XML file is placed.

When defining a project in Eclipse, a `main.xml` file is generated for us. Listing 8.1 is based on that generated file with an added Button. The file `main.xml` exists in the `/res/layout` directory. If you were working on an app for a phone and for Google TV, you might use additional layout directories. Those include layout-land for defining layouts used in landscape mode. Other alternative directories include layout-small, layout-large, and layout-xlarge. The directory `/res/layout-xlarge-land/` would be used for an extra large screen in landscape mode. This facilitates using one APK across multiple devices.

In the examples in this hour, we'll use the default directory `/res/layout`. Figure 8.1 shows the resource file directory structure, our layout in visual mode, and a list of properties for the TextField we defined.

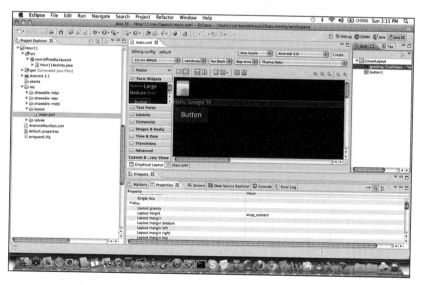

FIGURE 8.1
Viewing and editing a layout in an Eclipse project.

Connecting the Layout to Code

Using the layout defined in Listing 8.1, we'll create a simple Activity to display the layout and interact with the Button and TextField. When the Button is pressed, we'll update the message in the TextField. The goal is to see the relationship between the code and the layout we defined.

Listing 8.2 defines an Activity called Hour8Activity. This activity defines a Button and a TextView and overrides the method OnCreate. OnCreate is an Activity method that is used to create the activity's view. The association between this code and the layout we defined occurs on line 7 with the call to setContentView. That tells the Activity to look for and use this layout file to display the activity. The parameter to setContentView is R.layout.main. If we look at the Activity class, we can see that it has a method called setContentView that takes a resource ID as a parameter. That is what we are doing in this case.

It's easy to do, and we can see the association in the name, but where did it get created? When we build an Android project, an R.java file is generated and includes these definitions. The build process associates the XML layout file with the resources and the code. The references to the resource IDs for the Button and TextField are created the same way. The resources ID R.id.button1 and R.id.greeting are generated during the build process.

LISTING 8.2 Coding an Activity Using the Layout

```
1:   public class Hour8Activity extends Activity {
2:       Button mButton;
3:       TextView mText;
4:       @Override
5:       public void onCreate(Bundle savedInstanceState) {
6:           super.onCreate(savedInstanceState);
7:           setContentView(R.layout.main);
8:           mText = (TextView)findViewById(R.id.greeting);
9:           mButton= (Button)findViewById(R.id.button1);
11:          mButton.setOnClickListener(new OnClickListener() {
12:            public void onClick(View v) {
13:               mText.setText("You clicked it!");
14:            }
15:         });
16:      }
```

Having associated the XML layout to the activity, we can tie the Button and TextField from that XML file to our variables in the code. That is done in lines 8 and 9 with the calls to findViewById. The findViewById method belongs to the Activity and gets the widgets defined in the XML file and creates a View that can be used in the Activity. We cast the View as needed to match the widgets used. In this case, we cast the view as a TextField and Button.

To show some interaction in our activity, we call the Button's `setOnClickListener`. We are defining an action to occur when the Button is clicked. This is an event-driven model where we are listening for the click event and deciding what happens when the click event occurs. Essentially, we are making something happen when the click happens.

The parameter to `setOnClickListener` is an `onClickListener`. It is defined in an inner class. That is, the `onClickListener` is defined on-the-fly and passed to the `setOnClickListener`. That pattern is often used. It is similar to JavaScript callback functions being defined on-the-fly. The code can be used where needed with a focus on what to do in the `onClick` method. Note that the View passed to the `onClick` method is the view that was clicked. We don't need that info in this case, but it can be useful.

In our `onClick` method, we update the TextView to say, "You Clicked It!"

Changing LinearLayout Properties

We'll change two common properties within the LinearLayout to see the effect. One property that can be set is the background. The background color can be set or a background image can be specified. The color is set with a hexadecimal value like HTML colors, so looking at HTML color charts is a good guide for choosing colors for an app.

Listing 8.3 reflects these changes to the `main.xml` file.

LISTING 8.3   Updating the LinearLayout XML file

```
1:   <?xml version="1.0" encoding="utf-8"?>
2:   <LinearLayout xmlns:android="http://schemas.android.com/apk/res/android"
3:      android:orientation="horizontal"
4:      android:background="#777777"
5:      android:layout_width="fill_parent"
6:      android:layout_height="fill_parent">
7:      <TextView android:layout_width="fill_parent"
8:         android:layout_height="wrap_content"
9:         android:text="Hello Google TV"
10:         android:id="@+id/greeting"/>
11:     <Button android:text="Button"
12:         android:id="@+id/button1"
13:         android:layout_width="wrap_content"
14:         android:layout_height="wrap_content" />
15:   </LinearLayout>
```

Line 3 in Listing 8.3 changes the orientation from vertical to horizontal. Line 4 adds the new background color.

We set the background to #777777, which is a light gray. You may also set the alpha value for the color—that is, the first two values for the color that set the opaqueness of the color. Using 00 will make a transparent color. Using FF will create an opaque color. So we can also use #FF777777. The alpha value is not required.

The color of the entire layout changes as expected, but something seems wrong with the change in orientation. By changing the orientation from vertical to horizontal, we expect the TextField and Button to be displayed as a row instead of a column, but the Button has disappeared completely! That is shown is Figure 8.2

The explanation lies in the details of the widgets. The TextView is set to a width of "fill_par-ent". It will fill the entire layout from left to right. When we changed the orientation on the layout, we did not account for that. The TextView is taking up the whole screen, and the Button is not in view.

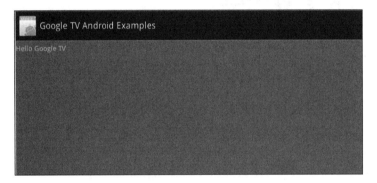

FIGURE 8.2
Layout with new background color, but with a missing Button.

The fix is to change the TextView width to "wrap_content". By making that change in Line 7, the TextField and Button are placed in a row we expected.

The fixed LinearLayout with a new background color and horizontal orientation is shown in Figure 8.3.

The interaction between layout attributes and widget attributes is explored further in the next section on laying out widgets.

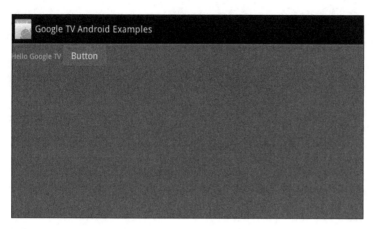

FIGURE 8.3
Layout with new background color and horizontal orientation.

Laying Out Widgets

As we saw in Listing 8.3, changing the properties of the layout may affect where widgets are placed on the screen. We'll look at padding and margin properties of widgets and illustrate how they affect the display.

Padding

Padding is the amount of space that is added to a side of a widget to give it more space on the screen. Padding often refers to the internal padding. For a standard Button, it is the space added between the button's text and sides of the button. Padding may be set for the whole widget or set specifically for the top, bottom, left, and right sides.

The correct unit to use to set padding is a **device-independent pixel**, referred to as a dip or dp within the XML layout. Device-independent pixels factor in screen resolution when displayed.

We'll modify our XML file to add two new buttons with padding set differently to highlight the effects.

Listing 8.4 defines three buttons. The first button has no padding property specified. The second button has its padding set to 20dp on line 14 by setting `android:padding="20dp"`. All sides of the button are padded with 20 device pixels. The third button has its padding set to 30dp for the right and left sides in lines 20 and 21. The right padding is set using `android:paddingRig ht="30dp"`.

The result is shown in Figure 8.4. To illustrate the padding, the orientation has been set back to `vertical`.

LISTING 8.4 Setting Button Padding

```
1:    <?xml version="1.0" encoding="utf-8"?>
2:    <LinearLayout xmlns:android="http://schemas.android.com/apk/res/android"
3:        android:orientation="vertical"
4:        android:background="#777777"
5:        android:layout_width="fill_parent"
6:        <Button android:text="Button"
7:          android:id="@+id/button1"
8:          android:layout_width="wrap_content"
9:          android:layout_height="wrap_content" />
10:       <Button android:text="Button"
11:         android:layout_height="wrap_content"
12:         android:layout_width="wrap_content"
13:         android:id="@+id/ButtonPadding"
14:         android:padding="20dp">
15:       </Button>
16:       <Button android:text="Button"
17:         android:layout_height="wrap_content"
18:         android:layout_width="wrap_content"
19:         android:id="@+id/ButtonSidePadding"
20:         android:paddingRight="30dp"
21:         android:paddingLeft="30dp">
22:       </Button>
23:   </LinearLayout>
```

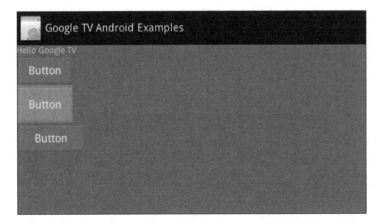

FIGURE 8.4
Buttons with padding set.

Layout Margins

Layout margins define the amount of space between a widget and the side of a parent container. To "push" a button down and to the right, you would set the margin from the top and the left of the layout. Listing 8.5 modifies the top and left margins for the first button in our layout definition.

LISTING 8.5 Setting Layout Margins

```
1:  <Button android:text="Button"
2:      android:id="@+id/button1"
3:      android:layout_width="wrap_content"
4:      android:layout_height="wrap_content"
5:      android:layout_marginTop="40dp"
6:      android:layout_marginLeft="120dp"/>
```

The result is shown in Figure 8.5. Because we are using a LinearLayout with vertical orientation, all the buttons are pushed down. By changing the `marginTop` property, the start of the column of buttons is also offset from the top. FrameLayouts and RelativeLayouts will show a different outcome when you set margins because the elements do not have the same relationship to each other as in a LinearLayout.

To assure that the screen does not appear too crowded, set reasonable margins on the widgets to give them space from the edges of the layout.

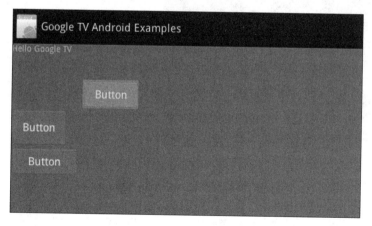

FIGURE 8.5
Button with margins set.

FrameLayout

A FrameLayout is a container that has no special rules for drawing widgets. By default, all widgets are drawn in the upper-left corner of the screen. That may not sound useful, but by using the layout margin, widgets can be placed anywhere. The FrameLayout is helpful when two widgets should be drawn on top of each other. For example, we might put a TextField on top of an image or use several images to draw shadows and highlights within the UI.

By changing the code in Listing 8.4 to use FrameLayout instead of LinearLayout, we get the result in Figure 8.6. The only change in the XML is to substitute FrameLayout for LinearLayout in the first and last lines. The button where we set the margins is shown in the middle of the screen. The others are piled in the upper-left corner.

Specifically, Button1 specified margins relative to the top of the screen and to left side of the screen by setting the attributes `marginTop` and `marginLeft`. By doing so, it retains the same position on the screen.

```
android:layout_marginTop="40dp"
android:layout_marginLeft="120dp"/>
```

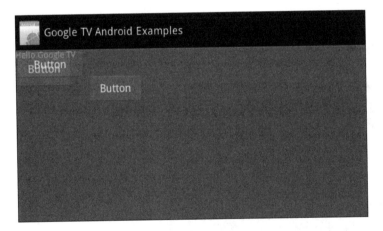

FIGURE 8.6
Using FrameLayout with the earlier example.

By setting margins for the other Buttons in this layout, we can fix the FrameLayout shown in Figure 8.5 so that the Buttons are not piled on top of each other. We will also include an image and show the Buttons on top of it. That is one way to take advantage of a FrameLayout.

Listing 8.6 sets the top margin for all buttons. Lines 6 to 10 create an ImageView as the first component on the page. The ImageView has the `src` value set to an image from the drawable folder. The image will be shown with buttons displayed on top of it.

By fixing the margins and adding the image, the layout presents the buttons so that they are usable and shows how we can use a FrameLayout to show components on top of each other.

LISTING 8.6   Fixing the FrameLayout

```
1:   <?xml version="1.0" encoding="utf-8"?>
2:   <FrameLayout xmlns:android="http://schemas.android.com/apk/res/android"
3:       android:layout_width="fill_parent"
4:       android:layout_height="fill_parent"
5:       android:orientation="vertical">
6:   <ImageView
7:       android:id="@+id/imageView1"
8:       android:layout_width="wrap_content"
9:       android:layout_height="wrap_content"
10:      android:src="@drawable/delessio_family_pool_1080" />
11:  <TextView android:layout_width="wrap_content"
12:      android:layout_height="wrap_content"
13:      android:text="Hello Google TV"
14:      android:id="@+id/greeting"/>
15:  <Button android:text="Button"
16:      android:id="@+id/button1"
17:      android:layout_width="wrap_content"
18:      android:layout_height="wrap_content"
19:      android:layout_marginTop="40dp"
20:      android:layout_marginLeft="120dp"/>
21:  <Button android:text="Button"
22:      android:layout_height="wrap_content"
23:      android:layout_width="wrap_content"
24:      android:id="@+id/ButtonPadding"
25:      android:padding="20dp" android:layout_marginTop="20dp"/>
26:  <Button android:text="Button"
27:      android:layout_height="wrap_content"
28:      android:layout_width="wrap_content"
29:      android:id="@+id/ButtonSidePadding"
30:      android:paddingRight="30dp" android:layout_marginTop="80dp"/>
31:  </FrameLayout>
```

Figure 8.7 shows the layout created by Listing 8.6. The ImageView is the first listed in the layout. That means it is in back of the other components. If we listed the ImageView last, it would cover the buttons.

FIGURE 8.7
Fixing the FrameLayout and adding an ImageView.

RelativeLayout

An alternative to the FrameLayout is the RelativeLayout. It has characteristics similar to the FrameLayout in that components can be placed on top of each other, but with the RelativeLayout it is possible to place components in relation to other components. In a FrameLayout, when we specify the `topMargin` for two buttons, we are indicating how far they are from the top of the parent. With a RelativeLayout, we can specify how far they are from each other.

For example, using RelativeLayout, one button can be placed to the left, right, top, or bottom of another button. A RelativeLayout can be very useful when creating complex user interfaces.

Listing 8.7 uses a RelativeLayout. It is similar to Listing 8.4, but RelativeLayout is used instead of LinearLayout. Additionally, the buttons in this example are positioned on the page relative to each other.

LISTING 8.7 Placing Buttons with RelativeLayout

```
1:     <Button android:text="Button"
2:         android:id="@+id/button1"
3:         android:layout_width="wrap_content"
4:         android:layout_height="wrap_content"
5:         android:layout_marginTop="40dp"
6:         android:layout_marginLeft="120dp"/>
7:     <Button android:text="Button"
8:         android:layout_height="wrap_content"
9:         android:layout_width="wrap_content"
```

```
10:         android:id="@+id/ButtonPadding"
11:         android:padding="20dp"
12:         android:layout_toRightOf="@+id/button1">
13:    </Button>
14:    <Button android:text="Button"
15:         android:layout_height="wrap_content"
16:         android:layout_width="wrap_content"
17:         android:id="@+id/ButtonSidePadding"
18:         android:paddingRight="30dp"
19:         android:paddingLeft="30dp"
20:         android:layout_below="@+id/ButtonPadding"
21:         android:layout_toRightOf="@+id/ButtonPadding">
22:    </Button>
```

The first button with id button1 is unchanged. The second button with id ButtonPadding is placed to the right of button1 in line 12. The third button with id ButtonSidePadding is placed below and to the right of the second button on lines 20 and 21. The result is shown in Figure 8.8.

Like FrameLayouts, RelativeLayouts also provide the capability to align widgets relative to the Parent Layout. We would align to the left side of the parent in the same way we did for a FrameLayout:

```
android:layout_alignParentLeft="20dp"
```

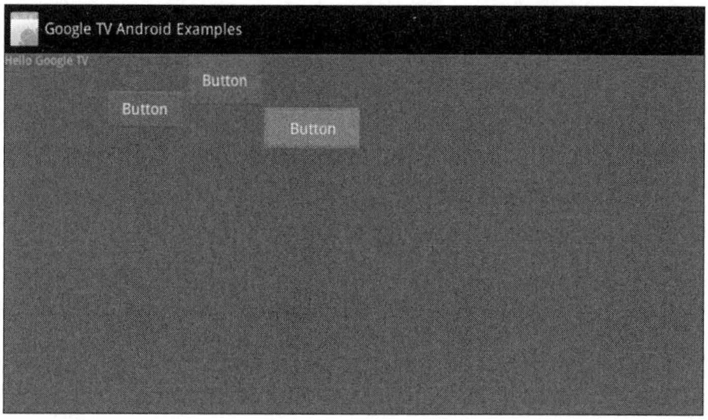

FIGURE 8.8
Using RelativeLayout with the earlier example.

When LinearLayouts and RelativeLayouts are used, the Android operating system takes the physical screen dimension into consideration when rendering the user interface. Because these layouts use components that are relative to each other, there is more opportunity for the system to optimize the experience. In a LinearLayout with vertical orientation, the spacing between components will reflect what the system considers to be an optimal layout. For that reason, LinearLayouts and RelativeLayouts are generally recommended.

▼ TRY IT YOURSELF

Implementing Layouts

In this hour, we implemented three types of layouts and set properties for both the layouts and widgets within the layouts. Using FrameLayout, implement a user interface with a button in each corner of the screen. Do the same with a RelativeLayout.

To do this using a FrameLayout, follow these steps:

1. Create a Layout file using FrameLayout.

2. Create four Buttons.

3. Set the topMargin and Left Margin of each Button so that the Buttons are placed in corners.

Summary

In this hour, we examined LinearLayout in detail as a way to understand how layouts work. Layouts are used to create user interfaces in Android by positioning widgets on the screen. Using padding and margins, we have significant control over the user interface. Examples using FrameLayout and RelativeLayout showed the properties of those layouts and how they are different.

Q&A

Q. What is Orientation used for?

A. Orientation defined the direction of the LinearLayout. Vertical creates a column, and horizontal creates a row. Orientation is not used in FrameLayouts or RelativeLayout.

Q. What is the difference between a FrameLayout and a RelativeLayout?

A. In a RelativeLayout, it is possible to position widgets relative to one another. That cannot be done in FrameLayout.

Q. What is the difference between setting a layout margin and padding?

A. Layout margins define the distance between a component and the edge of the layout. Padding pads the size of the component. Depending on the component, this can have different effects.

Workshop

Quiz

1. What does "dp" stand for?
2. What is the relationship between a LinearLayout and a ViewGroup?
3. How would you position a Button 100 pixels from the top of the device screen?

Answers

1. A device independent pixel can be referred to as "dip" or "dp." It is important to use device independent pixels to assure that the layout you design displays in the same way on devices with different screen sizes and densities.
2. A LinearLayout extends the ViewGroup class. A ViewGroup is a View in Android that contains other views.

3. Set the margin to be 100 device pixels from the top of the screen using `android:layout_marginTop="100 dp"`.

Exercises

1. Modify the code in Listing 8.7 to place the buttons on top of each other vertically and to align them so that their left sides match up. The result will be three buttons lined up on top of each other.

2. Try using one layout within another; specifically, create a LinearLayout with vertical orientation. Add a FrameLayout and a Button. Then add an ImageView to the FrameLayout.

Optimizing UI Components for Google TV

What You'll Learn in This Hour:

▶ How to use form widgets like buttons, EditViews, and AutoCompleteTextViews

▶ How to use ImageViews in advanced ways

▶ How to add interaction to videos with VideoViews

▶ How to put button overlays on a video

In this hour, you learn about the different types of components that we can use in our Google TV apps. We'll look at options for collecting data in form-style widgets. Then we'll dive into what can be done with images and videos using ImageViews and VideoViews. We'll cover complex visual designs and interactions with these elements.

Form Widgets

Widgets fall into the general category of form widgets. When we fill out a form on paper or on a website, we add text, choose check boxes, and are guided by labels and instructions. We'll consider several types of form widgets and modify their look and feel by setting properties and changing styles.

Styling TextViews

In Hour 8, "Using Android Layouts for Your Google TV App," we used a standard TextView as a label. The only properties we set were `LayoutWidth` and `LayoutHeight`. We used `fill_parent` and `wrap_content` for those values. There are more properties that can be set. We'll look at several in Listing 9.1. Properties can be set directly in the XML Layout file or through the Android Visual Tool in Eclipse.

LISTING 9.1   Adding Style to a TextView

```
 1:   <TextView
 2:       android:textAppearance="?android:attr/textAppearanceLarge"
 3:       android:layout_height="wrap_content"
 4:       android:layout_width="wrap_content"
 5:       android:id="@+id/textView1"
 6:       android:text="Large">
 7:   </TextView>
 8:   <TextView
 9:       android:layout_height="wrap_content"
10:       android:layout_width="wrap_content"
11:       android:id="@+id/textView4"
12:       android:textSize="32sp"
13:       android:textStyle="bold"
14:       android:textColor="#ff0000"
15:       android:text="RED with 32dp Size Bold">
16:   </TextView>
```

Two TextViews are defined in Listing 9.1. On line 2, the first TextView sets an attribute called `textAppearance`. The value ends with `textAppearanceLarge`. That sets this TextView to have default settings for many values, but to display large text.

In the second TextView, properties are set directly. In lines 11 to 14, attributes are set for size, style, and color. The `textSize` attribute has value "32sp". sp stands for scale-independent pixels. It is similar to device pixels but should be used for text. It takes into consideration the device's screen density and any preferences that the user has set for font size. The `textColor` attribute is set using a hexadecimal value for red.

Figure 9.1 shows the two TextViews from Listing 9.1 and two other TextViews that have `textAppearance` set to small and medium using `textAppearanceSmall` and `textAppearanceMedium` for values.

FIGURE 9.1
Showing the TextViews.

The `textAppearance` attribute in Listing 9.1 is set to `?android:attr/textAppearanceL-arge`. It is known as a platform style because it is included in Android platform distributions. The Android platform includes a large number of styles and themes that can be used in applications. They are defined in the Android source in a file called `styles.xml` and `themes.xml`.

It may seem daunting to look at the Android source code, but it can be viewed online. You can find the `styles.xml` file here: https://github.com/android/platform_frameworks_base/blob/master/core/res/res/values/styles.xml

What we find looking at the `styles.xml` file is that `textAppearanceLarge` has a simple definition. It sets the `textSize` attribute to 32sp. For your apps, it may be worthwhile to explore platform styles or even to define your own styles and themes. Two benefits of using platform styles for Google TV are that they will provide a consistent user interface across apps and that the device they are displayed on is taken into account. That is, platform styles will always use device independent definitions.

Using Buttons

In Hour 8, we used a button to change the text displayed on a TextView. We also set the padding value. We'll consider more attributes of buttons, look at creating a custom button, and cover the concept of events and listeners.

Button Attributes

In Listing 9.2, the text size and color is set for the first button. In the second button, a drawable is used. The drawable is the default icon for Android apps. In the code in Listing 9.3, we'll use the second button to hide the first. We'll also provide interaction between the drawable and the buttons.

LISTING 9.2 Adding Drawables to a Button

```
1: <Button android:id="@+id/button1"
2:    android:layout_width="wrap_content"
3:    android:layout_height="wrap_content" android:text="Button 1"
4:    android:textColor="#ff0000"
5:    android:textSize="32sp"
6:    android:textStyle="bold">
7: </Button>
8: <Button android:text="Button"
9:    android:id="@+id/button2"
10:    android:layout_width="wrap_content"
11:    android:layout_height="wrap_content"
12:    android:drawableLeft="@drawable/icon">
13: </Button>
```

NOTE

Bitmap and Drawable Defined

A Drawable in Android refers to anything that can be drawn. Shapes or bitmaps can both be made into drawables. A Drawable is an abstract class whose subclasses include a `ShapeDrawable` and a `BitmapDrawable`.

Figure 9.2 shows the buttons that were defined in Listing 9.2.

The IDs of the buttons defined in Listing 9.2 are `button1` and `button2`. In button2, the `drawableLeft` attribute has the value `@drawable/icon`. This indicates that the `icon.png` file in the drawable directory in the project is used.

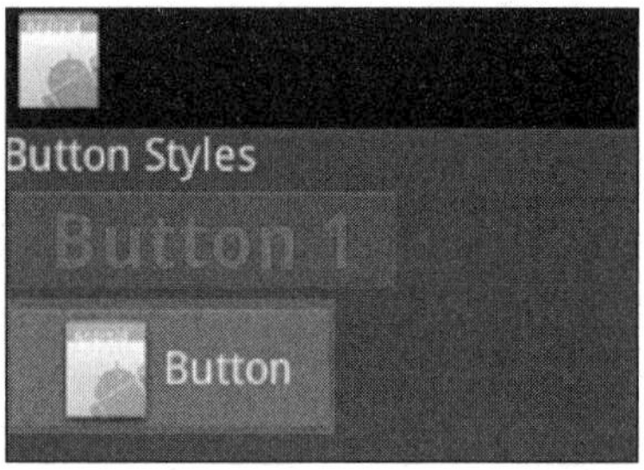

FIGURE 9.2
Using Styles and Drawables within Buttons.

We'll make one change to the layout and then work on the capability to change Button attributes from within the code. The change to the layout will be to add a new drawable for button2. To populate the drawable, we'll import two images into the drawable-mdpi directory. That directory refers to medium-density images. We'll use it as our default.

For Google TV, try using high-density images and placing them in the drawable-hdpi directory. Density refers to dots per inch, or dpi. Medium resolution is in the 150 to 200dpi range, and high resolution is in the 200 to 300dpi range.

Now we will have two drawables that we can use for button2. Our goal is to make button 1 disappear when we click button2. At the same time, we'll switch images and change the text on button2. That is done in the next section.

Changing Button Attributes Through Code

The Activity has been set up to have two Buttons declared: a `mButton1` and `mButton2`. There are also two `Drawables` defined as `mX` and `mCheck`. As in earlier examples, we get the `Buttons` using a call to `findViewById`:

```
mButton1= (Button)findViewById(R.id.button1);
```

The Drawable image files are on the resource directory for the project. To assign a Drawable field in the code, we call the `getResources` method to get the Drawable that we specify by its resource ID:

```
mCheck = getResources().getDrawable( R.drawable.check );
```

The work of the app is done in the `onClickListener` for button2. The `onClickListener` for button2 is shown in Listing 9.3

In line 3 of Listing 9.3, we check to see whether mButton1 is visible. The call to `getVisibility` returns the visible state of the button. That is compared to the constant `View.VISIBLE`. A view can be either visible, invisible, or gone. An invisible view is not seen, but it still takes up space in the layout. A view that is gone is not visible, and it does not take up any space in the layout; it is as though the view does not exist.

If mButton1 is visible, we make it invisible, and vice versa. We also change mButton2 depending on the case. In lines 5 and 9, the text is changed. In lines 6 and 10 the drawable image on the button is changed. The call to `setCompoundDrawablesWithIntrinsicBounds` takes four parameters that indicate drawables for left, top, right, and bottom. Choosing mButton2 flips between two displays.

LISTING 9.3 Updating Button Attributes Within Code

```
1:  mButton2.setOnClickListener(new OnClickListener() {
2:      public void onClick(View v) {
3:      if (mButton1.getVisibility() == View.VISIBLE){
4:        mButton1.setVisibility(View.INVISIBLE);
5:        mButton2.setText("Invisible");
6:        mButton2.setCompoundDrawablesWithIntrinsicBounds(mX, null, null, null);
7:      }else{
8:        mButton1.setVisibility(View.VISIBLE);
9:        mButton2.setText("Visible");
10:       mButton2.setCompoundDrawablesWithIntrinsicBounds(mCheck, null, null, null);
11:     }
12:   }
13: });
```

Figure 9.3 shows both states of the app. When button1, the visible button, is pressed, we change the state to say invisible and hide button1. The button is still active and can change the state back to the original display.

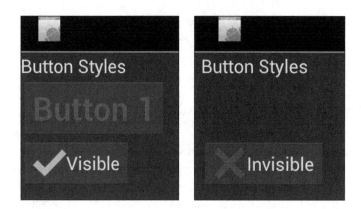

FIGURE 9.3
Flipping between button displays.

Events and Listeners

We have used the `onClickListener` several times to show interaction in an app when a button is clicked. In general, we can think of listeners as the piece of the code that responds to an event. In this case, the event is a button click. There are many types of events and corresponding listeners. For a `ListView`, there will be an event when an item is selected. For an `EditView`, there is an listener for changes.

Different views have different listeners. The pattern in Listing 9.3 of associating an event with a listener in an inner class is common. You can define separate classes for listeners if that makes sense for your app.

EditView and AutoCompleteView

An `EditView` is a simple input field. When the user selects the field, the keyboard is displayed. All Google TVs have keyboard entry. In general, we want to minimize the amount of typing in our apps. The AutoCompleteTextView helps with this. In an `AutoCompleteTextView`, when the user begins typing an entry, the full word is displayed.

EditView

Listing 9.4 shows the layout definition for an EditView.

LISTING 9.4 EditView Layout

```
1: <EditText
2:    android:hint="Enter some text"
3:    android:id="@+id/editText1"
4:    android:inputType="text"
5:    android:layout_marginTop="10dp"
6:    android:layout_height="wrap_content"
```

```
7:    android:layout_width="match_parent">
8: </EditText>
```

Line 2 specified the hint for the EditView. That is the text that will appear in the EditView to prompt the user for an entry. It will be overwritten when the user enters text. In line 4, the inputType is specified as "text". If inputType is not specified, the EditView will be displayed as a multiline field. Pressing Enter will add a new line to the input area. By specifying input-Type, the EditView shows as a single line input field. The Enter key will move the cursor to the next field on the screen.

AutoCompleteTextView

Listing 9.5 shows the layout definition for an AutoCompletTextView. There are no real differences from an EditView.

LISTING 9.5   AutoCompleteView Layout

```
1: <AutoCompleteTextView
2:    android:hint="This is an auto complete view"
3:    android:layout_height="wrap_content"
4:    android:layout_width="match_parent"
5:    android:id="@+id/autoCompleteTextView1"
6:    android:layout_marginTop="10dp">
7: </AutoCompleteTextView>
```

The autocomplete functionality is done in code. For autocomplete to work, a list of possible values must be provided. The AutoCompleteTextView is tied to an array of Strings to be displayed as possible options. This is shown in Listing 9.6.

LISTING 9.6   AutoCompleteTextView App Code

```
1: public class Hour9EditViewActivity extends Activity {
2: AutoCompleteTextView mAuto;
3: EditText mEdit;
4: String[] values = {"one", "two", "three", "one hundred", "one thousand" };
5: @Override
6:    public void onCreate(Bundle savedInstanceState) {
7:        super.onCreate(savedInstanceState)
8:        setContentView(R.layout.edit_layout);
9:        mEdit= (EditText)findViewById(R.id.editText1);
10:       mAuto= (AutoCompleteTextView)findViewById(R.id.autoCompleteTextView1);
11:       ArrayAdapter autoAdapter = new ArrayAdapter<String>
12:            (this,android.R.layout.simple_dropdown_item_1line,values);
13:       mAuto.setAdapter(autoAdapter);
14:    }
15:}
```

The new parts of Listing 9.6 occur in lines 11 to 13. An ArrayAdapter called `autoAdapter` is declared. It is passed an Android platform resource called `simple_dropdown_item_1line` and the String Array variable values defined on line 4. The list of values will display in the AutoCompleteTextView. The `simple_dropdown_item_1line` defines how a single item will be displayed. In line 13, the `autoAdapter` variable is tied to the AutoCompleteTextView with a call to `setAdapter`.

In this code, we've associated an array of String values with an Adapter, and we've tied that Adapter to the view on the screen. The result is that when a user starts typing "one" in the field, the possible values of one, one hundred, and one thousand will be displayed, as in Figure 9.4.

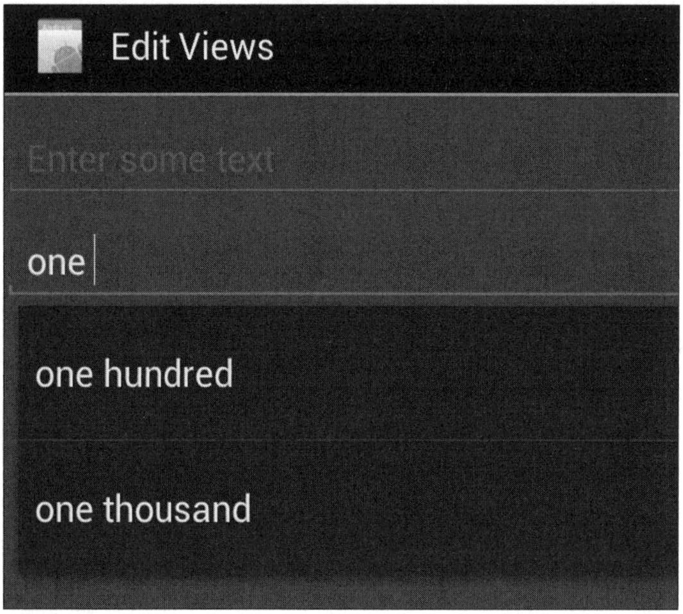

FIGURE 9.4
Entering "one" in an AutocompleteTextView shows a list of possible results

ProgressBars

ProgressBars are widgets that indicate an activity in progress. Typically, we will show a circle with a spinning animation. ProgressBars are handy when the user needs to wait for something to happen. Examples include performing a search or downloading a set of images.

Using the `setVisible` method that we covered in Listing 9.3, we can show ProgressBars as needed. Listing 9.7 defines a basic ProgressBar, and Figure 9.5 shows the result.

LISTING 9.7   Defining a ProgressBar

```
1: <ProgressBar android:id="@+id/progressBar1"
2:     android:layout_height="wrap_content"
3:     android:layout_width="wrap_content"
4: </ProgressBar>
```

FIGURE 9.5
A typical ProgressBar.

Using ImageViews

ImageViews contain images. The images displayed in ImageViews may be included in the draw-able folders within the project, they may be read from bitmap images in files, and they may even be bitmap images that we create on-the-fly. We'll examine how we can change how an image is displayed using ImageView properties and then make further changes via code in the app.

ScaleTypes

The `scaleType` property in an `ImageView` can give different effects to the same image. In Listing 9.8, we set the `scaleType` of an `ImageView` to `fitXY`. The image will be fit into the dimensions set by the width and height.

In this case, we will set the layout width and height to 100dp. Because we set `scaleType` for `fitXY` on line 3, we have the effect of shrinking the image to fit as shown in Figure 9.6.

Using `CENTER_CROP` as `scaleType` will center and crop the image. `CENTER_INSIDE` will center the image and not crop it.

LISTING 9.8   Setting ScaleType to fitXY for an ImageView

```
1: <ImageView
2:   android:layout_width="200dp"
3:   android:scaleType="fitXY"
4:   android:layout_height="200dp"
5:   android:src="@drawable/bbbsplash"
6:   android:id="@+id/bbb" >
7: </ImageView>android:layout_alignParentLeft="true"
```

FIGURE 9.6
Using scaleType set to fitXY

By setting `scaleType` to `centerInside` and the layout width and height to `wrap_content`, we get a completely different effect. The XML for the ImageView is shown in Listing 9.9.

LISTING 9.9   Setting ScaleType to centerInside for an ImageView

```
1: <ImageView
2:   android:layout_width="wrap_content"
3:   android:scaleType="centerInside"
4:   android:layout_height="wrap_content"
5:   android:src="@drawable/bbbsplash"
6:   android:id="@+id/bbb">
7: </ImageView>android:layout_alignParentLeft="true"
```

The resulting ImageView is shown in Figure 9.7.

Setting Alpha

The alpha value in an image defines how transparent it is. ImageViews have a `setAlpha` method for updating this value. The parameter to `setAlpha` is an integer between 0 and 255. Adjusting these values changes how transparent the image is and can give the effect of the image being faded. For a completely transparent image, the alpha value is zero. A completely transparent image would be invisible. The opposite is an image that is completely opaque with a setting of 255. In Listings 9.10, line 4 changes the alpha value for image.

LISTING 9.10   Setting Alpha Value Through Java Code

```
1: mAlpha= (Button)findViewById(R.id.changeAlpha);
2: mAlpha.setOnClickListener(new OnClickListener() {
3: public void onClick(View v) {
4:    mCheck1.setAlpha(60);
5: }
6:);
```

FIGURE 9.7
Using ScaleType set to centerInside

Drawing a Bitmap Directly

There may be times in developing your app when it makes sense to create an image on-the-fly. To do that, you create a Bitmap image, get the Canvas object associated with the bitmap, and then draw on that canvas. In Listing 9.11, line 5 defines a new bitmap and line 6 creates a Canvas object from that bitmap. Using the canvas, we can paint new objects into the image. The Paint object contains the attributes used for drawing on the canvas. On line 9, we write the word "hello" on the canvas for this bitmap. It will be displayed in the ImageView.

Remember, we could also define a TextView on top of an ImageView. Similarly, we could place one ImageView on top of another and make it visible or invisible. Those methods of composing a user interface may eliminate the need to create images directly.

LISTING 9.11 Creating a Bitmap Through Java Code

```
1: mAlpha= (Button)findViewById(R.id.changeAlpha);
2: mAlpha.setOnClickListener(new OnClickListener() {
3: public void onClick(View v) {
4:    mCheck1.setAlpha(60);
5:    Bitmap imageBitmap = Bitmap.createBitmap(120, 120, Bitmap.Config.ARGB_8888);
6:    Canvas canvas = new Canvas(imageBitmap);
7:    Paint p = new Paint();
8:    p.setTextSize(24);
9:    canvas.drawText("hello", 10, 20, p);
10:    mCheck2.setImageBitmap(imageBitmap);
11: }
12:);
```

Using VideoViews

VideoViews play videos. Incorporating videos should be a great part of Google TV apps. We'll look at a video that is served from a web URL and played in the app. We'll add our own controls for controlling the video, including a seekbar that indicates how much of the video has been played. In our example, the controls will remain showing on the video. We have seen how to make controls appear and disappear, so that concept could also be applied. An action can be taken when a video is clicked. Several listeners associated with VideoViews tell us when a video is ready to start and when it has completed. We'll examine how to set up these listeners in our apps.

A VideoView layout will often be very simple. Listing 9.12 shows a typical example. The code to play and control a video is more complex and interesting.

LISTING 9.12 VideoView Layout

```
1: <VideoView android:id="@+id/VideoView01"
2:    android:layout_height="fill_parent"
3:    android:layout_width="fill_parent">
4: </VideoView>
```

Loading a Video

After we declare our VideoView, we need to give the view a video to play, and then we need to start the video. To tie a video to the VideoView, a video is read from a local file or from a remote server. In both cases, we can use the setVideoUri of the VideoView. That method takes a

URI as a parameter. We can create a URI from a String. Listing 9.13 shows a VideoView being set to play a video hosted on a website. The listing assumes that a VideoView was declared as mVideoView.

LISTING 9.13 Assigning a Video to a VideoView

```
1: String videoToPlay = "http://bffmedia.com/bigbunny.mp4";
2: Uri videoUri = Uri.parse(videoToPlay);
3: mVideoView.setVideoURI(videoUri);
```

We could use the same code for reading a file from the SD card. Line 1 would change to include the location of a file:

```
String videoToPlay= Environment.getExternalStorageDirectory()+
"/Android/data/com.bffmedia/videos/bigbunny.mp4";
```

`Environment.getExternalStorageDirectory()` refers to the location of the SD card.

Starting, Pausing, and Positioning a Video

For controlling a video, the VideoView includes methods called `start`, `pause`, and `seekTo`. The `start` and `pause` methods start and stop the video. The `seekTo` method will position the video at a specific location and is based on milliseconds. If we call `seekTo` with 10,000 we will position the video at the tenth second. We can get the current position and duration of the video with the methods `getCurrentPosition` and `getDuration`. To skip ahead 10 seconds in the video, we would use

```
mVideoView.seekTo(mVideo.getCurrentPosition + 10000);
```

Listening for the States of a VideoView

Two listeners are unique to a VideoView. They are the `onPreparedListener` and the `OnCompletionListener`. Videos do not start playing immediately. First, they are downloaded and buffered. That is where the `onPreparedListener` comes in. We can do something in our user interface before the video begins. When it is prepared we can do something else. Often we will show a ProgressBar before the video starts and then hide it in the `onPreparedListener`.

The `onCompletionListener` is triggered when the video is done playing. It is an opportunity to repeat the video, start a new video, or change the user interface to prompt the user about what to do next.

Putting Button Overlays on a Video

Using a RelativeLayout or FrameLayout, we know that we can place widgets on top of each other. That provides a way to put controls on a video. We will create a FrameLayout that contains a VideoView and two LinearLayouts for holding controls. We include a ProgressBar to show before the video starts playing, a SeekBar to show the video progress, and buttons to control the video. In this case, the controls are present while the video plays. It is possible to set an onClickListener for the VideoView to show and hide the controls.

Using a SeekBar

A SeekBar is an Android widget that shows progress as a circle moving on a straight line. That is, it is precisely like a progress indicator on a TV or YouTube video. It shows what percentage of the video has been shown and how much is left to show.

To use a SeekBar, the minimum value of the timeline is 0, and we set a maximum value. Then we set the progress along the bar and the display updates proportionately. If we set the max to 100 and increment progress from 0 to 100, we'll observe the bar moving from left to right until it is complete.

For a video, a relationship exists between the SeekBar and the length of the video in seconds. We set the maximum value in the SeekBar to the duration of the video in seconds. Assuming we have a SeekBar defined as seekTimeline, we set the maximum value to the duration of the video that we get from the VideoView:

```
seekTimeline.setMax(mVideoView.getDuration());
```

As the video progresses, we want to update the SeekBar. We do this using a thread that checks the video progress and updates the SeekBar accordingly.

In Listing 9.14, we define a *runnable* or background thread that checks for the existence of the VideoView and in line 4 updates the SeekBar progress indicator to the value of the video's current position. Because the maximum value of the SeekBar is set to the duration of the video, this shows the correct relative position. Line 5 tells the UpdateProgress class to run again in .2 seconds. On line 5, frame is the variable that contains the FrameLayout. A postDelayed call can be attached to any widget.

The onResume method of the Activity is defined in line 10. On line 12, it initiates the UpdateProcess class. There is additional housekeeping in the onPause method in Line 16. We want to stop the thread from being called, so we call removeAllCallbacks.

LISTING 9.14 Incrementing the SeekBar with Video Progress

```
1: private Runnable UpdateProgress=new Runnable() {
2:   public void run() {
3:     if (mVideoView!=null) {
4:       seekTimeline.setProgress(mVideoView.getCurrentPosition());
5:       frame.postDelayed(UpdateProgress, 200);
6:     }
7:   }
8: };
9: @Override
10:protected void onResume() {
11:  super.onResume();
12:  frame.postDelayed(UpdateProgress, 200);
13:}
14:@Override
15:public void onPause() {
16:  frame.removeCallbacks(UpdateProgress);
17:  super.onPause();
18:}
```

We can use the SeekBar to find a particular spot in the video. The concept is the same, except we'll use the position of the SeekBar to set the position of the video. A SeekBar has an `onSeek-BarChangeListener` that we'll implement for this purpose. There are three methods, shown in Listing 9.15, that we must implement for listener.

LISTING 9.15 Changing Video Position from SeekBar

```
1: seekTimeline.setOnSeekBarChangeListener(new   OnSeekBarChangeListener(){
2:   public void onProgressChanged(SeekBar seekBar, int progress,
3:     boolean fromUser) {
4:     if (!fromUser) return;
5:   }
6:   public void onStartTrackingTouch(SeekBar seekBar) {}
7:   public void onStopTrackingTouch(SeekBar seekBar) {
8:     mVideoView.seekTo(seekTimeline.getProgress());
9:   }
10:});
```

We do nothing with `onStartTrackingTouch` method, but we must include it. It is on line 6 of Listing 9.15. In the `onProgressChanged` method, we ignore changes that are not from the user. That method is defined on line 2. All the work is done in the `onStopTrackingTouch` method. It indicates that the user has stopped moving the SeekBar. At that point, we read the position of the SeekBar and position the video at the point in time. That is all done in line 8.

Listing 9.15 does not account for other things that may be happening in the app. If the video is paused or being changed by rewinding, we would want to check that status and handle it for our app.

Implementing Rewind

We can implement rewind functionality using techniques similar to those that we used for the SeekBar. We'll have a rewind button and a Boolean that tells us whether we are currently rewinding. If we are rewinding and we choose the Pause button, for example, we will want to stop rewinding and pause by calling

```
mVideoView.pause();
```

For Rewind, we'll implement a thread very similar to the one that set video position on the SeekBar. That is done in Listing 9.16.

LISTING 9.16 Rewinding a Video

```
1: private Runnable Rewind=new Runnable() {
2:   public void run() {
3:     if (mVideoView!=null && mRewind==true) {
4:       int current = mVideoView.getCurrentPosition();
5:       if (current <=0 ){
6:         mVideoView.seekTo(0);
7:         seekTimeline.setProgress(0);
8:       }else{
9:         mVideoView.seekTo(current-200);
10:        seekTimeline.setProgress(mVideoView.getCurrentPosition());
11:        frame.postDelayed(Rewind, 100 );
12:     }
13:   }
14:  }
15:};
```

Listing 9.16 has a few differences from Listing 9.15. In line 3, we check to see if we have a VideoView and if we are rewinding. Next, in lines 4 and 5, we check to see if we've rewound past the beginning of the video. If we have, we set the video and SeekBar position to 0. If we are rewinding and have not reached the beginning of the video, we continue to rewind. Line 9 rewinds the video .2 seconds. Line 10 puts the SeekBar in the same position. Line 11 tells the thread to run again in .1 seconds. So we'll keep rewinding until we get to the beginning or until mRewind is set to false. We rewind the video by 2 seconds for every 1 second of actual elapsed time, so we are rewinding at double-speed.

Figure 9.8 shows the VideoView with the controls defined.

FIGURE 9.8
VideoView UI with controls on a TV.

TRY IT YOURSELF ▼

Using UI Components to Play a Video

In this hour, we implemented many types of widgets that can be used in Google TV apps. In particular, we covered details on working with ImageViews and VideoViews. Using layouts and the visibility properties of view, create a UI that plays a video and then swaps in an ImageView when the video is complete. Use an `onCompleteListener` and keep the image hidden until the video is over.

To do this, follow these steps:

1. Create a FrameLayout that contains a VideoView and an ImageView.

2. Set the initial visibility value of the ImageView to `View.GONE`.

3. Follow the example in the hour and play a video in the VideoView.

4. Implement an `onCompleteListener` for the VideoView.

5. In the `onCompleteListener`, set the visibility of the VideoView to `View.GONE` and set the visibility of the ImageView to `View.VISIBLE`. That will have the effect of showing an image when the video completes.

Summary

In this hour, we examined many widgets and examined their associated listeners to get a full understanding of both their visual properties and their functionality. Widgets have common characteristics like width, height, and visibility. Many widgets also have specialized capabilities. The `AutoCompleteTextView` can be used to prefill form fields, for example. We examined the relationship between UI components and event listeners that fire and allow us to act on events such as button clicks or changes in text of position on a seekbar.

ImageViews are used to display images, and VideoViews load and show videos. In this hour, we showed how to load images and create our own. We understand how to load a video and how to control the video within a VideoView.

Q&A

Q. **What is the difference between a Drawable and a Bitmap?**

A. A Drawable refers to anything that can be drawn, whereas a bitmap is a specific instance of a bitmap image. It is possible to create a Drawable with a set of shape commands in an XML file.

Q. **What is the relationship of an Adapter to UI components?**

A. Adapters tie data to UI components. For the AutoCompleteTextView, an Adapter contained the list of words to display when a user starts typing.

Q. **How much control do we have for a video in a VideoView ?**

A. Before the video plays, we have control by setting the VideoView's `onPrepared` listener. After the video completes, we have control via the VideoViews onComplete listener. While the video is playing, we can get information on the current position of the video using the VideoView's `getCurrentPosition` method. That will tell where the video is in milliseconds.

Workshop

Quiz

1. What does a hint do in an EditView?

2. If we have an original image that was 100 pixels wide and 100 pixels tall, and we put it into an ImageView with width set to 50dp, height set to 100dp, and scaleType set to `FIT_XY`, what would it look like?

3. We used buttons to change text fields and make widgets appear and disappear. How would you use a seekbar to change the value in a TextField?

Answers

1. A hint is text that is prefilled in the EditView. It can be typed over.

2. The image will be squished in from the sides. It will be twice as tall as it is wide.

3. Use the SeekBar's `OnSeekBarChangeListener` to detect changes. Then get the progress value from the SeekBar and update the TextField with that value. To update the TextField use the `setText` method.

Exercises

1. Implement a SeekBar that changes the text in a TextField.

2. Implement a sample app with an EditView, Button, and AutoCompleteTextView. Use the EditView and Button to populate a String array that is used by the AutoCompleteView. You will need to update the array and set the adapter with each update.

Organizing Google TV Apps Using the ActionBar

What You'll Learn in This Hour:

▶ How to implement an ActionBar

▶ How to add Tab Controls

▶ How to use MenuItems and ActionItems

▶ How to implement a LeftNavBar

The ActionBar was introduced in Android 3.0 (HoneyComb). It provides a convenient way to include tabs and other navigation elements in a tablet or GoogleTV app. The ActionBar is present throughout the life of the app. This hour covers creating an ActionBar with common elements. It then introduces the left navigation bar, which is built using a special library specifically for GoogleTV.

Implementing an ActionBar

The ActionBar is a UI element that is generally the main point of interaction for user navigation. When users want to jump from one part of your application to another, they will engage with the ActionBar to make that happen. The ActionBar can include tabs, action items, drop-down lists, and a menu.

An ActionBar is tied to a specific activity and is especially powerful when combined with fragments within a single activity.

We will create an ActionBar using common elements. To focus on the ActionBar, the action tied to each element is a short alert message indicating the action. When we create a tab called Tab 1, selecting it will display Tab 1. The code for this is shown in Listing 10.1.

LISTING 10.1   Creating the ActionBar

```
 1:   import android.app.ActionBar;
 2:   import android.app.Activity;
 3:   public class GTVActionBar extends Activity {
 4:     @Override
 5:       public void onCreate(Bundle savedInstanceState) {
 6:         super.onCreate(savedInstanceState);
 7:         setContentView(R.layout.gtvdemo);
 8:         final ActionBar actionBar = getActionBar();
 9:         actionBar.setDisplayShowTitleEnabled(false);
10:         actionBar.setNavigationMode(ActionBar.NAVIGATION_MODE_TABS);
11:       }
12:   }
```

Listing 10.1 creates a new class called `GTVActionBar` that is an Activity. Within the `onCreate` method, our ActionBar is created with the call to `getActionBar()`. That method is included in the `Activity` class. It creates an empty ActionBar for our use. Line 7 calls `setContentView` to associate this activity with a specific layout defined in an XML resource file. In this case, the layout resource contains a single LinearLayout.

In Lines 9 and 10, two additional properties of the ActionBar are set. The title of the ActionBar is not shown, and the navigation mode is set to `ActionBar.NAVIGATION_MODE_TABS`. That is required to display tabs in the ActionBar.

There are two other navigation modes: `ActionBar.NAVIGATION_MODE_STANDARD` defines a standard ActionBar with an icon and a title. `ActionBar.NAVIGATION_MODE_LIST` can be used to define a drop-down list-style navigation for the ActionBar.

At this point, the ActionBar is defined within the Activity but will not show anything. Our goal was to make the ActionBar shown in Figure 10.1.

Figure 10.1 shows an app icon, three tabs, a help icon, and a menu section. The icon is the home button for the application. Both the help icon and menu options are defined as Android *MenuItems* in the code. We'll look at each of these elements separately, beginning with tabs.

In Figure 10.1, the question mark for Help can be referred to as an ActionItem. It is shown in the ActionBar itself and when the menu is displayed.

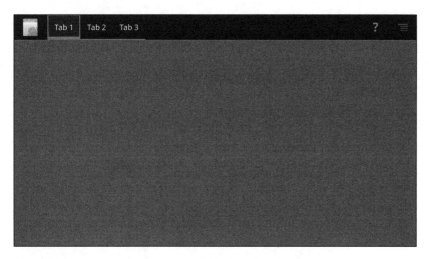

FIGURE 10.1
ActionBar with tabs and MenuItems.

Adding Tabs

Adding Tabs requires several steps. We create the tabs, add the tabs to the ActionBar, and create a `TabBarListener` where the actions associated with each tab are defined.

LISTING 10.2   Adding Tabs to the ActionBar

```
1:     import android.app.ActionBar;
2:     import android.app.Activity;
3:     import android.app.ActionBar.Tab;
4:     public class GTVActionBar extends Activity {
5:         Tab mTab1;
6:         @Override
7:         public void onCreate(Bundle savedInstanceState) {
8:             super.onCreate(savedInstanceState);
9:             setContentView(R.layout.gtvdemo);
10:            final ActionBar actionBar = getActionBar();
11:            actionBar.setDisplayShowTitleEnabled(false);
12:            actionBar.setNavigationMode(ActionBar.NAVIGATION_MODE_TABS);
13:            mTab1= actionBar.newTab().setText("Tab 1")
14:                    .setTabListener(new DemoTabListener());
15:                actionBar.addTab(mTab1);
16:        }
17:        private class DemoTabListener implements ActionBar.TabListener {
18:            public DemoTabListener() {
19:            }
```

```
20:        @Override
21:        public void onTabReselected(Tab tab, FragmentTransaction ft) {
22:        }
23:        @Override
24:        public void onTabSelected(Tab tab, FragmentTransaction ft) {
25:        }
26:        @Override
27:        public void onTabUnselected(Tab tab, FragmentTransaction ft) {
28:        }
29:     }
30:  }
```

In line 3 of Listing 10.2, we import the package required for defining tabs, and in line 5, we declare a variable called mTab1 to hold the tab. A new tab is defined and assigned to mTab1 in lines 13 and 14. The newly defined tab is added to the ActionBar in line 15.

When we examine how the tab is defined, we see a call to the ActionBar's newTab() method. An ActionBar is created in the Activity before a tab is created. Two additional things occur as the tab is defined: The text for the tab is set and will be displayed in the tab, and a TabListener for the tab is also set. The TabListener has the job of associating actions with the tab. This method of adding attributes by setting properties is known as the *builder pattern*.

The class DemoTabListener in Listing 10.1 implements the ActionBar.TabListener interface. An interface requires that specific methods must be implemented. For the ActionBar.TabListener, those methods are onTabSelected, onTabReselected, and onTabUnselected. In DemoTabListener, these methods are defined as required, but they do not do anything. If a tab changes from being unselected to selected, the onTabSelected method is called. If a selected tab is reselected, the onTabReselected method is called. When a selected tab changes to unselected, the onTabUnselected method is called.

There are cases where each of these methods can be helpful, but it can make sense to implement them with no real functionality. If a tab opens a dialog window, we may want to check whether the window is displayed when the user reselects the same tab. If it has been closed, it should be re-opened when the tab is reselected. Because it is possible to create custom views for tabs, we could use the onTabUnselected method to change how a tab looks, depending on the selected state.

Two parameters are passed to the TabListener. One is the tab that was acted on, and the other is a FragmentTransaction. Fragments are covered in detail in Hour 11, "Understanding Activities and Fragments in a Complex App." FragmentTransactions manage how Fragments are used within an app. To build a shell of an application with an ActionBar, we do not need to be concerned about the FragmentTransactions.

Adding ActionItems and MenuItems

In Figure 10.1, we see a question mark icon in the ActionBar and menu choices named Menu Option 1 and Menu Option 2. The question mark is an icon for accessing the help section of the app. Items shown like this in the ActionBar are referred to as *ActionItems*. ActionItems and things that appear in the menu are both really *MenuItems*. The difference is how they are displayed.

Listing 10.3 declares a variable for a MenuItem on line 5. Listing 10.4 defines the MenuItem. Similar to creating tabs, to create MenuItems we import the required packages and declare a MenuItem field called `mItem1`.

LISTING 10.3   Declaring the MenuItems

```
1:    import android.view.Menu;
2:    import android.view.MenuItem;
3:    import android.app.Activity;
4:    public class GTVActionBar extends Activity {
5:      MenuItem mItem1;
```

Unlike the ActionBar and tabs, MenuItems are not created in an Activity's `onCreate` method. There are two methods used to create a menu and to act on that menu. Those methods, shown in Listing 10.4, are `onCreateOptionsMenu` and `onOptionsItemSelected`.

LISTING 10.4   Defining MenuItems

```
1:    public boolean onCreateOptionsMenu(Menu menu) {
2:      super.onCreateOptionsMenu(menu);
3:      mItem1= menu.add("Menu Option 1");
4:      mItem1.setShowAsAction(MenuItem.SHOW_AS_ACTION_NEVER);
5:      return true;
6:    }
7:    public boolean onOptionsItemSelected(MenuItem item){
8:      if (item == mItem1){
9:      }
10:     return true;
11:   }
```

The field `mItem1` is defined in line 3 by adding it to the menu. Note that the menu is passed as a parameter to the `OnCreateOptionsMenu` method. The menu is tied to the activity. The MenuItem is added and set to display "Menu Option 1." Line 4 specifies how `mItem1` will be displayed. It is set to `MenuItem.SHOW_AS_ACTION_NEVER`. How a MenuItem is displayed is defined in the `setShowAsAction` method. The difference between an ActionItem and a MenuItem is based on what is set in the `setShowAsAction` method. We defined `mItem1` as a MenuItem.

To define the Help ActionItem, we include an icon in the definition and set the action to show as `MenuItem.SHOW_AS_ACTION_ALWAYS`. That is done in Listing 10.5 on line 5.

LISTING 10.5   Defining an ActionItem

```
1:    public boolean onCreateOptionsMenu(Menu menu) {
2:       super.onCreateOptionsMenu(menu);
3:       mItem3 = menu.add("Menu Option 3");
4:       mItem3.setIcon(android.R.drawable.ic_menu_help);
5:       mItem3.setShowAsAction(MenuItem.SHOW_AS_ACTION_ALWAYS);
```

An ActionItem is shown in the ActionBar itself with an icon. A MenuItem is shown as part of a list of MenuItems. In Figure 10.1 the question mark for Help is an ActionItem. The menu is on the right side of the ActionBar.

When the menu is selected, the MenuItems shown in Figure 10.2 are displayed. Note that the Help icon shows both in the ActionBar and in the list of MenuItems.

Line 4 in Listing 10.5 adds an icon to the MenuItem. The icon is a drawable resource that is included in the Android distribution. You can include your own drawable resources as well. The action is set to display as `MenuItem.SHOW_AS_ACTION_ALWAYS`.

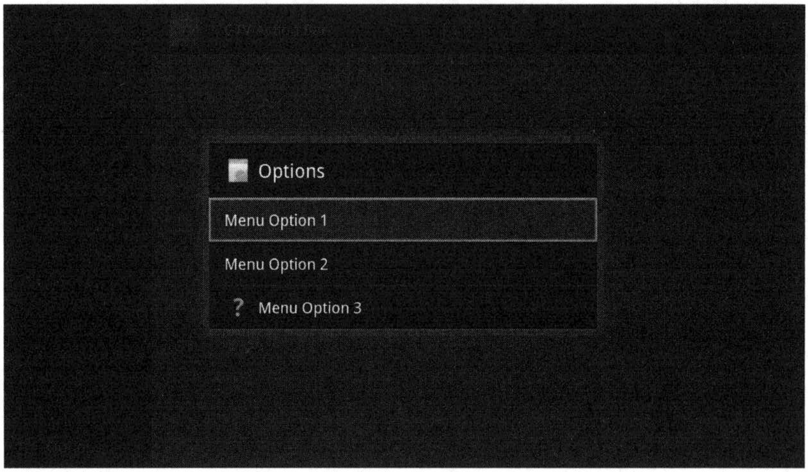

FIGURE 10.2
ActionBar showing MenuItems.

Other options for displaying MenuItems include `SHOW_AS_ACTION_IF_ROOM`, which will display on the ActionBar if there is room or in the menu if there is not. The option `SHOW_AS_ACTION_WITH_TEXT` will display as text even if an icon is associated with the MenuItem.

Using the LeftNavBar Library

All of the aspects of the ActionBar that we have covered so far are useful for both Android Tablets and Google TV. Because TVs are always in landscape mode and navigation should be easy with a remote control, an extension of the ActionBar called the LeftNavBar was created. It is used in the same way as the ActionBar and is recommended for Google TV.

Figure 10.3 shows a LeftNavBar.

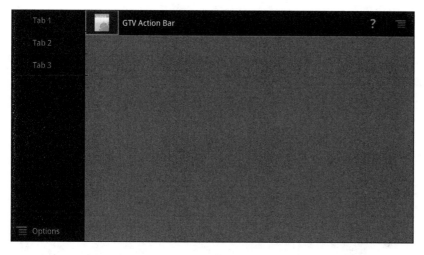

FIGURE 10.3
LeftNavBar showing tabs and menu.

The LeftNavBar puts the tabs on the left side of the screen, taking advantage of a TV's layout and size. In this example, the ActionBar also shows on the top of the screen.

It is possible to remove the ActionBar from the top of the screen. To do that, we set an option in the Android Manifest file for this project. The Android Manifest is an XML file that defines the properties of our application. To suppress the top ActionBar, we would set the Android theme to the style called `noTitleBar`:

```
android:theme="@android:style/Theme.NoTitleBar"
```

The LeftNavBar relies on an Android Library that can be found online here: http://code.google. com/p/googletv-android-samples/source/browse/#git:LeftNavBarLibrary. This is a GIT repository for the library. You can retrieve the code using a GIT command-line client or other GIT tools. You can also browse the source code online at the URL.

If you are using Eclipse, add the LeftNavLibrary project. The project is a library and cannot be run directly. To add the project, choose to create a new Android project and then choose to create that project from existing source. Browse to the folder where you saved the LeftNavLibrary project and choose it.

We will add the LeftNavLibrary to our project. To add a library using Eclipse, choose the project properties. Then choose Android, and you will see an option to add a library. When you choose to add, you should see the LeftNavLibrary project that was imported. Choose it. See Figure 10.4.

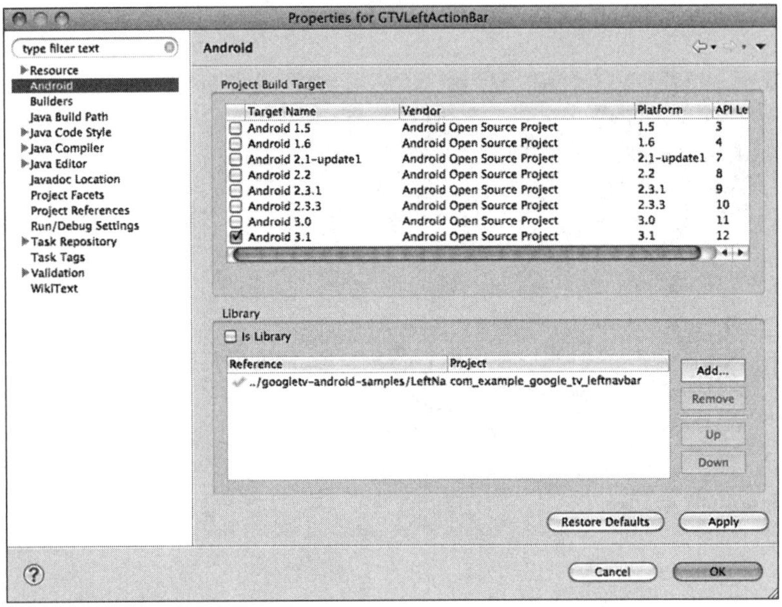

FIGURE 10.4
Adding a library to your project.

Putting It All Together

Listing 10.6 combines what has been covered in this hour to show an activity that includes a LeftNavBar with tabs, MenuItems, and an ActionItem. For each action defined, a call is made to a show a *Toast* message. Toast is similar to an alert message in JavaScript. It displays a brief message onscreen. Unlike an alert message, a Toast message does not require an acknowledgement from the user. A brief message is shown and then fades away.

LISTING 10.6   Creating an Activity with LeftNavBar, MenuItems, and an ActionItem

```
1:    package com.bffmedia.gtv.leftnav;
2:    import com.bffmedia.gtv.leftnav.R;
3:    import com.example.google.tv.leftnavbar.LeftNavBar;
```

```
4:    import com.example.google.tv.leftnavbar.LeftNavBarService;
5:    import android.app.ActionBar;
6:    import android.app.ActionBar.Tab;
7:    import android.app.Activity;
8:    import android.app.FragmentTransaction;
9:    import android.os.Bundle;
10:   import android.view.Menu;
11:   import android.view.MenuItem;
12:   import android.view.View;
13:   import android.widget.Toast;
14:
15:   public class GTVLeftActionBar extends Activity {
16:     Tab mTab1;
17:     Tab mTab2;
18:     Tab mTab3;
19:     MenuItem mItem1;
21:     MenuItem mItem2;
22:     MenuItem mItem3;
23:     private LeftNavBar mLeftNavBar;
24:
25:     @Override
26:     public void onCreate(Bundle savedInstanceState) {
27:       super.onCreate(savedInstanceState);
28:       setContentView(R.layout.gtvdemo);
29:       final LeftNavBar actionBar = (LeftNavBarService.instance()).
30:       getLeftNavBar((Activity) this);
31:       mTab1=actionBar.newTab().setText("Tab 1").setTabListener(new
              DemoTabListener());
32:       mTab2=actionBar.newTab().setText("Tab 2").setTabListener(new
              DemoTabListener());
33:       mTab3=actionBar.newTab().setText("Tab 3").setTabListener(new
              DemoTabListener());
34:       actionBar.setDisplayShowTitleEnabled(false);
35:       actionBar.setDisplayShowHomeEnabled(false);
36:       actionBar.setNavigationMode(ActionBar.NAVIGATION_MODE_TABS);
37:       actionBar.addTab(mTab1);
38:       actionBar.addTab(mTab2);
39:       actionBar.addTab(mTab3);
40:   }
```

In Listing 10.6, the LeftNavBar ActionBar is defined in lines 29 and 30. On Lines 34 and 35, the ActionBar title and home icon are disabled. This can be slightly confusing because we see these things displayed in Figure 10.2. This code has disabled these items in the LeftNavBar; they are still displayed in the default ActionBar at the top of the screen. If we chose to disable the top navigation by setting the Android Theme to noTitleBar in the Android Manifest file, we would not see this top ActionBar. An option is to use LeftNavBar and not suppress the home icon, but to suppress the top ActionBar via the manifest file.

If you did include the Home icon in the LeftNavBar and wanted to make it clickable you would set up an onClickListener using setOnClickHomeListener as follows:

```
mLeftNavBar.setOnClickHomeListener(new View.OnClickListener() {
```

Adding Actions to MenuItems and Tabs

Listing 10.7 defines MenuItems within the ActionBar, as was done earlier. The code for onOptionsItemSelected has expanded to include displaying a Toast message for each MenuItem.

LISTING 10.7   Adding the MenuItems

```
1:    public boolean onCreateOptionsMenu(Menu menu) {
2:       super.onCreateOptionsMenu(menu);
3:       mItem1= menu.add("Menu Option 1");
4:       mItem1.setShowAsAction(MenuItem.SHOW_AS_ACTION_NEVER);
5:       mItem2 = menu.add("Menu Option 2");
6:       mItem2.setShowAsAction(MenuItem.SHOW_AS_ACTION_NEVER);
7:       mItem3 = menu.add("Menu Option 3");
8:       mItem3.setIcon(android.R.drawable.ic_menu_help);
9:       mItem3.setShowAsAction(MenuItem.SHOW_AS_ACTION_ALWAYS);
10:      return true;
11:   }

11:   public boolean onOptionsItemSelected(MenuItem item){
12:      if (item == mItem1){
13:         Toast.makeText(getBaseContext(),   "Menu 1",
14:         Toast.LENGTH_LONG).show();
15:      }
16:      if (item == mItem2){
17:         Toast.makeText(getBaseContext(),   "Menu 2",
18:         Toast.LENGTH_LONG).show();
19:      }
20:      if (item == mItem3){
21:         Toast.makeText(getBaseContext(),   "Menu 3",
22:         Toast.LENGTH_LONG).show();
23:      }
24:      if (item.getItemId()== android.R.id.home) {
25:         Toast.makeText(getBaseContext(),   "Home Icon",
26:         Toast.LENGTH_LONG).show();
27:      }
28:      return true;
29:   }
```

In addition, we see something new in line 24. The item ID of the selected MenuItem, specified by item.getItemId(), is compared to a resource named android.R.id.home. That is the name that is reserved for the home icon in the top ActionBar. Had we used the home icon in the LeftNavBar, we would have used the setOnHomeListener that we covered earlier.

Listing 10.8 shows the implementation of the ActionBar's TabListener. This has been set up in a way that is very similar to the MenuItems. When a tab is selected, a Toast message is displayed.

The result is shown in Figure 10.5.

LISTING 10.8 Adding the TabListener

```
1:     private class DemoTabListener implements ActionBar.TabListener {
2:         public DemoTabListener() {
3:         }
4:         @Override
5:         public void onTabSelected(Tab tab, FragmentTransaction ft) {
6:             if (tab ==mTab1){
7:                 Toast.makeText(getBaseContext(),  "Tab 1", Toast.LENGTH_LONG).show();
8:             }
9:             if (tab ==mTab2){
10:                 Toast.makeText(getBaseContext(),  "Tab 2", Toast.LENGTH_LONG).show();
11:             }

12:             if (tab ==mTab3){
13:                 Toast.makeText(getBaseContext(),  "Tab 3", Toast.LENGTH_LONG).show();
14:             }
15:         }
16:         @Override
17:         public void onTabUnselected(Tab tab, FragmentTransaction ft) {}
18:         @Override
19:         public void onTabReselected(Tab tab, FragmentTransaction ft) {}
21:     }
20: }
```

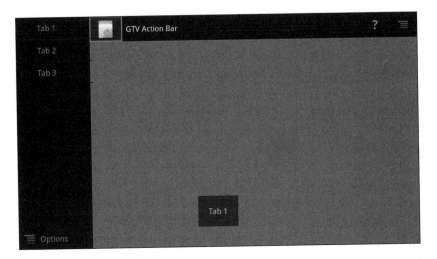

FIGURE 10.5
Clicking a tab displays a Toast message.

Organizing Your GoogleTV App

Tabs, MenuItems, and ActionItems provide multiple options for organizing the structure of your Google TV app. In most cases, the LeftNavBar is recommended to take advantage of the layout of a TV and to simplify navigation using a remote control. Tab use will be common for this purpose. MenuItems and ActionItems will be used much less frequently, but may be useful for your needs.

One typical case will be to have an ever-present LeftNavBar that works with content that is shown in the right side of the screen. The LeftNavBar will be for navigation and moving through the app, and the right display area will be used for content.

In other cases, app navigation will be used to access content, but that content will then take over the whole screen.

Thinking about the content areas of your app and the navigation areas will help when making design decisions.

Summary

In this hour, we examined an ActionBar in detail. ActionBars are available on Android tablets running HoneyComb and on Google TVs. They can include Tabs, ActionItems, and MenuItems. We implemented each of these with minimal code to make it easier to understand the overall structure of the application including options for navigation. Based on the layout of a GoogleTV, a library for LeftNavBars was created. We showed how to download that library and use it in an app.

Q&A

Q. How can ActionBars help in organizing an app?

A. ActionBars include tabs, ActionItems, and MenuItems. Each of these UI elements can navigate to another part of your app or take some other action. You can organize your app by thinking about the functions and content areas in your app and mapping them to elements in the ActionBar.

Q. What is the difference between an ActionItem and a MenuItem?

A. In code, both an ActionItem and a MenuItem are defined as part of the menu, and are both defined as MenuItems The difference is in how they are displayed. An ActionItem is displayed in the ActionBar itself. To specify the display, we use the `setShowAsAction` method.

Q. Why use a LeftNavBar when developing for Google TV?

A. The reason to use a LeftNavBar is the layout of a TV screen. Because TVs are in landscape mode, there is more room horizontally than vertically. The idea of the LeftNavBar is to take advantage of that space. The LeftNavBar is an Android Library. It must be downloaded and installed as a library project. At that point, it can be included in other Android projects.

Workshop

Quiz

1. In addition to `onTabSelected`, what are the two other methods that must be implemented in a TabListener?

2. An ActionBar is defined by calling the method `getActionBar()`. In what class is the method `getActionBar()` defined?

3. An ActionBar includes a method called `setNavigationMode`. If that method is called with a parameter of `ActionBar.NAVIGATION_MODE_TABS`, what happens?

Answers

1. A TabListener must implement three methods. They are `onTabSelected`, `onTabReselected`, and `onTabUnselected`.

2. The method `getActionBar()` is defined in the Activity class.

3. By setting the navigation mode in an ActionBar to `NAVIGATION_MODE_TABS`, we tell the ActionBar to display tabs.

Exercises

1. Modify the code in this hour to display tabs that are meaningful to an app that you are thinking of creating.

2. Modify the code in this app to include more than five MenuItems. Set two of those MenuItems to display as ActionItems.

Understanding Activities and Fragments in a Complex App

What You'll Learn in This Hour:

▶ How the Activity life cycle works

▶ What are Fragments?

▶ How to swap Fragments in an Activity

▶ How to use an ActionBar with Fragments

In this hour, you learn the details of the Activity life cycle and the relationship between Fragments and Activities. We explain Fragments in detail and show how to incorporate them into Google TV apps. Fragments make it easier to create sophisticated user interfaces. We'll use two Fragments in an Activity to understand the fundamentals of how they work. Then we'll create an app with more complex navigation using Fragments and an ActionBar.

Understanding the Activity Life Cycle

We've been using Activities in our apps since Hour 7, "Android and Google TV." In Hour 7, we said that it was useful to consider an Activity to be the full screen view in which the user interacts with the app. In this section, we will take a detailed look at the Activity life cycle. Activities are created, paused, and destroyed.

All Fragments are associated with an Activity. After examining the Activity life cycle, we'll look at how Fragments and Activities work together. One or more Fragments can live within an Activity. Fragments can be thought of as a subsection of the user interface that is used by the Activity.

Creating an Activity Life Cycle App

Listing 11.1 defines an Activity and the methods that are called throughout the Activity life cycle. The onCreate method was created when we created our app in Eclipse. The following methods were added: onStart, onResume, onPause, and onDestroy.

The Activity life cycle is important because Android is a multitasking operating system. Your Activity may be running when a user decides to do something else. When your app is running, but not visible, the onPause method runs. If you show your app and then choose the Back button on your Android device and back out of the app, your Activity is paused and then destroyed. That might be an opportunity to save or log critical information. For a TV app, the onPause method might be a good time to turn off the volume if your app plays media. The onResume method that fires when the Activity is back in focus could be a good place to reset the volume.

Fragments also have life cycle. Understanding the life cycle concept for both Activities and Fragments can be helpful in debugging a complex app or understanding where to look when something unexpected occurs in development.

LISTING 11.1 Showing Activity Life Cycle

```
1:  package com.bffmedia.hour11;
2:  import android.app.Activity;
3:  import android.os.Bundle;
4:  import android.util.Log;
5:  public class Hour11Activity extends Activity {
6:      private static final String TAG = "Hour11Activity";
7:      /** Called when the activity is first created. */
8:      @Override
9:      public void onCreate(Bundle savedInstanceState) {
10:     Log.v(TAG, "onCreate");
11:         super.onCreate(savedInstanceState);
12:         setContentView(R.layout.main);
13:     }
14:     @Override
15:     public void onStart() {
16:     Log.v(TAG, "onStart");
17:         super.onStart();
18:     }
19:     @Override
20:     public void onResume() {
21:     Log.v(TAG, "onResume");
22:         super.onResume();
23:     }
24:     @Override
25:     public void onPause() {
26:     Log.v(TAG, "onPause");
27:         super.onPause();
28:     }
29:     @Override
30:     public void onDestroy() {
31:     Log.v(TAG, "onDestroy");
32:         super.onDestroy();
33:     }
34: }
```

In Listing 11.1 the idea of logging is introduced. In line 4, the package `android.util.log` is imported. That makes the classes in the log package available to this app. Line 6 defined a static String called `TAG`. It is used in subsequent calls to the `Log.v` method.

In the modified code, we override the methods that are part of the Activity life cycle and log them with a tag and a String indicating the name of the current method. When the method is called, this info will be included in a log file.

Using Logcat to Check Results

Logcat is part of DDMS. Within Eclipse, we can choose the DDMS perspective. From there, the logcat window can be maximized to view what is happening on the device, as shown in Figure 11.1. In our case, the device is the AVD we defined earlier. When the app is started, we see several entries for Hour11Activity.

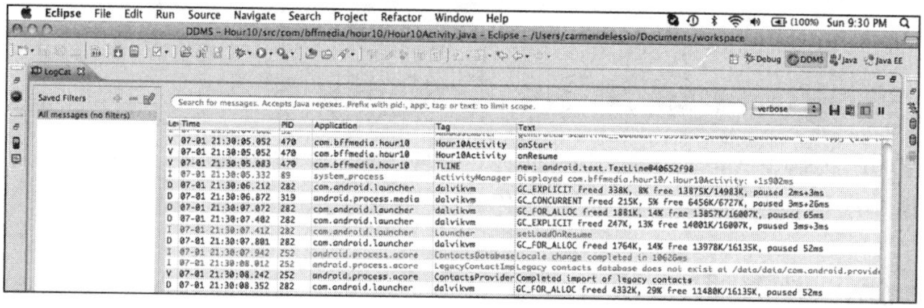

FIGURE 11.1
Logcat for starting the Activity.

While the app is running, choose the Back button in the emulator. The Hour11 app is now no longer visible. The methods `onPause` and `onDestroy` run as this occurs. We see these events logged in Figure 11.2.

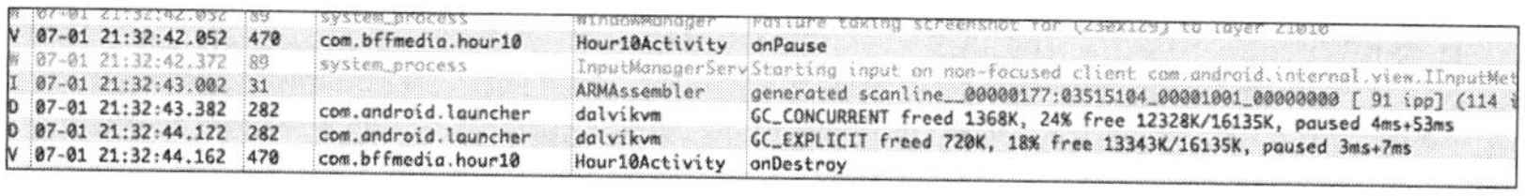

FIGURE 11.2
Logcat for ending the Activity.

Understanding Fragments

Fragments are sections of full UI functionality on a screen. They were introduced in Android 3.0 Honeycomb, which runs on Android tablets and Google TV. Before Fragments, the user interface for an Android app was made up of activities, layouts, and components like Buttons and TextViews. Activities load Fragments as part of the user interface. This adds a level of flexibility to creating apps and makes it possible to create an app with one Activity and multiple Fragments.

One reason Fragments were introduced was to make it easier to create apps that worked well on small devices, such as phones, as well as on larger devices, such as tablets and televisions. On a phone, you might use one Fragment in an Activity. On a tablet or TV, you might combine several Fragments within the Activity to take advantage of the larger display area.

Like activities, Fragments have a life cycle. They are started, paused, and destroyed. Fragments always live within an Activity, and whatever happens in the Activity happens in the Fragment. If an Activity is destroyed, all the Fragments within the Activity are also destroyed. You can consider Fragments to be subactivities with their own components, inputs, and interactions.

In this hour, we'll implement Fragments by creating a Layout and Class for each Fragment.

Swapping Fragments in an Activity

To create an Activity with a Button that swaps two Fragments takes a good amount of setup work, but it is a good way to understand how to use Fragments.

Creating Fragment XML Layouts

The layout for the Activity created in this section will have a horizontal LinearLayout that holds two vertical LinearLayouts. The left layout contains a single button, and the right layout is empty. We will use that right layout as the container for our Fragments. That is, we will add Fragments to the empty layout on the right. Figure 11.3 shows the relationship between the two layouts.

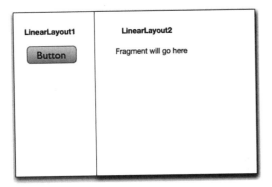

FIGURE 11.3
Layout for the Activity.

The two fragments that we will drop into the right side of the app are very similar to each other. Listing 11.2 shows the layout for our first fragment. The layout for the second fragment is nearly identical, except for the Text property in the `TextView`. The second fragment layout is named `two_fragment.xml` and the text for the TextView reads, "Layout for fragment 2."

LISTING 11.2   Layout for Fragment (one_fragment.xml)

```
1:  <?xml version="1.0" encoding="utf-8"?>
2:  <LinearLayout xmlns:android="http://schemas.android.com/apk/res/android"
3:      android:layout_width="fill_parent"
4:      android:layout_height="fill_parent"
5:      android:orientation="vertical">
6:  <TextView
7:      android:textAppearance="?android:attr/textAppearanceLarge"
8:      android:layout_height="wrap_content"
9:      android:layout_width="wrap_content"
10      android:id="@+id/textView1" android:text="Layout for fragment 1">
11: </TextView>
12: </LinearLayout>
```

Creating Fragment Java Classes

The Fragment classes that we create will be very simple. They will extend the class Fragment and create a view. The View will be created from the layout file created. For example, the class `FragmentOne.java` will create a View from the layout shown in Listing 11.2.

Listing 11.3 shows the code required for a Fragment that inflates a View. The `onCreateView` method is overridden and returns the View.

LISTING 11.3   Inflating a View (FragmentOne.java)

```
1: import android.app.Fragment;
2: import android.os.Bundle;
3: import android.view.LayoutInflater;
4: import android.view.View;
5: import android.view.ViewGroup;
6: public class TwoFragment extends Fragment    {
7:    @Override
8:    public View onCreateView(LayoutInflater
9:         inflater, ViewGroup container, Bundle savedInstanceState) {
10:    View v = inflater.inflate(R.layout.one_fragment, container, false);
11:    return v;
12:  }
13: }
```

In line 10 of Listing 11.3, a View is created using the layout we defined. The View is returned from the onCreateView method. The code to create a second Fragment is nearly identical. The name of the second Fragment class is FragmentTwo.java and the only difference in the code is that it inflates the layout R.layout.two_fragment. The two Fragments will be created in the calling Activity.

We've defined a Layout for the Activity and a simple Layout and Class for each Fragment. The work of putting this together will occur in the Activity class. We'll initially display the first Fragment. When the button is clicked, we'll check which Fragment is currently being displayed and display the other one. If we are displaying the OneFragment class, we'll display the TwoFragment class, and vice versa. Listing 11.4 shows the complete Activity code for swapping fragments. In Line 9, there is a call to getFragmentManager(). That will return a FragmentManager that handles Fragment transactions. From the FragmentManager, we call the beginTransaction method.

The result is that we have defined a FragmentTransaction called ft. We define what we want to happen with the Fragment within the FragmentTransaction. Specifically, we add a Fragment, set how the transition is displayed, and commit the FragmentTransaction.

LISTING 11.4   **Activity Code for Swapping Fragments**

```
1: public class Hour11Activity extends Activity {
2:    Button mButton1;
3:    @Override
4:    public void onCreate(Bundle savedInstanceState) {
6:       super.onCreate(savedInstanceState);
7:       setContentView(R.layout.main);
8:       FragmentOne of = new FragmentOne();
9:       FragmentTransaction ft = getFragmentManager().beginTransaction();
10:      ft.add(R.id.linearLayout2, of, "one");
11:      ft.setTransition(FragmentTransaction.TRANSIT_FRAGMENT_FADE);
12:      ft.commit();
13:      mButton1= (Button)findViewById(R.id.button1);
14:      mButton1.setOnClickListener(new OnClickListener() {
15:      public void onClick(View v) {
16:        Fragment showing = getFragmentManager().
17:                           findFragmentById(R.id.linearLayout2);
18:       if (showing.getTag().equalsIgnoreCase("one")){
19:         FragmentTwo tf = new FragmentTwo ();
20:         FragmentTransaction ft = getFragmentManager().beginTransaction();
21:         ft.replace(R.id.linearLayout2, tf, "two");
22:         ft.setTransition(FragmentTransaction.TRANSIT_FRAGMENT_FADE);
23:         ft.commit();
24:       }else{
25:         FragmentOne of = new FragmentOne ();
26:          FragmentTransaction ft = getFragmentManager().beginTransaction();
```

```
27:          ft.replace(R.id.linearLayout2, of, "one");
28:          ft.setTransition(FragmentTransaction.TRANSIT_FRAGMENT_FADE);
29:          ft.commit();
30:       }
31:     }
32:  });
33: }
```

In Listing 11.4, we create an instance of OneFragment and display it. In lines 8 to 14, we create the Fragment and a FragmentTransaction. In line 10, the Fragment is added to the container identified by resource R.id.linearLayout2. That is, our new Fragment is dropped into our LinearLayout. The last parameter to the FragmentTransaction's add method is a String called a tag. The tag allows us to refer to this Fragment later by tag name. We can set how the Fragment transitions into the Layout. In Listing 11.4 on line 27 we set the transition to FragmentTransaction.TRANSIT_FRAGMENT_FADE, which is a simple fade-in display. We then commit the FragmentTransaction. Lines 8 to 14 actually display a FragmentOne in linearLayout2.

Lines 14 to 28 show the onClickListener code for the Button. The logic is to determine which Fragment is showing and to display the other Fragment. If an instance of FragmentOne is showing, we will show a FragmentTwo.

Line 16 gets an instance of the Fragment showing on linearLayout2 using a call to findFragmentById. The id in this case is the LinearLayout that contains the Fragment. Because we gave the Fragment a tag, we can retrieve that tag in Line 17 with a call to getTag. At that point, if the tag is "one", we create a Fragment of class FragmentTwo and replace the current Fragment. We give the FragmentTwo a tag of "two".

We added the first Fragment to the layout. In subsequent calls, we call replace in the FragmentTransaction to replace the current Fragment. Replace is called in lines 20 and 26.

Using the Back Button with Fragments

A feature of Android and Google TV is the hardware or software Back button on the device. A Back button appears on the keypad remote for Google TV devices. One potentially difficult thing about handling Activities in Android is understanding what will happen when the Back button is clicked.

Things are a little different with Fragments. In Listing 11.4, we have one Activity. No matter how many times we switch Fragments, if we touch the Back button on our device, the Activity will stop. We are on the first Activity of the app, and the Back button takes us out of it.

Fortunately, with Fragments, there is an easy solution. We'll add our Fragments to the backstack. We do this with a call to the FragmentTransaction's addToBackStackMethod. This causes the Fragment state to be remembered. If the Back button is pressed, the previous Fragment shown will appear. The `addToBackStack` method takes a String as a parameter that acts as a reference for the transaction. It can be null. We can implement Back button functionality modifying the code in Listing 11.4 to contain a call to `addToBackStack` before each commit:

```
ft.addToBackStack("one fragment");
```

Adding UI Components to a Fragment

So far in this hour, we have added Fragments to an Activity and shown how we can change the Fragments in a layout. Now we can expand the Fragment code to include widgets. For this example we'll give the Fragment its own Button. We'll use that new Button to flip from one Fragment to another.

The layout and code will be similar to Listings 11.2 and 11.3 for the `FragmentOne` class. For the layout, we will add a new Button. That is, in the XML layout file `one_fragment.xml` that we use with `FragmentOne`, we will add Button. Listing 11.5 shows the `onCreateView` that is used in `FragmentOne` to define the Button and implement the `onClickListener`.

LISTING 11.5 Adding Buttons with Actions to a Fragment View

```
1: @Override
2: public View onCreateView(LayoutInflater inflater,
3:          ViewGroup container, Bundle savedInstanceState) {
4:    View v = inflater.inflate(R.layout.one_fragment, container, false);
5:    mButton1= (Button)v.findViewById(R.id.button1);
6:    mButton1.setOnClickListener(new OnClickListener() {
7:    public void onClick(View v) {
8:       FragmentTwo tf = new FragmentTwo();
9:       FragmentTransaction ft = getFragmentManager().beginTransaction();
10:      ft.replace(R.id.linearLayout2, tf, "two");
11:      ft.setTransition(FragmentTransaction.TRANSIT_FRAGMENT_FADE);
12:      ft.addToBackStack("fragment two");
13:      ft.commit();
14:   }
15: });
16: return v;
17:}
```

Listing 11.5 creates a View for the Fragment as we did in Listing 11.3. In addition, we add a Button to the View. On line 5, we use the familiar `findViewById` method. There is an important difference: When we use this method with an Activity, we can call it directly. See line 13 of Listing 11.4 as an example.

In this case, when we call `findViewById` within a Fragment, it is called as method of the View we defined. The `View v` is defined in line 4 and a Button is added to it in line 5 with the call to `findViewById`. At a high level, it is easy to see this as adding a Button to the Fragment. The `OnClickListener` for the Button swaps out `FragmentOne` and replaces it with `FragmentTwo`. Because we are in `FragmentOne`, we do not need to check what the current Fragment is.

TRY IT YOURSELF ▼

Adding a TextView to a Fragment

Adding a TextView to a Fragment is like adding a Button:

1. Add the TextView in the XML Layout file.

2. Define the TextView in the Java code. This will be similar to the Button code of Listing 11.5.

Activity Visibility in a Fragment

We now have an Activity that switches between 2 Fragments and a Fragment that loads another Fragment. There is redundant code in what we have done. Let's look at how we can streamline what we have and consolidate some code. In doing do, we'll learn more about the relationship between and Activity and a Fragment.

We said that a Fragment was something like a subactivity. Fragments have their own life cycle of events, but are also subject to the related Activity's events. If an Activity is paused or destroyed, the Fragments within that Activity are paused and destroyed. Further, we can access the Activity's data and methods from within a Fragment.

The Fragment life cycle includes a method called `OnActivityCreated`. This method is fired when the Fragment is associated with the Activity that created it. It is called after the Fragment's `onCreateView` method and before its `onStart` method. It is the first time that we know which Activity created the Fragment. One thing we can do in the `OnActivityCreated` method is to get the Activity info that created the Fragment. That can be very helpful if we want to get data or other info from the Activity to use in our Fragment.

In Listings 11.4 and 11.5 we are doing the same thing. When a user touches a button, we are swapping in different Fragments. We can consider a consolidated version of this code where we add methods into the Activity to show each Fragment. It would be ideal, if we could call the Activity's method from the Fragment. We'll show how to do that.

Listing 11.6 is functionally equivalent to the Activity we defined in Listing 11.4. The code adds a Fragment and implements a Button to check which Fragment is displaying and swaps

Fragments. Two new methods are introduced in lines 17 and 19. These new methods are called showFragmentOne and showFragmentTwo. Their job is to do the Fragment swapping.

LISTING 11.6 New Methods for the Activity

```
1: public class Hour14ActivityConsolidated extends Activity {
2: Button mButton1;
3: @Override
4: public void onCreate(Bundle savedInstanceState) {
5:    super.onCreate(savedInstanceState);
6:    setContentView(R.layout.main);
7:    FragmentOne of = new FragmentOne();
8:    FragmentTransaction ft = getFragmentManager().beginTransaction();
9:    ft.add(R.id.linearLayout2, of, "one");
10:   ft.setTransition(FragmentTransaction.TRANSIT_FRAGMENT_FADE);
11:   ft.commit();
12:   mButton1= (Button)findViewById(R.id.button1);
13:   mButton1.setOnClickListener(new OnClickListener() {
14:   public void onClick(View v) {
15:     Fragment showing = getFragmentManager().findFragmentById(R.id.linearLayout2);
16:     if (showing.getTag().equalsIgnoreCase("one")){
17:       showFragmentTwo();
18:     }else{
19:       showFragmentOne();
20:     }
21:   }
22: });
23:}
```

The code for showFragmentTwo is shown in Listing 11.7. The code for showFragmentOne is similar. The method showFragmentTwo swaps in FragmentTwo. The method showFragmentOne swaps in FragmentOne.

LISTING 11.7 Activity Method to Show a Fragment

```
1: public void showFragmentTwo(){
2:    FragmentTwo tf = new FragmentTwo();
3:    FragmentTransaction ft = getFragmentManager().beginTransaction();
4:    ft.replace(R.id.linearLayout2, tf, "two");
5:    ft.setTransition(FragmentTransaction.TRANSIT_FRAGMENT_FADE);
6:    ft.addToBackStack("fragment two");
7:    ft.commit();
8: }
```

Because our Button on FragmentOne shows FragmentTwo, it would be ideal to call the method defined in Listing 11.6 from FragmentOne. To do that, we would need to have access to the Activity and to the method showFragmentTwo. The code to do that is in Listing 11.8.

LISTING 11.8 Calling an Activity Method from a Fragment

```
1: @Override
2: public View onCreateView(LayoutInflater inflater,
3:           ViewGroup container, Bundle savedInstanceState) {
4:   View v = inflater.inflate(R.layout.one_fragment, container, false);
5:   mButton1= (Button)v.findViewById(R.id.button1);
6:   mButton1.setOnClickListener(new OnClickListener() {
7:   public void onClick(View v) {
8:     ((Hour11ActivityConsolidated)
9:       FragmentOne.this.getActivity()).showFragmentTwo();
10:  }
11: });
12: return v;
13:}
```

The code in Listing 11.8 is functionally equivalent to Listing 11.5. A Button is defined, and when it is clicked, FragmentTwo replaces FragmentOne. Line 2 defines the onCreateView for FragmentOne.

In line 8 the Fragment calls the Activity's showFragmentTwo method. There is a lot going on in that single line of code. We'll look at it from the inside out. First, there is a reference to FragmentOne.this. FragmentOne is the current class and FragmentOne.this tells us to refer to that class. That is required because the code is being called from the onClickListener. We are defining the OnClickListener class on-the-fly. The this keyword within the OnClickListener code refers to the OnClickListener itself and not the Fragment.

Fragments include a method called getActivity that returns the Activity that the Fragment is associated with. A call to getActivity will return an instance of an Activity class. We want to use the showFragmentTwo method that we defined in the Hour11ActivityConsolidated class. To do that, we must cast the Activity returned from getActivity to an Hour11ActivityConsolidated Activity.

After we have the Fragment, get the Activity, and cast the Activity to an Hour11ActivityConsolidated Activity, we can call the showFragmentTwo method.

Overall, this technique lets us refer to data and call Activity methods from the Fragments within the Activity.

Using Fragments with ActionBar

This is a good opportunity to combine what we have learned about Fragments this hour and what we learned about the ActionBar in Hour 10, "Organizing Google TV Apps Using the ActionBar." The goal is to make an app that uses ActionBar tabs to switch between Fragments.

Basic ActionBar with Fragments

We'll leverage the work done in this hour in Listing 11.6. We'll implement an ActionBar that calls either the showFragmentOne or ShowFragmentTwo method when the user selects a tab. In Listing 11.9, we create an ActionBar with two tabs. We'll use these tabs to show the Fragments.

LISTING 11.9   Creating an ActionBar with Two Tabs

```
1:  public void onCreate(Bundle savedInstanceState) {
2:  super.onCreate(savedInstanceState);
3:  setContentView(R.layout.main);
4:  final ActionBar actionBar = getActionBar();
5:  mTab1= actionBar.newTab().setText("Show Fragment 1")
6:                          .setTabListener(new DemoTabListener());
7:  mTab2= actionBar.newTab().setText("Show Fragment 2")
8:                          .setTabListener(new DemoTabListener());
9:  };
```

In Listing 11.10, we implement an ActionBar.TabListener and implement the onTabSelected and onTabReselected Methods. For the first tab we call show showFragmentOne, and for the second tab we call showFragmentTwo.

When using a TabListener, the onTabSelected method fires when the tab is first shown, so showFragmentOne is called when the Activity is set up and the tab is added. So the Fragment is added when the tab is added. No distinction needed to be made between the add and replace methods of the FragmentTransaction.

Figure 11.4 shows an ActionBar with Tabs and Fragments.

LISTING 11.10   Implementing ActionBar.TabListener

```
1:  @Override
2:  public void onTabSelected(Tab tab, FragmentTransaction ft) {
3:    if (tab ==mTab1){
4:      showFragmentOne();
5:    }
6:    if (tab ==mTab2){
7:      showFragmentTwo();
8:    }
9:  }
```

```
10: @Override
11: public void onTabUnselected(Tab tab, FragmentTransaction ft) {
12:   if (tab ==mTab1)
13:     if (mFragmentOne != null) {
14:       ft.hide(mFragmentOne);
15:     }
16:     if (tab ==mTab2)
17:       if (mFragmentTwo != null) {
18:         ft.hide(mFragmentTwo);
19:       }
20: }
21: public void onTabReselected(Tab tab, FragmentTransaction ft) {
22: }
```

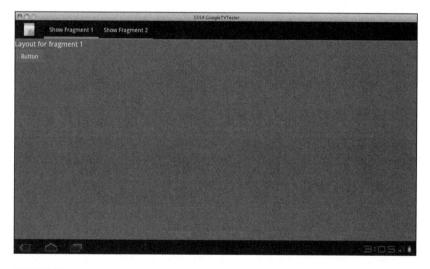

FIGURE 11.4
ActionBar shown with Fragments.

Using the FragmentTransaction Parameter

The code in Listing 11.10 accomplishes the objective of using ActionBar tabs with Fragments, but in line 2 of Listing 11.10, notice that the onTabSelected method is being passed a FragmentTransation. We are not currently using it, but we can take advantage of this FragmentTransaction as we work with Fragments.

The FragmentTransaction passed to the ActionBar.TabListener methods does not specify which Fragment to use. The FragmentTransaction is there as a convenience for development. There are restrictions on how the passed FragmentTransaction can be used.

First, the `commit` method cannot be called from the code we implement with this `FragmentTransaction`. Commits are handled within the `ActionBar.TabListener`. Second, the `addToBackStack` method may not be used. These Fragments are not added to the backstack.

With those restrictions in place, we implement the `ActionBar.TabListener` with a different strategy. Our two Fragments are defined as class variables for the listener. When Tab 1 is selected by the user, we check to see if `FragmentOne` has been defined. If it has, we show it in the Activity. If it has not been defined, we define it and display it. The selection code appears on the `OnTabSelectedListener`. We take care of removing the Fragment on the `OnTabUnselected` Listener. That is shown in Listing 11.11.

LISTING 11.11   TabListener onTabSelected Method

```
1: private class DemoTabListener implements ActionBar.TabListener {
2: FragmentOne mFragmentOne;
3: FragmentTwo mFragmentTwo;
4: @Override
5: public void onTabSelected(Tab tab, FragmentTransaction ft) {
6: if (tab ==mTab1){
7:    if (mFragmentOne == null) {
8:      mFragmentOne = new FragmentOne();
9:      ft.add(R.id.actionBarLayout, mFragmentOne, "one");
10:   } else {
11:     ft.show(mFragmentOne);
12:   }
13:}
14: if (tab ==mTab1){
15:    . . .
```

In line 2 of Listing 11.11, `mFragmentOne` is declared as a class variable. In lines 6 to 10, if Tab 1 is selected, a check is made to see if `mFragmentOne` is null. If it is not null, it is instantiated. In line 10 it is added to the Activity in the layout identified by the resource `R.id.actionBarLayout`. If `mFragment` is not null, it is shown with the call to the `FragmentTransaction`'s show method in line 11. The code for `mFragmentTwo` follows the same logic.

We need to handle removing the Fragments when another Tab is selected. In this case, we do that by hiding the Fragment when the tab is unselected. A tab is unselected when another tab is selected. The code for `onTabUnselected` is shown in Listing 11.12.

LISTING 11.12   TabListener onTabUnselected Method

```
1: @Override
2: public void onTabUnselected(Tab tab, FragmentTransaction ft) {
3:    if (tab ==mTab1)
```

```
4:      if (mFragmentOne != null) {
5:          ft.hide(mFragmentOne);
6:      }
7:   if (tab ==mTab2)
8:      if (mFragmentTwo != null) {
9:          ft.hide(mFragmentTwo);
10:     }
11: }
12:}
```

This works great, and we are not creating new Fragments each time a tab is selected. But we have introduced an issue. In our code for FragmentOne in Listing 11.6, we implement a Button that switched Fragments. In that case, we replaced the current Fragment when the Button was pressed. That will not work for us now because the code for the onTabListener in Listing 11.11 depends on knowing the state of the loaded Fragments.

Fortunately, there is a simple way to handle this case. We can say that we want a Button click in FragmentOne to behave precisely the same way as selection "Tab 2" in the Activity. We can do that by simulating a tab click in the FragmentOne code. We add a new method to the Activity to do this, as shown in Listing 11.13. The tab is defined in the class variable mTab2. Line 2 calls the select method for that tab. Calling the clickTabTwo method will select the tab, and the OnTabListener will fire.

LISTING 11.13   Defining a Click Method

```
1: public void clickTabTwo(){
2:    mTab2.select();
3: }
```

We then change the FragmentOne code to call this method. Line 8 in Listing 11.14 calls the method defined on Listing 11.13.

LISTING 11.14   Using the Click Method Within Activity

```
1: @Override
2: public View onCreateView(LayoutInflater inflater,
3:         ViewGroup container, Bundle savedInstanceState) {
4:    View v = inflater.inflate(R.layout.one_fragment, container, false);
5:    mButton1= (Button)v.findViewById(R.id.button1);
6:    mButton1.setOnClickListener(new OnClickListener() {
7:    public void onClick(View v) {
8:      ((Hour11ActivityActionBarFT) FragmentOne.this.getActivity()).clickTabTwo();
9:    }
10: });
11: return v;
12:}
```

Summary

In this hour, we introduced Fragments and demonstrated how they work in an Activity using multiple layouts and an ActionBar. Fragments provide a convenient way to create and work with complex user interfaces. We introduced the `FragmentManager` to add, replace, show, and hide Fragments using `FragmentTransactions`. We defined methods in an Activity and used those methods in the Fragments loaded by the Activity.

Q&A

Q. **What are some similarities and differences between an Activity and a Fragment?**

A. Activities are usually full-screen areas of user interaction. Activities have a life cycle that includes being created, paused, and destroyed. Fragments are associated with an Activity and can be considered a subactivity. Fragments have their own user interfaces and can be added to and removed from Fragments. Multiple Fragments can be used within an Activity.

Q. **How do you create a View for a Fragment?**

A. To create a View for a Fragment you call the Fragment's `onCreateView` method and return a View. The View can include any UI components, such as TextViews or Buttons. Actions like `onClickListeners` may be added to the Buttons. An XML Layout file can be inflated to create the View.

Q. **Fragments can be used with ActionBars, but are there any limitations?**

A. Yes, two limitations exist in this case. The `FragmentTransaction` commit method may not be called, and any Fragments used must not be added to the backstack.

Workshop

Quiz

1. What is the backstack for Fragments?

2. What method would you call to get the Activity that created a Fragment?

3. What methods of an ActionBar `TabListener` include a `FragmentTransaction` as a parameter?

Answers

1. The backstack is used to hold Fragments that have been added with a call to the `FragmentTransaction`'s `addtoBackStack` method. After being added to the stack, these fragments will be shown in reverse order when a user touches Back.

2. Fragments have a `getActivity` method for getting the Activity that they are associated with. The method will return an Activity class that you can cast to an Activity defined in the app.

3. All the methods that must be implemented are passed a `FragmentTransaction`. The methods are `onTabSelected`, `OnTabReselected`, and `OnTabUnselected`.

Exercises

1. Implement an Activity that contains three Fragments and three ActionBar tabs.

2. Create a new layout for at least one of these Fragments. Add Buttons to the Layout to navigate between Fragments.

HOUR 12
Using Specialized Fragments

What You'll Learn in This Hour:

▶ How to Display a DialogFragment

▶ How to use a ListFragment

▶ How to create GridView and Gallery Fragments

In this hour, you learn about two specialized Fragments. They are `DialogFragments` and `ListFragments`. `DialogFragments` are used to create dialog windows that allow users to interact with the app. `ListFragments` are a convenient way to show a user a list of information. Additionally, you'll learn about `GridViews` and `Gallery` views. GridViews and Gallery views can act as alternative displays for a list, but require us to build our own Fragments.

DialogFragments

Dialogs enable user interaction without losing context. When a dialog window is displayed, it usually contains a short message and one or two choices. Keeping dialogs very simple is particularly important in a Google TV app. The user has a remote and not a keyboard and is generally consuming content rather than entering information. We'll create a `DialogFragment` with a short message and Yes and No buttons. Our goals are to display the dialog, get the user decision, and then customize the message, so we can use this class for any yes or no questions in the app.

Opening and Closing a DialogFragment

We create a Layout for the `DialogFragment` the same way we did for other Fragments. The Layout contains a `TextView` and two buttons. We'll also need a place in our Activity to open this Dialog, so we'll create a Layout with a Button to open the Dialog.

The `DialogFragment` class that we'll create is very similar to the other Fragment classes that we have created. Listing 12.1 creates the `DialogFragment` class. Line 1 extends the `DialogFragment` class. As in other examples, we override the `OnCreateView` method to set up the display for this Fragment. The implementation of the Yes and No buttons closes the dialog window on lines 12 and 18 by calling the `DialogFragment`'s dismiss method.

LISTING 12.1   Creating a DialogFragment Class

```
1: public class YesNoDialogFragment extends DialogFragment  {
2:    Button mYes;
3:    Button mNo;
4:    @Override
5:    public View onCreateView(LayoutInflater inflater,
6:            ViewGroup container, Bundle savedInstanceState) {
7:     View v = inflater.inflate(R.layout.yes_no_fragment, container, false);
8:     getDialog().setTitle("Quick Question");
9:     mYes = (Button)v.findViewById(R.id.yes);
10:    mYes.setOnClickListener(new OnClickListener() {
11:      public void onClick(View v) {
12:        YesNoDialogFragment.this.dismiss();
13:      }
14:    });
15:    mNo = (Button)v.findViewById(R.id.no);
16:    mNo.setOnClickListener(new OnClickListener() {
17:      public void onClick(View v) {
18:        YesNoDialogFragment.this.dismiss();
19:      }
20:    });
21:    return v;
22:  }
23:}
```

To use the Fragments we defined in Hour 11, "Understanding Activities and Fragments in a Complex App," we displayed the Fragments in Layouts with calls to either add or replace methods of the `FragmentTransactionManager`. We'll do something similar to show the `YesNoDialogFragment`.

Figure 12.1 shows what the `YesNoDialogFragment` looks like after it is opened.

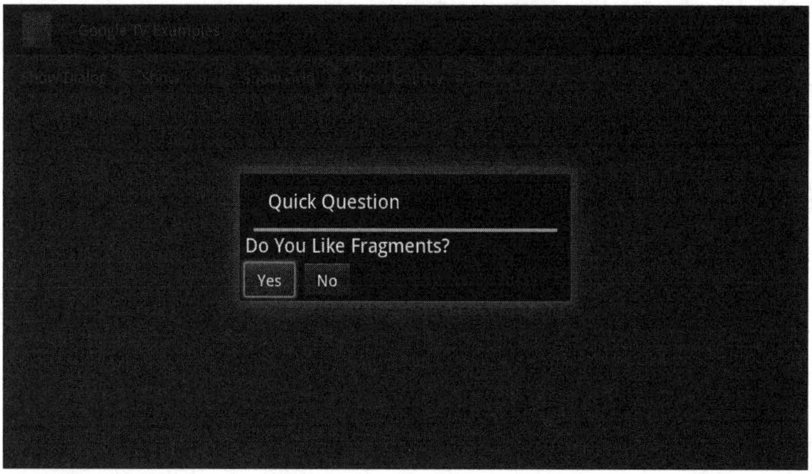

FIGURE 12.1
Displaying the YesNoDialogFragment.

In our Activity, we will add a Button and implement an `OnClickListener` to instantiate and open the Dialog. Listing 12.2 shows the code that does this. Line 4 defines a new `YesNoDialog` and line 5 displays the `DialogFragment`.

LISTING 12.2   Opening a DialogFragment

```
1: mButton1= (Button)findViewById(R.id.button1);
2: mButton1.setOnClickListener(new OnClickListener() {
3:   public void onClick(View v) {
4:     YesNoDialogFragment yesNoDialog = new YesNoDialogFragment();
5:     yesNoDialog.show(getFragmentManager(), "yes_no_dialog");
6:   }
7: });
```

Getting Data from the DialogFragment

In a typical use of a `DialogFragment`, a window opens, the user makes a choice, the window closes, and the choice from the window is acted on. In Listings 12.1 and 12.2, the code just opens and closes the window. To act on the choices made in the window, we must set up communication between the window and the Activity.

The goal is to have the Activity display YES or NO based on the choice made in the YesNoDialogFragment. We'll do this by adding a Listener Interface to the YesNoDialogFragment. When the Activity opens the DialogFragment, it will specify which listener to use. Another way to say this is: the YesNoDialogFragment will call the listener method supplied by the Activity when a selection has been made.

Listing 12.3 shows the changes to the YesNoDialogFragment class.

LISTING 12.3 Adding a Listener Interface to a DialogFragment

```
1: public class YesNoDialogFragment extends DialogFragment  {
2:    Button mYes;
3:    Button mNo;
4:    YesNoListener mListener;
5:    public interface YesNoListener {
6:      public void ready(String answer);
7:    }
8:    public YesNoDialogFragment( YesNoListener yesNoListener) {
9:      super();
10:     this.mListener = yesNoListener;
11:   }
```

In lines 5 to 7 an interface is created that defines a YesNoListener with a single method called ready. The ready method takes a String parameter called answer. This is what we will ultimately use to pass the selected answer back to the calling Activity. We declare a class variable called mListener of this type in line 4. In line 8, we change the constructor of the YesNoDialogFragment class to access a YesNoListener as a parameter. In line 10, the parameter passed to the constructor is assigned to the class variable mListener. A constructor is a method that defines a class. Some classes have more than one constructor.

The Activity will create a YesNoListener to use and pass it to the YesNoDialogFragment constructor. That YesNoListener's ready method will fire when the answer is selected. We implement that by calling the ready method in the YesNoDialogFragment class. When the Yes button is selected, we'll pass the String "yes" to the ready method.

The code to do this for the onClickListener method for the Yes button is shown in Listing 12.4. In line 4, the ready method of the YesNoReadyListener that was passed to the constructor is called.

LISTING 12.4 Calling the Listener Ready Method

```
1: mYes = (Button)v.findViewById(R.id.yes);
2: mYes.setOnClickListener(new OnClickListener() {
3:    public void onClick(View v) {
4:      mListener.ready("yes");
```

```
5:      YesNoDialogFragment.this.dismiss();
6:    }
7: });
```

We'll have to change the Activity class to add the changes that correspond to the changes made in the `DialogFragment`. That means we must create a listener and pass it in the constructor. The code to open the `DialogFragment` is nearly identical to the code in Listing 12.2. Instead of declaring the `yesNoDialog` with no parameters, we pass along a new listener:

```
YesNoDialogFragment yesNoDialog = new YesNoDialogFragment(new PostDialogListener());
```

`PostDialogListener` is a class that we defined within our Activity. It implements the `YesNoDialogListener` interface. In our case, we'll display the answer from the `DialogFragment` in a `TextView`. Listing 12.5 defines the `YesNoListener` class.

In line 3 of Listing 12.5, we override the ready method of the `YesNoListener`. That method was defined in the `YesNoListener` interface in Listing 12.3.

LISTING 12.5   **Creating a Listener in the Activity**

```
1: private final class PostDialogListener implements YesNoListener {
2:    @Override
3:    public void ready(String answer) {
4:        mTextView.setText(answer);
5:    }
6: }
```

The calling Activity has the responsibility to create the listener and to open the `YesNoDialogFragment`. The `YesNoDialogFragment` must have a constructor to accept the listener, an interface that defines the listener, and functionality that calls the listener's ready method.

Using Bundles to Pass Data

The `YesNoDialogFragment` can be useful in many situations. It could pass data to the window to display a custom message above the Yes and No buttons. One way to do this would be to create a constructor for the class that takes a `String` parameter and displays that `String` in a `TextView`. That would work well.

Another option is to pass arguments to the `DialogFragment` using a `Bundle`. A `Bundle` is a class that acts as a `Bundle` of data. It contains data elements of different types that can be retrieved by a key name. In this case, we will pass a `String` from the Activity to the Fragment. `Bundles` can be used for other data types, as well.

Listing 12.6 shows a Button onClick method to pass data to a YesNoDialogFragment using a Bundle. The Bundle is declared in line 3 and a String is added to the Bundle in line 4. Line 5 ties the Bundle to the Fragment with the call to setArguments.

LISTING 12.6   Passing Data in the Activity

```
1:public void onClick(View v) {
2:   YesNoDialogFragment yesNoDialog = new YesNoDialogFragment(new
3:   PostDialogListener());
4:   Bundle args = new Bundle();
5:   args.putString("QUESTION", "Do you like Fragments?");
6:   yesNoDialog.setArguments(args);
7:   yesNoDialog.show(getFragmentManager(), "yes_no_dialog");
8:}
```

The Fragment can now access the data being passed by the Activity to the Fragment via the Bundle. That will occur in the onActivityCreated method of the Fragment. The onCreateView method fires first. There we define a new TextView called mQuestionText. The Bundle is read in the onActivityCreated method, and the TextView is populated. This is shown in Listing 12.7.

LISTING 12.7   Read Data in the Fragment

```
1: public void onActivityCreated(Bundle savedInstanceState) {
2:    super.onActivityCreated(savedInstanceState);
3:    Bundle b = this.getArguments();;
4:    String question=b.getString("QUESTION");
5:    mQuestionText.setText(question);
6: }
```

ListFragments

A ListFragment is another specialized Fragment class that simplifies the use of Fragments when we want to display a list of items. ListFragments are an easy-to-use replacement for ListViews. Later in this hour, we examine Gallery views and GridViews. Those components provide alternatives to a list for displaying a related set of data. They are similar to a standard ListView class.

For the example, we will display a String Array of data. We'll add a Button and a LinearLayout to the layout file for our Activity. Clicking the Button will populate the new LinearLayout with a ListFragment class that we'll create.

We'll create a ListFragment class called ArrayListFragment. Listing 12.8 shows the entire class. Notice that there is no onCreateView method. A ListView is inherent in the ListFragment class.

That means that a ListView is created by the system. There is no need to explicitly create a ListView in the onCreateView method. That also means that ListFragments are used only for creating and showing lists.

LISTING 12.8 Defining a ListFragment Class

```
1: import android.app.ListFragment;
2: import android.os.Bundle;
3: import android.view.View;
4: import android.widget.ListView;
5: import android.widget.Toast;
6: import android.widget.ArrayAdapter;
7: public class ArrayListFragment extends ListFragment  {
8:   private String[] mInfo = {"one", "two", "three", "four", "five"};
9:   @Override
10:   public void onActivityCreated(Bundle savedInstanceState) {
11:      super.onActivityCreated(savedInstanceState);
12:      setListAdapter(new ArrayAdapter<String>(getActivity(),
13:      android.R.layout.simple_list_item_1, mInfo));
14:   }
15:   @Override
16:   public void onListItemClick(ListView l, View v, int position, long id) {
17:     Toast.makeText(this.getActivity(), mInfo[position], Toast.LENGTH_SHORT).
show();
18:   }
19:}
```

In line 8, the String Array mInfo is defined. It is used as the data for the ArrayAdapter defined on lines 7 and 8. An onListItemClick method for the ListFragment is defined in line 16. A Toast message will open and display the selected String from the mInfo Array.

Figure 12.2 shows the ListFragment.

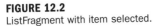

FIGURE 12.2
ListFragment with item selected.

The `ListFragment` is displayed by clicking a Button in the Activity. In this case, we treat the `ListFragment` like any other Fragment and display it with calls to a `FragmentTransaction`. The Activity layout contains a `LinearLayout` that we use for displaying the Fragment. Listing 12.9 shows the `onClick` method of the Button's `onClickListener`

LISTING 12.9   Displaying a ListFragment Class

```
1: public void onClick(View v) {
2:    ArrayListFragment aListFragment = new ArrayListFragment();
3:    FragmentTransaction ft = getFragmentManager().beginTransaction();
4:    ft.replace(R.id.linearLayout1, aListFragment, "list");
5:    ft.commit();
6: }
```

Grids and Galleries

There are no specific classes like `ListFragment` for making `GridView` and `Gallery` Fragments, but we can create useful Fragments with these components. `GridView` and `Gallery` are the class names of the components that we will use to create the Fragments. When we use these views to create Fragments, the result will be very similar to the `ListFragment`. In Listing 12.8 we used a `String Array` to populate a `ListFragment` with data. We'll use the same method to demonstrate creating a Fragment to hold a `GridView` and to hold a `Gallery`.

Creating a Fragment with a GridView

A GridView displays data in a grid containing columns and rows. It is very easy to create a Fragment that shows only a GridView. We can then place the new Fragment wherever we want it in our design. To create the Fragment, we will use a Layout that contains only a GridView. Our Fragment class will use that layout to define the View in the onCreateView method. In the onActivityCreated method, we'll populate the GridView in the same way we populated a list in the ListFragment. Listing 12.10 defines the necessary layout.

LISTING 12.10   Layout for a GridView (grid_fragment.xml)

```
1: <?xml version="1.0" encoding="utf-8"?>
2: <GridView
3:   xmlns:android="http://schemas.android.com/apk/res/android"
4:   android:layout_width="fill_parent"
5:   android:numColumns="4"
6:   android:layout_height="fill_parent" >
7: </GridView>
```

On line 5, the property for the number of columns to display is set. We'll use this GridView to create a new GridFragment class. Listing 12.11 defines a Fragment using the layout defined in Listing 12.10.

LISTING 12.11   Creating a GridView Fragment

```
1: import android.app.Fragment;
2: import android.os.Bundle;
3: import android.view.LayoutInflater;
4: import android.view.View;
5: import android.view.ViewGroup;
6: import android.widget.ArrayAdapter;
7: import android.widget.GridView;
8:
9: public class GridFragment extends Fragment   {
10:   GridView mGrid;
11:   private String[] mInfo = {"one", "two", "three", "four", "five"};
12:   @Override
13:   public void onActivityCreated(Bundle savedInstanceState) {
14:     super.onActivityCreated(savedInstanceState);
15:     mGrid.setAdapter(new ArrayAdapter<String>(getActivity(),
16:     android.R.layout.simple_list_item_1, mInfo));
17:   }
18:   @Override
19:   public View onCreateView(LayoutInflater inflater,
20:     ViewGroup container, Bundle savedInstanceState) {
```

```
21:    mGrid  = (GridView) inflater.inflate(R.layout.grid_fragment, container,
false);
22:    return mGrid;
23:  }
24:}
```

On line 10, we declare a variable called mGrid of type GridView. In the onCreateView method on line 21, mGrid is populated by inflating the GridView layout. The view returned from the onCreateView method is mGrid.

In the onActivityCreated method, on lines 15 and 16, we set an ArrayAdapter for the GridView that we defined in the onCreateView method. This part of the code is very similar to the ListFragment code in Listing 12.8.

We display this Fragment using the same methods as previously. A grid will be displayed.

Figure 12.3 shows the GridFragment defined in Listing 12.11 shown within a layout.

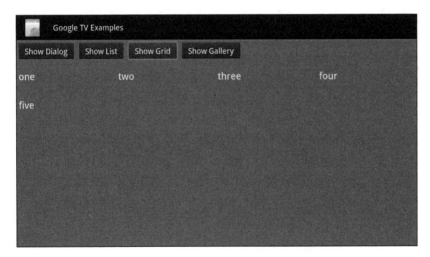

FIGURE 12.3
A GridView as a Fragment.

Creating a Fragment with a Gallery

A Gallery displays data in a view that can be scrolled through horizontally. This is ideal for a photo gallery app where the goal is to show images and swipe through them. In this case, we'll use the same model as previously and set up a Gallery populated by the data in a String Array. The code and layout are very similar to what we used for creating a GridView

Fragment. At a high level, we use a Gallery widget instead of a GridView and then implement the same code. Listing 12.12 is very similar to Listing 12.10, but instead of using a GridView, we use a Gallery. In both cases, the idea is to create a layout with a single component. That layout will be used in the onCreateView method of the Fragment. The job of the Fragment is to populate the view with data.

LISTING 12.12 Layout for a Gallery (gallery_fragment.xml)

```
1: <?xml version="1.0" encoding="utf-8"?>
2: <Gallery
3: xmlns:android="http://schemas.android.com/apk/res/android"
4: android:layout_width="fill_parent"
5: android:layout_height="fill_parent" >
6: </Gallery>
```

Listing 12.13 creates a class called GalleryFragment. This class will show a String Array as a horizontal row using the Gallery view.

The data for the GalleryFragment is defined on line 3. On line 7, the onActivityCreated method sets the adapter to an ArrayAdapter using this data. The onCreateView method on line 11 creates a Gallery view and returns it.

LISTING 12.13 Creating a GalleryFragment

```
1:  public class GalleryFragment extends Fragment    {
2:      Gallery mGallery;
3:      private String[] mInfo = {"one", "two", "three", "four", "five"};
4:      @Override
5:      public void onActivityCreated(Bundle savedInstanceState) {
6:        super.onActivityCreated(savedInstanceState);
7:        mGallery.setAdapter(new ArrayAdapter<String>(getActivity(),
8:        android.R.layout.simple_list_item_1, mInfo));
9:      }
10:     @Override
11:     public View onCreateView(LayoutInflater inflater,
12:       ViewGroup container, Bundle savedInstanceState) {
13:       mGallery = (Gallery) inflater.inflate(R.layout.gallery_fragment,
14:           container, false);
15:       return mGallery;
16:     }
17: }
```

Figure 12.4 shows the result of the GalleryFragment. Each String is shown taking up nearly the entire width of the screen. When the users clicks the next visible String, the clicked String slides into view. In this case, when the user clicks the "f" on the right side of the screen, the word "five" will slide across the screen and land where the word "four" is shown.

FIGURE 12.4
A Gallery view as a Fragment.

▼ TRY IT YOURSELF

DialogFragments

DialogFragments can be powerful for collecting info and displaying information. Create a DialogFragment with a listener that collects a String in an EditField. If the user clicks OK in the Dialog, display the String in the Activity. If the user clicks Close, then just close the Dialog. This will be similar to the `YesNoDialogFragment`, but there are differences in the layout of the DialogFragment and in the listener that will need to be created.

To do this, follow these steps:

1. Create a DialogFragment similar to the `YesNoFragment`.

2. Create your own XML Layout file for the Fragment and include an EditView and OK button.

3. Create a listener interface within the DialogFragment. The interface will pass back whatever is entered in the EditView.

4. Create an Activity with a Button that opens the DialogFragment. The Activity must implement the listener that was defined in the DialogFragment.

Summary

In this hour, we examined DialogFragments in detail and showed how to implement a `ListFragment`. We created other Fragments based on a `GridView` and `Gallery` Fragments. We saw how these Fragments are created and used in similar ways.

Q&A

Q. **How is a DialogFragment different from a Fragment?**

A. A DialogFragment is shown as an independent window. Fragments are generally embedded within layouts in an Activity. As a window, DialogFragments are opened with a show method and are closed by calling dismiss. In the `YesNoDialogFragment` we used `YesNoDialogFragment.this.dismiss()` to close the window.

Q. **Why would you create a listener interface in a DialogFragment?**

A. The listener interface is a way for the DialogFragment to provide data back to the calling Activity. The Activity implements the listener and passes it to the DialogFragment. If the DialogFragment calls the listener, information can be passed back to the Activity. The listener defined in the Activity acts as a callback for the Dialogfragment.

Q. **What is the purpose of the onCreateView method in a Fragment?**

A. The `onCreateView` method creates a view for the Fragment to display. For the GalleryFragment and GridFragment, we returned a `GridView` and `Gallery` widget for the view

Workshop

Quiz

1. What method is used to display a DialogFragment?

2. Which of the following classes that we covered in this hour does not directly implement an `onCreateView` method?

    a. GridFragment

    b. ListFragment

    c. YesNoDialogFragment

3. In what view would we set the number of columns?

Answers

1. A DialogFragment has a show method. For the `YesNoDialogFragment`, we created a variable called `yesNoDialog` and then called the show method.

   `YesNoDialogFragment yesNoDialog = new YesNoDialogFragment();`

   `yesNoDialog.show(getFragmentManager(), "yes_no_dialog");`

2. The answer is b. A `ListFragment` has an inherent `ListView`. In the other Fragments, a view needed to be created for use with a call to `onCreateView`. That is not done for the `ListFragment` because it already has a `ListView`.

3. A `GridView` has columns. The number of columns can be set in the layout for the `Gridview`.

Exercises

1. Implement an Activity with a DialogFragment that collects data in a String. Return the String to the Activity from the DialogFragment and add it to an array of Strings. Update a ListFragment on the Activity with the new data. You can keep this simple and limit the numbers of entries in the list.

2. Create an Activity with two LinearLayouts. In one, implement a `ListFragment`. When a user clicks an item in the `ListFragment`, change the Fragment displayed in the second layout. Use any Fragments we have created in Hours 10 or 11 for display.

Handling D-Pad and Key Events

What You'll Learn in This Hour:

▶ How to design for the D-Pad

▶ How to control focus on UI controls

▶ How to handle key events

Google TV remotes always have a keyboard, a cursor or mouselike device, and directional keys known as a D-Pad. The expectation is that by using the up, down, left, and right directional keys, the user can quickly navigate through the app. In this hour, you learn how to create apps that use remote control keys for navigation

Designing for the D-Pad

Whether the Google TV remote looks like a traditional computer keyboard or like a combination remote control and game controller, specific features will always be available. If that were not the case, app development would be impossible. As developers, we rely on standard features to code against. Google TV provides that. We can rely on the remote to have a keyboard, cursor, and D-Pad.

The D-Pad is the set of directional keys available on a Google TV remote. On the Logitech Revue, the D-Pad is on the lower-right part of the keyboard underneath the trackpad. It is diamond-shaped and surrounded by Back, Home, Favorite, and Picture-in-Picture keys. On the Sony Blu-Ray Disc Player, the D-Pad is in the upper-left corner of the remote. It is a circle and can be easily used with one hand. Figure 13.1 shows the D-Pad on the Logitech Revue and Sony remotes. The Logitech Review is on the left and Sony on the right.

Your app should be designed with the D-Pad as the primary form of navigation. Quick clicks for direction and OK or Enter to make a selection are the most common actions.

FIGURE 13.1
D-Pads on two remote controls.

The D-Pad provides left, right, up, and down keys. The best design to take advantage of this is a grid. D-Pad interactions should be fast, easy, and intuitive. A grid visually reinforces the capabilities of the D-Pad and should be used when possible.

Navigation in your app should be easy to learn. There may be little to learn in a grid design, but even in a more complex design you can do some things to reinforce the navigation scheme to the user. Selected items should be highlighted or otherwise set off from other elements on the page. When an item has focus or is selected, it should be clear. Ensure that arrow keys can be used to navigate to all controls on the screen. Consider whether a loop makes sense. That is, should hitting the down arrow on the last control take you to the first control?

Figure 13.2 shows an example of grid-based navigation where the selections are highlighted as the user navigates through the user interface.

FIGURE 13.2
Navigating with a D-Pad.

Controlling Focus

In most cases, the default navigation for an Android-based Google TV will work fine without modification. Sometimes, with testing, you will find that things do not work quite as expected. In other cases, you may have a "quirky" design that does not work well with the default navigation scheme.

Figure 13.3 represents the case of a quirky design layout. By default, hitting the right arrow will take focus through Button 1, Button 2, Button 4, and then Button 6. At Button 6, the left arrow would be used to get to Button 5.

The desired navigation is shown in Figure 13.4. This example navigates from Button 1 to Button 6 in the numerical order of the buttons. Clicking the right arrow on Button 6 will navigate to Button 1.

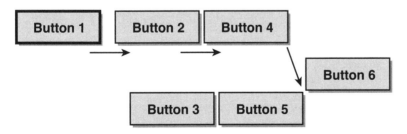

FIGURE 13.3
Default navigation shown by arrows.

The desired navigation is implemented within the XML layout file by specifying the details for focus for each element on the page. We can set focus for left, right, up, and down actions.

That is done by specifying the android:nextFocusLeft, android:nextFocusRight, android:nextFocusDown, and android:nextFocusUp values for each element.

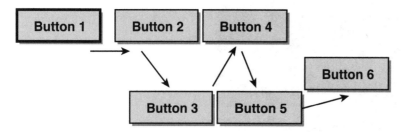

FIGURE 13.4
Desired navigation shown by arrows.

The value is set to the control that should receive focus next. For example, the android:nextFocusRight value for Button 2 is Button 3. Listing 13.1 shows these values for Button 1 and Button 2.

LISTING 13.1 Setting Navigation Focus in an XML Layout

```
 1: <Button
 2:    android:id="@+id/button1"
 3:    android:layout_width="wrap_content"
 4:    android:layout_height="wrap_content"
 5:    android:layout_alignParentLeft="true"
 6:    android:layout_below="@+id/textView1"
 7:    android:text="Button 1"
 8:    android:nextFocusLeft="@+id/button6"
 9:    android:nextFocusDown="@+id/button2"
10:    android:nextFocusRight="@+id/button2"
11:
12: />
13:
14: <Button
15:    android:id="@+id/button2"
16:    android:layout_width="wrap_content"
17:    android:layout_height="wrap_content"
18:    android:layout_below="@+id/textView1"
19:    android:layout_toRightOf="@+id/button1"
20:    android:text="Button 2"
21:    android:nextFocusDown="@+id/button3"
22:    android:nextFocusRight="@+id/button3"
23:    android:nextFocusUp="@+id/button1"
24:    android:nextFocusLeft="@+id/button1"
25: />
```

Programming D-Pad Key Events

Detecting D-Pad key events is done in an onKeyDown(int keyCode, KeyEvent event) method. The first parameter, keyCode, indicates which key has been pressed and can be referred to by a constant value from the KeyEvent class as

KeyEvent.KEYCODE_DPAD_DOWN

In addition to up, down, left, and right keys, we can refer to the center of the D-Pad as

KeyEvent.KEYCODE_DPAD_CENTER

Media keys and other keyboard keys can be intercepted in the onKeyDown event. Media keys include the actions: pause, play, stop, fast-forward, rewind, next, and previous. Table 13.1 shows typical representations of these media keys on the Google TV remote control.

TABLE 13.1 Media Keys and Values

Action	Keycode Constant	Keyboard Symbol
Start Playback	KeyEvent.KEYCODE_MEDIA_PLAY	▶
Pause Playback	KeyEvent.KEYCODE_MEDIA_PAUSE	❚❚
Stop Playback	KeyEvent.KEYCODE_MEDIA_STOP	■
Next	KeyEvent.KEYCODE_MEDIA_NEXT	▶❙
Fast-forward	KeyEvent.KEYCODE_MEDIA_FAST_FORWARD	▶▶
Previous	KeyEvent.KEYCODE_MEDIA_PREVIOUS	❙◀
Rewind	KeyEvent.KEYCODE_MEDIA_REWIND	◀◀

In this next code example, we'll implement the onKeyDown method for an Activity. Many views and controls support the onKeyDown method, but Fragments do not. It is possible to implement the KeyEvent.Callback interface on a Fragment to make the onKeyDown method available in the Fragment. One problem is that the Activity that contains the Fragment may consume the keyEvent before it gets to the Fragment. If there are any UI controls in your Activity, those controls will consume the keyEvents for navigation. One option is to handle the onKeyDown method within the Activity itself.

Implementing the onKeyDown Method

The structure of an onKeyDown method is very simple. It includes a switch statement to handle which key has been pressed.

Listing 13.2 shows the first case in a switch statement to handle keycodes. In lines 4 and 5, the media rewind key and the D-Pad left key are specified. If either of those keys is pressed, the String "LEFT CLICK" will be printed.

LISTING 13.2 Switch Based on KeyCode

```
1: @Override
2: public boolean onKeyDown(int keyCode, KeyEvent event) {
3: switch (keyCode) {
4:        case KeyEvent.KEYCODE_MEDIA_REWIND:
5:        case KeyEvent.KEYCODE_DPAD_LEFT: {
6:            System.out.println ("LEFT CLICK");
7:            break;
8:        }
```

We'll create an app that does something a little more interesting with the D-Pad controls. We'll use the left, right, up, and down arrow keys to draw short lines on the TV screen when pressed. The effect is to turn the TV into a version of the Etch-A-Sketch.

Creating a View for Drawing

To do that, we will create a new type of View called the DpadImageView by extending the ImageView class. By doing so, we are given access to a Canvas in the onDraw method of our new DpadImageView class. The DpadImageView class will not handle key events directly. Instead, it will have public methods called right, left, up, and down that can be used by other classes.

We will create an Activity that implements the onKeyDown method. Each time a relevant key is pressed, the Activity will call one of the DpadImageView's new methods. Those methods will determine a new position on the screen to draw a short line. The coordinates will be added to an ongoing list, and all will be drawn in the onDraw method.

Listing 13.3 defines a new class called DpadImageView. Line 1 defines the new class as an extension of ImageView. The logic of this new View is to have an internal ArrayList of coordinates that are used to draw the view. The inner class Coordinate is defined in lines 47 to 54. A Coordinate consists of publicly available x and y integer values.

LISTING 13.3   Extending ImageView

```
1:  public class DpadImageView extends ImageView {
2:     int x = 0;
3:     int y = 0;
4:     int newX = 0;
5:     int newY = 0;
6:     static int INTERVAL = 8;
7:     ArrayList<Coordinate> drawing = new ArrayList<Coordinate>();
8:     public DpadImageView(Context context) {
9:        super(context);
10:       drawing.add(new Coordinate(0,0));
11:    }
12:   public void right(){
13:      newX =x+INTERVAL;
14:      newY = y;
15:      drawing.add(new Coordinate(newX, newY));
16:   }
17:   public void left(){
18:      newX =x-INTERVAL;
19:      newY = y;
20:      drawing.add(new Coordinate(newX, newY));
21:   }
22:   public void up(){
23:      newX =x;
24:      newY = y-INTERVAL;
25:      drawing.add(new Coordinate(newX, newY));
26:   }
27:    public void down(){
28:       newX =x;
29:       newY = y+INTERVAL;
30:       drawing.add(new Coordinate(newX, newY));
31:    }
32:   @Override
33:   public void onDraw(Canvas canvas) {
34:      Paint paint = new Paint();
35:      paint.setStrokeWidth(INTERVAL);
36:      for (int i=0; i < drawing.size()-1; i++){
37:          canvas.drawLine(
38:                          drawing.get(i).x,
39:                          drawing.get(i).y,
40:                          drawing.get(i+1).x,
41:                           drawing.get(i+1).y,
42:                            paint);
43:      }
44:      x= newX;
45:      y= newY;
46:    }
```

```
47:    private class Coordinate {
48:      public int x;
49:      public int y;
50:      public Coordinate(int newX, int newY) {
51:      x = newX;
52:      y = newY;
53:    }
54:  }
55:}
```

DpadImageView contains four methods representing the possible directions: left, right, up, and down. When any of those methods is called, a new Coordinate is added to the growing ArrayList named drawing that was declared on line 7. For example, in the method right(), a newX value is defined by adding 8 to the old x value. The new coordinate is added to drawing.

The onDraw method defined in lines 32 to 46 reads all the coordinate values from drawing and draws lines between them. The onDraw method is called when DpadImageView is first created and when it needs to be redrawn. In this case, we force the DpadImageView to be redrawn by calling the method invalidate() from our Activity. In this example, the new View DpadImageView and the Activity work closely together to give the expected result.

Handling Keys Pressed in the Activity

When a key is pressed in the Activity, the appropriate method is called in DpadImageView. For example, the right D-Pad key causes the right() method to be fired. The DpadImageView is redrawn after each key press with the invalidate call.

The Activity defined in Listing 13.4 displays our new DpadImageView and implements the onKeyDown method. In lines 10 to 31, key presses are detected and acted upon. The Activity works in tandem with the DpadImageView. On line 12, the left D-Pad key is detected. In Line 13, the DpadImageView left() method is called. After each key is detected, the DpadImageView is invalidated. That occurs on line 29. The onKeyDown event returns true to indicate that the key event has been handled.

LISTING 13.4   Activity with OnKeyDown Implemented

```
1:    public class Hour13ActivityDpad extends Activity {
2:      DpadImageView mDpadView;
3:      @Override
4:      public void onCreate(Bundle savedInstanceState) {
5:        super.onCreate(savedInstanceState);
6:        setContentView(R.layout.dpad);
```

```
7:        mDpadView = (DpadImageView)findViewById(R.id.imageView1);
8:      }
9:      @Override
10:     public boolean onKeyDown(int keyCode, KeyEvent event) {
11:       switch (keyCode) {
12:         case KeyEvent.KEYCODE_DPAD_LEFT: {
13:           mDpadView.left();
14:           break;
15:         }
16:         case KeyEvent.KEYCODE_DPAD_RIGHT: {
17:           mDpadView.right();
18:           break;
19:         }
20:         case KeyEvent.KEYCODE_DPAD_DOWN: {
21:           mDpadView.down();
22:           break;
23:         }
24:         case KeyEvent.KEYCODE_DPAD_UP: {
25:           mDpadView.up();
26:           break;
27:         }
28:       }
29:      mDpadView.invalidate();
30:      return true;
31:     }
32: }
```

To use the new DpadImageView, we are required to put it into our XML layout file. Listing 13.5 shows that. Note that the full class name is used in the layout definition.

LISTING 13.5   Layout Including DpadImageView

```
1:   <com.bffmedia.hour13.DpadImageView
2:       android:id="@+id/imageView1"
3:       android:layout_width="match_parent"
4:       android:layout_height="match_parent"
5:       android:src="@drawable/icon" />
```

The result is an app that responds to D-Pad directional key events by allowing the user to draw on the screen. Figure 13.5 shows the results of drawing with D-Pad.

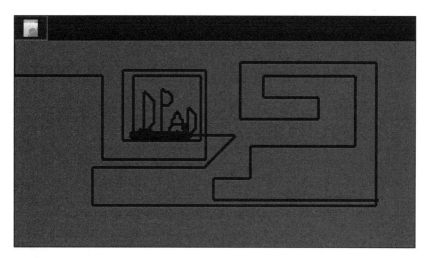

FIGURE 13.5
Drawing with D-Pad.

▼ TRY IT YOURSELF

Using the D-Pad

Change the code for the D-Pad drawing program to implement an action when the center of the D-Pad is pressed. When the user presses the center button, clear the picture.

1. Determine which key to use to represent the center of the D-Pad.

2. Detect that the center of the D-Pad has been pressed.

3. Clear the drawing. Because all coordinates are drawn each time in the `onDraw` method, one way to do this is to clear the `ArrayList` of coordinates named `drawing`.

Summary

In this hour, you learned about D-Pad and media keys on Google TV. You learned how to control navigation between components like buttons by specifying focus for a set of UI controls and by handling key presses directly. Those key presses might be D-Pad controls, media keys, or other keys.

Q&A

Q. What are some layout considerations for Google TV navigation?

A. The D-Pad has left, right, up, and down keys that can be used for easy navigation. Having UI components lined up makes it natural to use these keys. The `GridView` lines up components automatically. It is also possible to set specific focus for components. That puts the developer in control of how keys work through the app.

Q. How are keys presses handled in an Activity?

A. The method `onKeyDown` will detect key presses in an Activity. The code can detect which key was entered and take an action.

Q. How are media keys similar to D-Pad keys?

A. Both media keys and D-Pad keys are represented by `KeyEvents`. The media key for PLAY is represented by `KeyEvent.KEYCODE_MEDIA_PLAY`. The D-Pad left key Is represented by `KeyEvent.KEYCODE_DPAD_LEFT`. The system sees the `KeyEvents` in the same way, the difference is in the values. Media keys and D-Pad keys are a logical way for us to categorize the keys.

Workshop

Quiz

1. What is an example of a media key?
2. What method is overwritten to draw on a Canvas in a view?
3. Where would you use `android:nextFocusLeft`?

Answers

1. Media keys include play, pause, rewind, and fast-forward.
2. The `onDraw` method is overwritten to draw on a Canvas in a View. This was implemented in the `DpadImageView` class.

3. An XML layout for the user interface is the place for `android:nextFocusLeft`. The `nextFocusLeft` property would be added on one control to indicate which control should receive focus when the user presses the left button on a D-Pad.

Exercises

1. Implement a new focus path for the buttons in Figure 13.3. The order should be Button 1, Button 3, Button 2, Button 4, Button 5, and then Button 6. Button 6 should navigate to Button 1.

2. Add media keys to the `onKeyDown` implementation in Listing 13.4. Code the next and previous keys to perform the same actions as right and left keys.

Accessing Remote Content for a Google TV App

What You'll Learn in This Hour:

- ▶ How to access and display remote images and videos
- ▶ How to fetch remote data
- ▶ How to parse JSON formatted data
- ▶ How to put the pieces together in an app

As a developer of Google TV apps, you are able to take advantage of a truly connected device. The TV is either directly or wirelessly connected to the Internet. You can be assured that those who use your apps will have a good Internet connection and the TVs are literally plugged in. That is different from developing an Android phone app where connectivity and battery life are important considerations.

In this hour, you will learn about accessing remote data. First, we'll examine receiving and displaying remote media like images and videos. Then we'll develop an app that communicates with an external API to provide app data. We'll communicate with Facebook's API to get a list of photos from a particular Facebook page, and then the app will randomly display one of those images.

Displaying Remote Images and Videos

In Hour 9, "Optimizing UI Components for Google TV," we displayed media using an ImageView and a VideoView. In this hour, we'll display images and videos in the same way, but the focus will be on working with remote media. For any remote media, we have the choice of making local copies to improve performance. It will take less time to read a local file than it will to remotely retrieve an image or a video. We know that users will have a good wireless connection on the TV, so making a decision about what to cache and what to retrieve remotely is an app-specific decision.

Web browsers read URLs and display the relevant pages. Typically we use a web browser to display HTML pages, but we know that if we give the browser a URL for a JPEG image, the browser will display that image. The browser retrieves the remote image and then displays it.

In this hour we retrieve and display an image from a URL. We'll download the image for the app within a Fragment and then display the Fragment in our Activity. In this case, the XML layout will contain only an ImageView that we will populate.

Getting the Bitmap from a Remote Image

If we work backward from the ImageView and examine the available methods, we will see that an ImageView contains a method called setImageBitmap. The parameter is a Bitmap image. We can then consider the methods available to create a Bitmap. Bitmaps can be created using the static class BitmapFactory. One of the methods in BitmapFactory is decodeStream, which takes an InputStream as a parameter. Given an InputStream named photoStream, we create a Bitmap using

```
Bitmap bm = BitmapFactory.decodeStream(photoStream);
```

Starting with a URL or an image, we can create an InputStream using the UrlConnection class. We turn the String into a URL and then open the connection to the URL. We can then request an InputStream to get data from the URL.

We put this all together in Listing 14.1. In line 1, mImageString is a String containing the URL for an image. We create the URL, connect to it, and create an InputStream. In line 5 we use a BitmapFactory to create a bitmap from the InputStream and assign it to the Bitmap mBitmap.

LISTING 14.1   Creating a Bitmap from a URL

```
1: URL imageUrl = new URL(mImageString);
2: URLConnection connection = imageUrl.openConnection();
3: connection.connect();
4: InputStream is = connection.getInputStream();
5: mBitmap = BitmapFactory.decodeStream(is);
```

So, the code for starting with a String of a URL that contains an image is straightforward, but to use the snippet in Listing 14.1, we must address important details about the structure of our Android program.

First, we are making a network connection to download the image. That operation can cause a delay. In Android 2.3, the concept of StrictMode was introduced. The purpose of StrictMode is to alert developers to common errors by throwing exceptions. The most common use of StrictMode is to keep disk and network operations off of the main UI thread. That means that we do not want to be doing a network operation, like downloading an image, on the same thread the user is engaging with to make decisions in the app.

If we put the snippet of code in Listing 14.1 in the Fragment's `onActivityCreated` method, we will receive this error:

```
android.os.NetworkOnMainThreadException
```

Using an AsyncTask for Background Downloads

We can use an `AsyncTask` class to download the image in the background. When the image is completely downloaded, we will display it in the ImageView. The code for downloading an image using `AsyncTask` is shown in Listing 14.2.

An `AsyncTask` class has several methods that we override to handle background tasks. Typically, we override the `doInBackground` and `onPostExecute` methods. We can also override the `onPreExecute` method. Our work to download the image will be done in the `doInBackground` method. In `OnPostExecute`, we'll show the Bitmap in the ImageView.

LISTING 14.2   Downloading an Image Using an AsyncTask

```
1:  private class LoadImage extends AsyncTask<String , String , Long > {
2:  ImageView mImageView;
3:  String  mImageString;
4:  Bitmap mBitmap;
5:  public LoadImage (ImageView v, String imageString){
6:    mImageView =v;
7:    mImageString = imageString;
8:  }
9:  @Override
10: protected void onPreExecute() {
11  }
12: @Override
13: protected void onPostExecute(Long result) {
14:   if (result==0){
15:     mImageView.setImageBitmap(mBitmap);
16:   }
17: }
18: @Override
19: protected Long doInBackground(String... params) {
20:   try {
21:     URL imageUrl = new URL(mImageString);
22:     URLConnection connection = imageUrl.openConnection();
23:     connection.connect();
24:     InputStream is = connection.getInputStream();
25:     mBitmap = BitmapFactory.decodeStream(is);
26:     return (0l);
27:   } catch (MalformedURLException e) {
28:     e.printStackTrace();
29:     return (1l);
30:   } catch (IOException e) {
31:     e.printStackTrace();
```

```
32:      return (11);
33:    }
34:  }
35: }
```

In Listing 14.2, the code to download and create a bitmap is in the doInBackgroundMethod in lines 21 to 26. If the bitmap is created and there are no exceptions, the method returns a 0 for success. That result is passed to the onPostExecute method. We cannot reference user interface objects like an ImageView in the doInBackground method, but that is permitted in the onPre-Execute and onPostExecute methods. In this case, we put the bitmap in the ImageView in the onPostExecute method.

The constructor for the class is on line 17. We will pass the ImageView and the String for the URL to this class. Listing 14.3 shows the code in the onActivityCreated method of the Fragment that is executed to populate the ImageView.

LISTING 14.3   Calling the AsyncTask for Background Image Loading

```
1:  public void onActivityCreated(Bundle savedInstanceState) {
2:      super.onActivityCreated(savedInstanceState);
3:      LoadImage li = new LoadImage(
4:          mImageView,"http://www.bffmedia.com/delessio_family_pool_1080.jpg");
5:      li.execute();
6:  }
```

▼ TRY IT YOURSELF

Displaying an Image from a URL

Using the code from Listings 14.1 to 14.3, create an Android Activity that downloads an image from your own website or some other site on the Web.

Here's how it works:

1. Determine the URL that you want to use.

2. Create an Android layout that contains an ImageView.

3. Create an Activity and define the ImageView.

4. Include the AsyncTask from Listing 14.2 in your Activity.

5. Load the ImageView using LoadImage.

Note that Listing 14.3 calls LoadImage from a Fragment. In this section, it is being called from an Activity.

Setting the Internet Permission

When we create Android projects there is an associated `AndroidManifest.xml` file. This XML file is responsible for many things, which we'll cover in detail in Hour 19, "Mastering the Android Manifest File." For now, we'll say that permissions for the app are set in the manifest file and that to access a remote file, we need to set the Internet Permission as follows:

```
<uses-permission android:name="android.permission.INTERNET"></uses-permission>
```

CAUTION

Setting Permissions for an App

The app will not run if the Internet Permission is not set. You will receive an error and may spend quite a bit of time tracking it down! Check permissions as an early step in testing the app.

Caching an Image Locally

In this example, the image to download is fairly large at 578 kilobytes. It takes approximately 3 seconds to download. We have the option to cache this image locally. That is, we can write the image to a file.

When we retrieve the image, first we will check to see if a local copy is available. If there is, we'll use it. If we find and use the cache image, it will display in less than one second, which is a perceptible difference for the user.

Listing 14.4 shows how to cache the image. The listing is based on the `doInBackground` method from Listing 14.2.

The new parts of the method attempt to read the image from a file. If the file has not been created and reading the file fails, the image is retrieved, the file is written for future use, and the bitmap is returned.

Lines 7 to 13 attempt to open and read the file to create the bitmap.

Lines 14 to 25 create the file if it does not exist and then creates the bitmap.

LISTING 14.4   Caching an Image for Performance

```
1:   protected Long doInBackground(String... params) {
2:       Date now = new Date();
3:       System.out.println("time start: " + now.getTime() );
4:       String imageFileName = mImageString.replace(":", "");
5:       imageFileName =imageFileName.replace("/", "");
6:       imageFileName =imageFileName.replace(".", "");
7:       File imageFile = new File(getActivity().getCacheDir(), imageFileName);
8:       OutputStream imageOS;
```

```
 9:   if (imageFile.exists()){
10:      mBitmap = BitmapFactory.decodeFile(imageFile.getAbsolutePath());
11:      System.out.println("Getting file from Cache");
12:      return 01;
13:   }
14:   try {
15:      imageFile.createNewFile();
16:      URL imageUrl = new URL(mImageString);
17:      URLConnection connection = imageUrl.openConnection();
18:      connection.connect();
19:      InputStream is = connection.getInputStream();
20:      mBitmap = BitmapFactory.decodeStream(is);
21:      imageOS = new BufferedOutputStream(new FileOutputStream(imageFile));
22:      mBitmap.compress(Bitmap.CompressFormat.JPEG, 100, imageOS);
23:      imageOS.flush();
24:      imageOS.close();
25:      return (01);
26:   } catch (MalformedURLException e) { . . .
```

Lines 2 and 3 mark the start time of the method. The `mImageString` is cleaned up to make a more readable filename. Line 7 declares a new `File`. The `getCacheDir` method returns a private directory where cached items can be stored for the app. We use it for the `File`. In Line 9, we check to see if the image file exists; if it does, we call the `BitmapFactory` method to read a `Bitmap` from a file and return 0.

If the file does not exist, we move to the `try` statement. In Line 15, we create a new empty `imageFile`. Lines 16 to 20 are unchanged; they retrieve and create the image from the remote URL. In line 21, we open an `OutputStream` that will be used to write out the image data. The file data is written in line 22 using the Bitmap compress method. The bitmap is written to the specified `OutputStream`. The `OutputStream` is flushed and closed. The image has now been downloaded and the file is available for the next time we need to retrieve this image.

Displaying a Video from a URL in a VideoView

We saw in Hour 9 that a VideoView can be used to play a remote video. Accessing a remote video is built in to the VideoView functionality. See Listing 9.13 where the `set-VideoURI` method is used to associate a remote video with a VideoView.

Fetching Remote Data

Now that our TV is a connected device, we can pursue integrating with existing services using their APIs. Our focus will be on how to retrieve and parse JSON data to use in our TV app. We'll use Facebook as our data source. Facebook provides its Graph API that allows us to retrieve data for our apps using a REST API. Many Facebook API calls require the user to be logged in. We'll use an API call that does not require authentication. That allows us to focus on retrieving and parsing the data.

Making an API Call

Although we are using Facebook as an example, many services provide interesting and useful APIs. Part of the work in using an API is to understand how to make a call to retrieve the data and what parameters to pass.

An *endpoint* for an API is the URL your app will use to communicate with the API. The endpoint for the Facebook Graph API is https://graph.facebook.com. If we have an ID for an object on Facebook, we can retrieve it by accessing https://graph.facebook.com/ID. Full documentation on the Graph API can be found here: http://developers.facebook.com/docs/reference/api/.

Facebook uses the Coca-Cola page as an example for demonstrating the Graph API. We'll do the same. The ID for that page is 99394368305. To retrieve data on the Coca-Cola Facebook page, we can use https://graph.facebook.com/99394368305/. Accessing that address in a web browser will show some details about the page.

For our app, we'll get a list of photos associated with this page. To do that, we'll use the URL https://graph.facebook.com/99394368305/photos. If we access this address in the browser, the result will look like Figure 14.1.

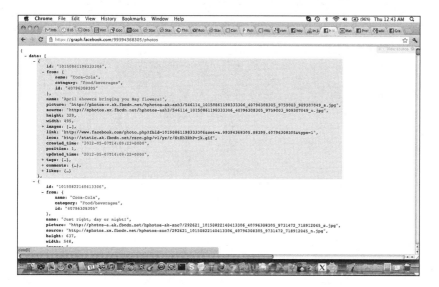

FIGURE 14.1
Facebook photo data for the Coca-Cola page.

Retrieving Data with HTTPUrlConnection

Our first goal is to make the data available at this URL available to our app. For that we'll use the HTTPUrlConnection class, which is used to access data on a remote URL. Google has provided very specific advice on what classes to use when retrieving data on Android. For Éclair and Froyo, Google recommends using Apache HTTP Client. For Gingerbread, HoneyComb, and future releases, use the HttpUrlConnection class. For GTV, we can be assured we are using a Honeycomb or newer OS, so HttpUrlConnection should be used.

We have all gone to a web page and received a 404 error to indicate that the page was not found on the server. 404 is the response code, and many possible response codes convey the failure or success of retrieving data. A 200 response indicates success. Using an HttpUrlConnection, we can get an InputStream of data and an Integer representing the response code. We'll check for a 200 response code.

The current goal of the app is to retrieve the data from https://graph.facebook.com/99394368305/photos and assign it to a String. We'll use the HttpUrlConnection class to create an InputStream. We'll check the response code and then read from the InputStream into a String. First we'll look at the snippet of code to do this; then we'll examine where it fits in with our Activity and Fragment structure.

In Listing 14.2, we used a URLConnection. As you can see in Listing 14.5, using the HttpUrlConnection class is nearly identical.

LISTING 14.5   Make an HttpUrlConnection Request and Read the Response

```
1:  HttpURLConnection connection = null;
2:  try {
3:      URL dataUrl = new URL("https://graph.facebook.com/" + mPageId + "/photos");
4:      connection = (HttpURLConnection) dataUrl.openConnection();
5:      connection.connect();
6:      int status = connection.getResponseCode();
7:      System.out.println("Response: " + status);
8:      InputStream is = connection.getInputStream();
9:      BufferedReader reader = new BufferedReader(new InputStreamReader(is));
10:     String responseString;
11:     StringBuilder sb = new StringBuilder();
12:     while ((responseString = reader.readLine()) != null) {
13:       sb = sb.append(responseString);
14:     }
15:     System.out.println("Data: \n" + sb);
16:     String photoData = sb.toString();
17: } catch (MalformedURLException e) { . . .
```

In Listing 14.5, we create an `HttpUrlConnection` and connect to it in lines 1 to 5. In line 6, we get the response code, but for now we just print it. Lines 8 to 16 get the data from the connection as an `InputStream` and convert it to a String. Each line is read and appended to a `StringBuilder`. Line 16 uses the `StringBuilder toString` method to place the complete downloaded message on the String `photoData`.

The Structure of This App

This code appears in an AsyncTask in our Activity. We are getting Facebook photo data in the background. For the full example of using this data, we'll make an app that downloads the data, parses the list of photos, and then shows a random photo from the set. For showing the photo, we'll use the Image viewing Fragment from earlier in this hour. We'll add a parameter that specifies the URL of the image to download. That URL will come from the Facebook data.

To review the structure of the app, the Activity will download the data in the background. When the data is available, a button will be enabled in the Activity UI. Clicking that button will randomly select the URL of an image. That URL will be passed to an `ImageViewFragment` to be displayed. As we click the button, random images from the set will be shown. To do that, we will need to parse the data that we have downloaded.

Using and Parsing JSON Formatted Data

JSON stands for JavaScript Object Notation. JSON began as a subset of the JavaScript language in the late 1990s, but it is a language-independent format for passing structured data in a human readable format. Most web services offer JSON as their data format.

JSON data is based on name/value pairs. We will see the name of a field paired with the value for that field. Listing 14.6 shows a snippet of the data returned from Facebook API.

LISTING 14.6   JSON Example

```
1:  {
2:  id: "10150861198333306",
3:  from: {
4:    name: "Coca-Cola",
5:    category: "Food/beverages",
6:    id: "40796308305"
7:  },
8:  name: "April showers bringing you May flowers!",
9:  picture: "http://photos-c.ak.fbcdn.net/hphotos-ak-
10: ash3/546114_10150861198333306_40796308305_9759003_909307049_s.jpg",
11: }
```

The JSON in Listing 14.6 represents a single JSON Object. Lines 3 to 6 represent an embedded object. So our photo object includes an embedded "from" object.

Creating a JSONObject

Listing 14.6 shows the data format for JSON. The Android platform includes a class for JSON called `org.json.JSONObject` to work with JSON. If we started with a String of data in JSON format, we would create a new `JSONObject` with the String as the parameter to the constructor:

```
JSONObject data = new JSONObject(photoData);
```

After we have a `JSONObject`, we can reference individual fields within the object using the name that we know. For example, in Listing 14.6, the id field has the value "10150861198333306". We can use the `getString` or `optString` method of a `JSONObject` to read this value. The benefit of `optString` is that no exception is thrown if the name we are seeking is not in the object. Given a `JSONObject` called data, we would read the value of id into a String using

```
String id=(String) data.optString("id");
```

Using a JSONArray

A `JSONArray` consists of an Array of JSON Objects. `JSONArrays` are surrounded by square brackets []. The Facebook photo data is returned as a single `JSONObject` that contains a `JSONArray` of `JSONObjects`.

As an example of a simple structure, Listing 14.7 shows a `JSONObject` that contains a `JSONArray` called data. Lines 2 and 9 begin and end the Array.

LISTING 14.7   JSONArray Structure

```
 1:  {
 2:  data: [
 3:    {
 4:      id: "1"
 5:    }
 6:    {
 7:      id: "2"
 8:    }
 9:  ]
10: }
```

Assume we start out with a String called `photoData` that contains JSON formatted data like that in Listing 14.7. Listing 14.8 loads the String into a `JSONObject` called data. In line 2, the

JSONArray photoArray is populated from the JSONObject. In lines 3 to 6, we ready each object from the JSONArray into a JSONObject and print the id field for that object.

LISTING 14.8 Loading and Reading a JSONArray

```
1:   JSONObject data = new JSONObject(photoData);
2:   JSONArray photoArray = data.optJSONArray("data");
3:   for(int i = 0; i < photoArray.length(); i++) {
4:     JSONObject photo= (JSONObject) photoArray.get(i);
5:     System.out.println (photo.optString("id");
6:   }
```

Parsing JSON

We will put together the info about the Facebook photo format, JSONObjects, and JSONArrays to create a new class called Photo.java. This will be a *plain old Java object (POJO)* for holding the data that we care about from the Facebook photo data. We'll create a constructor that takes a JSONObject with photo data and loads our object. We'll also create a constructor that will take the full data that Facebook returns and create an ArrayList of Photo objects for our use in the app.

Listing 14.9 creates the Photo class with four fields; id, name, source, and picture. In lines 6 to 11, we define a constructor that creates a Photo object from a JSONObject. Each field in the Photo object is populated with a field from the JSONObject. The JSONObject may contain many fields that we do not care about. In this case, we took four fields. We will use the source field to show the image.

LISTING 14.9 Making a Photo Object from a JSONObject

```
1:   public class Photo extends Object{
2:   String id;
3:   String name;
4:   String source;
5:   String picture;
6:   public Photo(JSONObject jsonPhoto) throws JSONException{
7:     this.id=(String) jsonPhoto.optString("id");
8:     this.source=(String) jsonPhoto.optString("source");
9:     this.name=(String) jsonPhoto.optString("name");
10:    this.picture=(String) jsonPhoto.optString("picture");
11  }
```

The method makePhotoList shown in Listing 14.10 is a method in the Photo class. It follows the model of Listing 14.8. Given a JSONObject that contains a JSONArray of JSONObjects with photo data, makePhotoList parses the data and returns an ArrayList of Photo objects.

Line 6 reads a JSONObject from the JSONArray. In line 7, we use the object to create a new Photo object.

LISTING 14.10   Making a Photo Array from a String

```
1:   public static ArrayList <Photo> makePhotoList (
2:           String photoData ) throws JSONException, NullPointerException {
1:     ArrayList <Photo> photos = new ArrayList<Photo>();
3:     JSONObject data = new JSONObject(photoData);
4:     JSONArray photoArray = data.optJSONArray("data");
5:     for(int i = 0; i < photoArray.length(); i++) {
6:       JSONObject photo=    (JSONObject) photoArray.get(i);
7:       Photo currentPhoto = new Photo (photo);
8:       photos.add(currentPhoto);
9:     }
10:    return photos;
11: }
```

Putting the Pieces Together in the App

The pieces to make our app are the Activity, the Photo object, and a Fragment that will display an image when passed the URL for that Image. In the Activity, we will have an AsyncTask that retrieves data from Facebook for a list of photos on the wall of the Coca-Cola page. After we have the data, we'll enable a Button on the Activity for viewing a random image from the group. When the user clicks that Button, we'll pick a random image from our Photo list and pass the URL to the Fragment for display.

Listing 14.11 shows the definition and constructor for an AsyncTask class called LoadPhotos.

LISTING 14.11   AsyncTask in Activity

```
1:     private class LoadPhotos extends AsyncTask<String , String , Long > {
2:     String  mPageId;
3:     Bitmap mBitmap;
4:     public LoadPhotos (String pageId){
5:       mPageId = pageId;
6:     }
7:     @Override
8:     protected void onPostExecute(Long result) {
9:       if (result==0){
10:        mButton2.setEnabled(true);
11:      }
12:    }
```

The constructor on line 4 is passed a parameter called pageId. In the onPostExecute method of this class we enable the button in the Activity. We do not want to do that until we have retrieved the data we need. The data is retrieved and loaded into an ArrayList in the doInBackground method shown in Listing 14.12.

LISTING 14.12   Retrieving Data in Background to Populate Photo Array

```
1:  @Override
2:  protected Long doInBackground(String... params) {
3:    HttpURLConnection connection = null;
4:    try {
5:      URL dataUrl = new URL("https://graph.facebook.com/" + mPageId + "/photos");
6:      connection = (HttpURLConnection) dataUrl.openConnection();
7:      connection.connect();
8:      int status = connection.getResponseCode();
9:      if (response!=200) return 1l;
10:     InputStream is = connection.getInputStream();
11:     BufferedReader reader = new BufferedReader(new InputStreamReader(is));
12:     String responseString;
13:     StringBuilder sb = new StringBuilder();
14:     while ((responseString = reader.readLine()) != null) {
15:       sb = sb.append(responseString);
16:     }
17:     String photoData = sb.toString();
18:     mPagePhotos = Photo.makePhotoList(photoData);
19:     return (0l);
20:   } catch (Exception e) {
21:       e.printStackTrace();
22:     return (1l);
23:   } finally {
24:     connection.disconnect();
25:   }
```

The code in Listing 14.12 is very similar to that in Listing 14.5. We retrieve the photo data and put it into a String called photoData. Because we created the Photo class to handle this data, we can use the Photo.makePhotoList method in line 18. At that point, we have successfully retrieved the data. The makePhotoList method will parse it and return an ArrayList of Photo objects. Those are assigned to the Activity class field mPagePhotos. When 0 is returned from this method, the onPostExecute method enables a Button to display an image from Facebook.

The code for the onClickListener for the Button is in Listing 14.13.

LISTING 14.13   Button onClickListener for Random Photo

```
1:  mButton2.setOnClickListener(new OnClickListener() {
2:    public void onClick(View v) {
3:      ImageViewFragment fbImg = new ImageViewFragment();
4:      Bundle args = new Bundle();
5:      int random = (int)(Math.random() * mPagePhotos.size());
6:      args.putString("URL", mPagePhotos.get(random).source);
7:      fbImg.setArguments(args);
8:      FragmentTransaction ft = getFragmentManager().beginTransaction();
9:      ft.replace(R.id.linearLayout1, fbImg, "Image from Facebook");
10:     ft.commit();
11:   }
12: });
```

We create an ImageViewFragment in line 3 of Listing 14.12. In line 5, a random number is generated in the range of the number of Photo objects in the ArrayList called mPagePhotos. We populated mPagePhotos in the AsyncTask called LoadPhotos. After we have the random number, we get the source field from the selected photos. The source field contains the URL of the image. We put it in a Bundle to be passed to a new ImageViewFragment.

The ImageViewFragment contains the LoadImage AsyncTask from Listings 14.2 to 14.4. There are minor changes required for the onActivityCreated method. We'll check to verify that we've been passed a URL. If we do not have one, we will show a default image. If we have been passed a URL, we will download it and display it. The LoadImage AsyncTask is unchanged, so we get the benefit of saving images to cache.

Listing 14.14 checks to see whether we have been passed a Bundle. If we have, it checks to see if we have been passed a URL to use as a parameter. The LoadImage AsyncTask uses the passed String if it is available.

Figure 14.2 shows the finished app showing the static photo and the buttons we defined.

LISTING 14.14   ImageViewFragment

```
1:  @Override
2:  public void onActivityCreated(Bundle savedInstanceState) {
3:    super.onActivityCreated(savedInstanceState);
4:    Bundle b = this.getArguments();
5:    String url = null;
6:    if (b!=null){
7:      url=b.getString("URL");
8:    }
9:    if (url==null){
10:     url = "http://www.bffmedia.com/delessio_family_pool_1080.jpg";
11:   }
12:   LoadImage li = new LoadImage(mImageView,url );
13:   li.execute();
14: }
```

FIGURE 14.2
Screenshot of the finished app.

Summary

In this hour, we covered retrieval and display of remote images in detail. In doing so, we worked with the URLConnection, Bitmap, and BitmapFactory classes to retrieve images and create Bitmaps. We also wrote Bitmaps to a file for faster loading.

To work with remote data, we built an app that retrieves a list of photos for a specified Facebook page. To create the app, we used the HTTPUrlConnection class to retrieve the data. We understood the JSON data format and parsed the data returned from Facebook. After the data was retrieved, we used our knowledge of remote image retrieval to get and display the relevant images.

Q&A

Q. What is the purpose of an AsyncTask?

A. An AsyncTask Class provides the capability to do background processing. In the example in this hour, we retrieved images and data by overriding the doInBackground method provided in AsyncTasks.

Q. What is the difference between using getString and optString in a JSONObject?

A. The getString method requires that the field being requested exists in the JSONObject. If it does not, an exception is thrown. The optString method will not throw an exception in this case.

Q. What is the responseCode in an HTTPUrlConnection used for?

A. The responseCode is an integer that indicates success or failure for the request. For example, a value of 200 means success, and a value of 404 means file not found.

Workshop

Quiz

1. Is it possible for a Fragment to use an AsyncTask?

2. If you have a snippet of JSON data, how would you distinguish between a JSONObject and a JSONArray?

3. How is an InputStream related to an HttpUrlConnection?

Answers

1. Yes, the ImageViewFragment in this hour uses an AsyncTask to retrieve image data and then display it. The image is retrieved in the `doInBackground` method and displayed by updating an ImageView in the `onPostExecute` method.

2. A `JSONObject` will be bounded by curly brackets `{}` and a `JSONArray` will be bounded by square brackets `[]`.

3. After a connection is made using an `HttpUrlConnection`, the data can be retrieved as an `InputStream`. For the example in this hour, we converted the `InputStream` to a String.

Exercises

1. In the Photo object, we populate a field called Name. This contains a caption for the image. Pass this caption to the ImageViewFragment and display it anywhere on that screen.

2. Add the field `createdTime` to the Photo object. Populate it with the value returned from Facebook in the JSON field named `created_time`. Optionally, pass this data to the ImageViewFragment and display it. This exercise will demonstrate the steps required to add data to the class and to populate that data.

Storing Data with SQLite

What You'll Learn in This Hour:

▶ How to organize data with tables

▶ How to manage a database with `SQLiteOpenHelper`

▶ How to add, delete, and update data

▶ How to use cursors to query data

▶ How to use a database with our app

SQLite is a small, fast, file-based database that is included with Android. In this hour, we'll build on our earlier work to understand how to use SQLite in our apps.

In Hour 14, "Accessing Remote Content for a Google TV App," we retrieved a list of photos in JSON format from a Facebook page. We parsed the JSON and randomly displayed a photo. In this hour, we take advantage of the SQLite Database included with Android to store that structured data. We'll build on this code in the next several hours when we cover ContentProviders and CursorLoaders to put together a full app using Facebook page photo data.

One advantage of having this data in the database is that it is immediately available to the user. In Hour 14, the data was fully retrieved before the Show Facebook Page Image button was enabled. With SQLite, after the initial database load, we can retrieve the data from the database without waiting for a new download.

Organizing a Database with Tables

At a basic level, a database stores information and provides a way for us to retrieve that data in a structured way. SQL stands for Structured Query Language and is the mechanism for data retrieval. We use queries to specify the data we want to retrieve. Data in a database is organized into tables.

A table is made up of items that form a logical group. In the photo data from Facebook, we used the returned JSON to create Photo objects that contained the photo's id, name, source, and picture info. It makes sense to start with that data to define a table.

A table can be thought of as having rows and columns. A column is similar to a heading on a spreadsheet, it defines the name of the data field. A row represents a data entry in the column. Multiple columns and rows compose a table.

Managing Data with SQLiteOpenHelper

Databases are opened and closed like files. To help manage the database, we will use the class SQLiteOpenHelper.

In Hour 14, we created a Photo class for handling basic photo data and a method to create Photo objects from JSON. We parsed the data that Facebook returns to load an array of Photo objects.

In this hour, we'll introduce a class to handle the database functionality for our app. We'll name the new class PhotoDBHelper. In PhotoDBHelper, we'll use a SQLiteDatabase class to handle the database, and we'll use an instance of the SQLiteOpenHelper class to take care of opening and closing the database. Listing 15.1 shows how the SQLiteOpenHelper is used.

LISTING 15.1   Using SQLiteOpenHelper

```
1:   private static final String DATABASE_NAME = "FB_PHOTOS";
2:   private static final String DATABASE_TABLE = "photo";
3:   private static final int DATABASE_VERSION = 3;
4:
5:   private static class DatabaseHelper extends SQLiteOpenHelper {
6:     DatabaseHelper(Context context) {
7:       super(context, DATABASE_NAME, null, DATABASE_VERSION);
7:     }
9:     @Override
10:    public void onCreate(SQLiteDatabase db) {
11:      db.execSQL(DATABASE_CREATE);
12:    }
13:    @Override
14:    public void onUpgrade(SQLiteDatabase db, int oldVersion, int newVersion) {
15:      db.execSQL("DROP TABLE IF EXISTS " + DATABASE_TABLE );
16:      onCreate(db);
17:    }
18: }
```

In line 5 of Listing 15.1, the static class DatabaseHelper is defined as an extension of the SQLiteOpenHelper class. The constructor in line 6 calls the super method on line 7. The parameters passed are context, DATABASE_NAME, null, and DATABASE_VERSION. DATABASE_NAME is a String and DATABASE_VERSION is an int defined on lines 1 and 3 of this listing. The super method indicates that the SQLiteOpenHelper constructor should be called.

DATABASE_VERSION represents the current version of the database. The version number starts at 1. If the DATABASE_VERSION in the constructor is larger than the current database version, the onUpgrade method will be called. The onUpgrade method on lines 14 to 17 drops the existing database table and makes a call to onCreate(db). The table is dropped in the code on line 15 using the SQLiteDatabase method db.execSQL. The SQL passed to this method is executed on the database.

The onCreate method defined on lines 10 to 12 defines the database with a call to db.execSQL.

The DATABASE_CREATE field passed as a parameter in line 11 is a String that defines how to create the table in the database. It is shown in Listing 15.2.

LISTING 15.2   Creating the Photo Database

```
1: private static final String DATABASE_CREATE =
2:    "create table photo (_id INTEGER PRIMARY KEY AUTOINCREMENT,"
3:    + "photo_id not null,"
4:    + "page_id not null,"
5:    + "name text,"
6:    + "source text,"
7:    + "picture text,"
8:    + "createdDate INTEGER,"
9:    + "modifiedDate INTEGER"
10: +");";
```

Listing 15.2 is the SQL used to create the table. In line 2 the table is created and the column _id is defined as an integer primary key that will autoincrement. We'll leave it to the SQLiteDatabase to handle incrementing this value. Including a field called _id is not strictly required when using SQLite and Android, but it is required when working with certain other Android classes, such as the CursorAdapter class. We'll use CursorAdapters in Hours 17 and 18.

The additional fields are what we will retrieve from Facebook. We are currently getting photos for one page, but we add a column for page_id so that we can ultimately query the database for more than one page. Note that we added the createdDate and modifiedDate as INTEGER. That INTEGER refers to the database integer. In our Java code, the matching type is a Long. We can add some restrictions on inserting data. For example, we can say that a field must not be null to be inserted.

This DatabaseHelper class takes care of creating and upgrading our database. All other methods are inherited from SQLiteOpenHelper. In the PhotoDBHelper class, we declare a field called mDbHelper of type DatabaseHelper. We use dDbHelper in three methods in our class; open, update, and close. They are shown in Listing 15.3.

LISTING 15.3   Open, Close, and Update

```
1:  public PhotoDBHelper open() throws SQLException {
2:    mDbHelper = new DatabaseHelper(mCtx);
3:    mDb = mDbHelper.getWritableDatabase();
4:    return this;
5:  }
6:  public void close() {
7:    if(mDbHelper!=null){
8:      mDbHelper.close();
9:    }
10: }
11: public void upgrade() throws SQLException {
12:   mDbHelper = new DatabaseHelper(mCtx); //open
13:   mDb = mDbHelper.getWritableDatabase();
14:   mDbHelper.onUpgrade(mDb, 1, 0);
15: }
```

We will need to open and close the database. When a call is made to the open method, a new DatabaseHelper class is instantiated. As we saw, this creates a database if needed and upgrades the database if the version number is larger. In line 3, a call is made to the SQLiteOpenHelper method getWritableDatabase, which will return a SQLiteDatabase object that we can read or write to. After we open the database, we need to close it. That is done on line 8 with a call to the close method. We saw in Listing 15.1 that a Context is passed to the DatabaseHelper class. The variable mCtx represents a value of type Context.

Adding, Deleting, and Updating Data

So far in this hour, we have focused on the structure of the database. We have defined a table and set up a way to open and close the database. With that done, we will focus on getting Photo objects into the database and learn how to update and delete entire rows.

Inserting a Photo

In Hour 14 we defined a Photo object, and we will start with a Photo object here. The goal is to insert this Photo object into the database. We must match fields in the object to columns in the database. The type of fields needs to match between the object and the database. Listing 15.4 shows the createPhoto method. A Photo object is passed as the only parameter. The create-Photo method inserts data for a new photo into the database.

LISTING 15.4 Inserting a Photo in the Database

```
1: public long createPhoto(Photo photoToCreate) {
2:    ContentValues initialValues = new ContentValues();
3:    if (photoToCreate.id!=null)
4:        InitialValues.put("photo_id", photoToCreate.id);
5:    if (photoToCreate.pageId!=null)
6:        initialValues.put("page_id", photoToCreate.pageId);
7:    if (photoToCreate.name!=null)
8:        initialValues.put("name", photoToCreate.name);
9:    if (photoToCreate.source!=null)
10:        initialValues.put("source", photoToCreate.source);
11:    if (photoToCreate.picture!=null)
12:        initialValues.put("picture", photoToCreate.picture);
13:    if (photoToCreate.createdDate!=0)
14:        initialValues.put("createdDate", photoToCreate.createdDate);
15:    if (photoToCreate.modifiedDate!=0)
16:        initialValues.put("modifiedDate", photoToCreate.modifiedDate);
17:    return mDb.insert(DATABASE_TABLE, null, initialValues);
18:}
```

In Listing 15.4 the `createPhoto` method is defined in line 1. A Photo object is passed as a parameter. We will use the contents of this photo object to add a row to the database.

In line 2 a `ContentValues` object called `initialValues` is instantiated. The `ContentValues` class is used to store data of different types. Data is put into a `ContentValues` object as a set of name/value pairs. The name is a String that acts as a key for retrieving the value from the `ContentValues` object. When you're working with a SQLiteDatabase, the `ContentValues` names are the names of the columns to add to the database. Note that in Listing 15.2, a column called `_id` was defined. The value was not passed in and will autoincrement with each row added.

We build a set of data to load by checking each value in the `photoToCreate` parameter. In line 17, the values in the `initialValues` `ContentValues` object are inserted into the database. If the insert is successful, the returned value will be the row id of the new photo record. If there is an error, -1 will be returned.

Updating a Photo

The method used to update photo data in the database is very similar to inserting a photo, but there are two key differences. For an update, we need to identify the photo that we want to update. That is not required for an insert. An insert creates a completely new record in the database. An update updates an existing record. Listing 15.5 shows the code for an update.

LISTING 15.5   Updating a Photo in the Database

```
1: public boolean updatePhoto(String id, Photo photoToUpdate) {
2:   ContentValues updateValues = new ContentValues();
3:   if (photoToUpdate.id!=null)
4:     updateValues.put("photo_id", photoToUpdate.id);
5:   if (photoToUpdate.pageId!=null)
6:     updateValues.put("page_id", photoToUpdate.pageId);
7:   if (photoToUpdate.name!=null)
8:   ...
9:   if (photoToUpdate.modifiedDate!=0)
10:    updateValues.put("modifiedDate", photoToUpdate.modifiedDate);
11: return mDb.update(DATABASE_TABLE, updateValues, "photo_id" + "=" + id, null) >
0;
12: }
```

In Listing 15.5, ContentValues are used to store the data that will be put into the database. This is very similar to the insert code in Listing 15.4. Two parameters are passed to the update-Photo method. The Photo object passed contains the data to load. The String passed as parameter id is the photo_id for the object, and we will use it to identify the photo to update.

Line 11 shows the update call. We pass a String representing the table, the ContentValues with the new data, and a String to represent the query to identify the record. That String is known as a whereClause. The last parameter to the mDb.update call is currently null. That parameter may contain an array of Strings.Array for arguments to be passed to the whereClause. The array of Strings would be declared as String[];

In this case, to update a photo record in the database, we find the record by passing the photo_ id value as a parameter. If the passed parameter matches the id of a record in the database, an update is performed. The type returned from this method is a Boolean. In Line 11, we see that the value returned is based on the result of the update statement being greater than 0. A result greater than 0 indicates that an update has occurred, and true will be returned, indicating success.

Deleting a Photo

Deleting a photo is very similar to updating a photo. We identify the row to delete and call the appropriate database method. The whereClause in this example is the same as in Listing 15.5. In Listing 15.6, we identify the row to delete based on the passed id matching the photo_id in the table.

LISTING 15.6   Deleting a Photo from the Database

```
1: public boolean deletePhoto(String photo_id) {
2:     return mDb.delete(DATABASE_TABLE, "photo_id" + "=" + photo_id, null) > 0;
3: }
```

Querying Data and Using Cursors

In this hour, we have used a whereClause to identify records to update or delete. The whereClause is key to constructing a SQL statement to retrieve data from a database.

After specifying the data to retrieve from the database, we need a way to work with the returned data. For example, if a query result includes 110 photos, we need a way to both iterate through the results and to work with a specific row of data. Cursors are used for this purpose. If we consider the resultset of our query to be a list of data rows, the cursor acts a pointer to a specific row.

To be very precise, the return value of a query is a Cursor. We work with that Cursor to get specific data.

Listing 15.7 shows the fetchByPageId method in the PhotoDBHelper class. Given the id of a Facebook page, this method retrieves the photos associated with the page and returns a Cursor.

LISTING 15.7   Getting Photos from the Database

```
 1: public Cursor fetchByPageId(String id) throws SQLException {
 2:    Cursor mCursor =
 3:      mDb.query(true, DATABASE_TABLE, PHOTO_FIELDS, "page_id" + "='" + id+"'",
 4:      null,
 5:      null, null, null, null);
 6:    if (mCursor != null) {
 7:       mCursor.moveToFirst();
 8:    }
 9:    return mCursor;
10:}
```

The query is done on lines 2 to 5. In line 3, we pass the first four parameters of the query method and leave the remainder as nulls. The passed parameters are called distinct, tables, columns, and selection. The distinct parameter is set to true and indicates that only unique rows should be returned. The Table parameter is set to DATABASE_TABLE and the Column parameter is set to PHOTO_FIELDS. These parameters specify the table to use and the columns that should be returned from that table. The selection parameter is a whereClause similar to what we used earlier. We want all the photos that have a page_id that matches our query.

Lines 3 and 5 contain five nulls for the remaining parameters to the query method. They are selectionArgs, groupBy, having, orderBy, and limit. These are all options supported in complex queries in SQLite databases.

When querying a database, we will often want to specify the order in which the data is returned. If we have a database of people, we might want to order the data by last name. We use the orderBy parameter to specify a column in the database for ordering data. If we had a row with both a firstName column and a lastName column, we could set the order by firstName or lastName in ascending or descending order. Listing 15.9 includes the orderBy parameter.

Limit specifies the limit on the number of rows to return. For complex queries, selectionArgs can be used as replacement values in the selection statement.

The groupBy and having parameters perform SQL GROUP BY and SQL HAVING clauses. A GROUP BY clause is useful when combining data. For example, we may have a database that includes multiple orders placed by customers. Customers can repeat in the rows in that database, so GROUP BY provides a way to group the orders by a customer. The HAVING clause acts like a whereClause for the GROUP BY clause. That is, the HAVING clause sets the criteria for the GROUP BY.

Listing 15.8 shows the definition of PHOTO_FIELDS that are used in line 3 of Listing 15.7.

LISTING 15.8 Defining the Photo Columns

```
1:  public static final String KEY_ROWID = "_id";
2:  public static final String[] PHOTO_FIELDS = new String[] {
3:    KEY_ROWID,
4:    "photo_id", // id of the photo
5:    "page_id",
6:    "name",
7:    "source",
8:    "picture",
9:    "createdDate",
10:   "modifiedDate"
11: };
```

Listing 15.9 is very similar to that in Listing 15.7, but in line 4, we specify the orderBy value. In Listing 15.9 the field photo_id will be used to specify the order of the returned data.

LISTING 15.9 Getting Photos from a Database in Specified Order

```
1: public Cursor fetchByPageIdDateOrder(String id) throws SQLException {
2:   Cursor mCursor =
3:     mDb.query(true, DATABASE_TABLE, PHOTO_FIELDS, "page_id" + "='" + id+"'",
4:     null,
5:     null, null, "photo_id DESC", null
```

Records are sorted in ascending order by default. To change that to descending order, we use the DESC as in line 5.

The query examples in Listings 15.7 and 15.9 both return a Cursor. We'll create a method to create a Photo object from a Cursor, and then we'll use these methods in our Activity to work with the remote data retrieval code from Hour 14.

In Listing 15.10 a Cursor is passed as a parameter to the getPhotoFromCursor method. The method will return a Photo object corresponding to the data where the Cursor is pointing. If the Cursor is pointing at the first record in the resultset, the Photo object returned will consist of data from the first record.

LISTING 15.10   Returning a Photo Object from a Cursor

```
1:   public static Photo getPhotoFromCursor(Cursor cursor){
2:       Photo photo = new Photo();
3:       photo.dbId = cursor.getLong(cursor.getColumnIndex("_id"));
4:       photo.id = cursor.getString(cursor.getColumnIndex("photo_id"));
5:       photo.name = cursor.getString(cursor.getColumnIndex("name"));
6:       photo.source = cursor.getString(cursor.getColumnIndex("source"));
7:       photo.picture = cursor.getString(cursor.getColumnIndex("picture"));
8:       photo.createdDate = cursor.getLong(cursor.getColumnIndex("createdDate"));
9:       photo.modifiedDate = cursor.getLong(cursor.getColumnIndex("modifiedDate"));
10:      return(photo);
11:  }
```

To do this, two methods from the Cursor class are used in each line. The method getColumn-Index is used to get a column number based on the name of the column. Then a call is made to get the value associated with that column. On line 3 the call is cursor.getLong. On line 4, the call is cursor.getString. This method assumes we know the names of the columns in the database and how they correspond to the Photo object class Each field in the Photo object defined in line 2 is populated from a value in the cursor. The Photo object is returned so it can be used in the app.

Using a Database in the App

We'll build on the app that was created in Hour 14 by using our new PhotoDBHelper class and creating a database of photos. We'll load the database when we retrieve data from Facebook. If a database is available with photo data, we'll immediately let the user interact with it by showing a random photo. The user will no longer need to wait for the download to complete.

The Button in the app that shows the random image will retrieve the image URL from the database.

Providing a Database of Photo Objects

In Hour 14, we used an AsyncTask to retrieve remote data in the background. After data was retrieved, we parsed the data and loaded it into an ArrayList of Photo objects. See Listing 14.12 for the details. To add a database to the app, we'll do exactly what we did in Hour 14, and then we'll load the Photos from the ArrayList directly into the database. We'll check to see of a record exists in the database. If it does we'll update it, if not we'll create a new record. That is done in Listing 15.11.

LISTING 15.11   Updating the Database from an ArrayList of Photo Objects

```
1:    String photoData = sb.toString();
2:    mPagePhotos = Photo.makePhotoList(photoData);
3:    long dbId;
4:    for (Photo currentPhoto : mPagePhotos) {
5:      currentPhoto.pageId = mPageId;
6:      Photo exists = photoDbHelper.fetchPhotoById(currentPhoto.id);
7:      if (exists==null){
8:        dbId = photoDbHelper.createPhoto(currentPhoto);
9:      } else{
10:       photoDbHelper.updatePhoto(exists.id, currentPhoto);
11:     }
12:   }
```

In Listing 15.11, on line 10, we use a variable called `photoDbHelper`. The `photoDbHelper` object was instantiated as type `PhotoDBHelper` as follows:

```
PhotoDBHelper photoDbHelper = new PhotoDBHelper(Hour15Activity.this);
```

The `PhotoDBHelper` object must be opened before we use it and then closed afterward.

Listing 15.11 is the snippet of code that updates the database. Lines 1 and 2 are the same as Listing 14.12. In lines 4 to 10, we iterate through each record in the ArrayList of photos and try to retrieve the record from the database using the id of the photo. The id is the Facebook-provided id. If the photo data does not exist in the database already, we add it to the database using a call to our `photoDbHelper` on line 8. If it does exist, we update it in line 10.

This provides us with a database of photo objects to use in our app. If we know there are records in the database for photos, we do not need to wait to enable the Button to show a Facebook photo.

Determining Whether Records Are Available

We'll use the `preExecute` method of the AsyncTask to check to see if records are available in the database. If records are available, we'll enable the Button immediately. Listing 15.12 shows the entire `onPreExecute` method.

LISTING 15.12   Checking the Database for Photos

```
1: protected void onPreExecute() {
2:    PhotoDBHelper photoDbHelper = new PhotoDBHelper(Hour15Activity.this);
3:    photoDbHelper.open();
```

```
4:    Cursor photoCursor = photoDbHelper.fetchByPageId("99394368305");
5:    if (photoCursor.getCount() >0){
6:      mButton2.setEnabled(true);
7:    }
8:    photoDbHelper.close();
9: }
```

Lines 2 and 3 declare a `PhotoDBHelper` object and open it. A Cursor is returned in line 4 with a call to the `PhotoDbHelper` method `fetchByPageId`. Our current goal is to determine if records exist in the database that we can use for showing a random image. In line 5, we use the `getCount` method to determine the number of records associated with the Cursor. If there are more than zero records, we enable the Button in the app that lets a user show a random image.

This lets the user interact with the app immediately. There is no perception of a performance lag while waiting for the data.

Selecting a Random Photo to Display

We'll change the Button `onClickListener` logic to select a random image to display. Listing 15.13 shows the entire Button `onClickListener`. The portions regarding the `ImageViewFragment` declaration and arguments to pass are the same as Listing 14.13.

LISTING 15.13   Using a Cursor to Select a Random Photo

```
1: mButton2.setOnClickListener(new OnClickListener() {
2:   public void onClick(View v) {
3:     ImageViewFragment fbImg = new ImageViewFragment();
4:     Bundle args = new Bundle();
5:     PhotoDBHelper photoDbHelper = new PhotoDBHelper(Hour15Activity.this);
6:     photoDbHelper.open();
7:     Cursor photoCursor = photoDbHelper.fetchByPageId("99394368305");
8:     int random = (int)(Math.random() * photoCursor.getCount()-1);
9:     photoCursor.moveToPosition(random);
10:    Photo randomPhoto =  PhotoDBHelper.getPhotoFromCursor(photoCursor);
11:    photoDbHelper.close();
12:    args.putString("URL", randomPhoto.source);
13:    fbImg.setArguments(args);
14:    FragmentTransaction ft = getFragmentManager().beginTransaction();
15:    ft.replace(R.id.linearLayout1, fbImg, "Image from Facebook");
16:    ft.commit();
17:  }
18:});
```

In lines 5 to 11, we retrieve a random Photo object from the database. In line 7, we create a Cursor with a call to the PhotoDBHelper method fetchByPageId. In line 8, we generate a random number between 0 and the number of records in the Cursor. If the cursor has five records, the random number will be between 0 and 4. We use the random number in line 9 to set the cursor on a particular row. With the cursor positioned at a random record, we create a corresponding Photo object in line 10. We then use the data from that Photo to display a random image in the fragment.

Summary

In this hour, we covered the basic functionality of a SQLite database. Using the same photo data that we used in Hour 14, we inserted and updated records into a SQLite database. To accomplish that, we created the PhotoDBHelper class to handle the opening and closing of the database and common queries. We gained an understanding of Cursors and how to use them in our apps.

Q&A

Q. What is SQLiteOpenHelper used for?

A. SQLiteOpenHelper handles creating and opening SQLite databases. It contains methods to upgrade the database when needed.

Q. Within a database, we can insert, update, and delete data. How are updates and deletes different from inserts?

A. With both deletes and updates, a record or records must already exist in the database. We select the records to act on and then perform the update or delete action. To select the records, we form a query with a whereClause. For an insert, a new record is inserted. There is no need to find an existing record.

Q. How is a whereClause used?

A. A whereClause is a SQL statement that specifies the matching criteria for the data to be returned. It is used to specify data for deletes, updates, and to return data to the app in a cursor.

Q. How is a Cursor used?

A. A Cursor is what is returned from a query. We can think of a Cursor as a pointer to the list of results. We can iterate through the entire list of results and we can get the data for a specific result.

Workshop

Quiz

1. How is DESC used?
2. What type of objects are returned by queries?
3. Is the field _id required to define a Table?

Answers

1. DESC is used in a ORDER BY clause to indicate descending order.

2. Cursors are returned by queries.

3. The field _id is not required to define a Table, but it is needed when working with other Android classes like CursorAdapter.

Exercises

1. Implement an ORDER BY clause in a query in the app. Test by replacing the random result in the app with the first result from the new query. Change the order by direction from DESC to ASC and verify that the opposite result is achieved.

2. Add a new field to the database. This can be a random field or an actual field returned from the Facebook API. Make note of all the places that must change and upgrade the database version.

Creating a Content Provider

What You'll Learn in This Hour:

▶ How to retrieve data with a URI
▶ How to build a Content Provider
▶ How to use PhotoProvider in our app
▶ How to use the Channel Provider

In Hour 15, "Storing Data with SQLite," we introduced SQLite and used cursors in our app to access data from the database. Content Providers can be thought of as a bridge between the database and the app. Content Providers work with any type of structured data. One reason to use a Content Provider is that it provides a way for other apps to access the data. That is what makes this a *content* provider. Another reason, which we will cover in detail in Hour 17, "Using Cursors and CursorLoaders," is that Content Providers can be used with the `CursorLoader` class to make it easy to update data in our Fragments and Activities.

The focus of this hour is to create our own Content Provider for the Facebook photo data that we introduced in Hour 14, "Accessing Remote Content for a Google TV App," and stored in a SQLite database in Hour 15. We'll update the sample apps to use a Content Provider to create a cursor with the data we expect.

It is important to remember that we can use Content Providers created by others. Google TV includes a specific content provider for TV Channels. The Channel Listing content provides cross-references call letters like MSNBC with a channel number. We'll examine the Channel Listing Content Provider in detail in Hour 20, "Using the Channel Listing Provider."

Using a URI for Data Retrieval

URI stands for Uniform Resource Identifier. Content providers use URIs to identify the data resources that they provide. We are all familiar with URLs of the format http://www.amazon.com. A URL, or Uniform Resource Locator, is an example of a URI that defines the network location of a specific resource.

The format of the URI should represent the data being returned. Content providers return cursors that may point to a single item or to a list of items. In our sample app, we are getting a list of Facebook photos based on the Facebook page id. So the end of our URI can be

`/page/99394368305`

URIs for Android content providers begin with *content://*. To create the full URI, we will add the *authority* and a meaningful *base path*. Authority is the creator of the ContentProvider, and the Android package name can be used here. In our example, the package name is `com.bffme-dia.content`. We are working with photos, so our base path name is `photos`. When we put this together, we get

`content://com.bffmedia.content/photos/page/99394368305`

We can also create a URI to access an individual photo that we identify by the Facebook photo id:

`content://com.bffmedia.content/photos/12345`

In this case, `12345` represents the id of a particular Facebook photo.

Building a ContentProvider

We have defined the URIs to use in our ContentProvider. We'll examine the process to build a ContentProvider in detail. Then we'll use the new ContentProvider in our app to get a cursor to a list of photo records.

The work will be in creating the new class `PhotoProvider` as an extension of ContentProvider. We'll build on this in Hours 17 and 18.

Methods Required in a ContentProvider

When we define a new class as an extension of ContentProvider, we are required to implement six methods. Four methods interact with the data managed by the ContentProvider. They are the `insert`, `update`, `delete`, and `query` methods. All must be implemented, but it is possible to create a provider without providing full functionality to these methods. That is, you can have stub methods if that fits your purpose. The two other methods are `onCreate` and `getType`. The `onCreate` method is used to initialize the ContentProvider. That initialization often means opening a database. The `getType` method indicates the type of data that the ContentProvider returns.

Listing 16.1 shows a ContentProvider that is not very useful, but that implements a stub for all required methods.

LISTING 16.1   The Shell of a ContentProvider

```
1: package com.bffmedia.content;
2: import android.content.ContentProvider;
3: import android.content.ContentValues;
4: import android.database.Cursor;
5: import android.net.Uri;
6: public class EmptyProvider extends ContentProvider {
7:    @Override
8:    public int delete(Uri uri, String selection, String[] selectionArgs) {
9:       return 0;
10:   }
11:   @Override
12:   public String getType(Uri uri) {
13:      return null;
14:   }
15:   @Override
16:   public Uri insert(Uri uri, ContentValues values) {
17:     return null;
18:   }
19:   @Override
20:     public boolean onCreate() {
21:     return false;
22:   }
23:   @Override
24:   public Cursor query(Uri uri, String[] projection, String selection,
25:                      String[] selectionArgs, String sortOrder) {
26:      return null;
27:   }
28:   @Override
29:   public int update(Uri uri, ContentValues values,
30:                  String selection,String[] selectionArgs) {
31:      return 0;
32:   }
33: }
```

Declaring the ContentProvider

We'll examine each section of the PhotoProvider class. Often field definitions are self-explanatory, but in the case of PhotoProvider we will benefit from going through the declarations and definitions. We'll declare static fields that correspond to the parts of our URI definition, and declare static fields that will be used in the getType method and elsewhere to make the code more readable.

A static UriMatcher will be declared. The job of the UriMatcher is to match the String pattern of a URI to a specific constant value as a convenience for development. Instead of String and pattern-matching logic to determine what action should be taken with a URI, we can use the UriMatcher and a switch statement to simplify the code. The UriMatcher is a convenience method created for this purpose.

When you create a ContentProvider, you'll see that there are many interconnected pieces. Listing 16.2 shows the PhotoProvider declarations and definitions starting with the `import` statements.

LISTING 16.2 PhotoProvider Declarations

```
1:  package com.bffmedia.content;
2:  import android.content.ContentProvider;
3:  import android.content.ContentResolver;
4:  import android.content.ContentUris;
5:  import android.content.ContentValues;
6:  import android.content.UriMatcher;
7:  import android.database.Cursor;
8:  import android.database.SQLException;
9:  import android.database.sqlite.SQLiteQueryBuilder;
10: import android.net.Uri;
11: public class PhotoProvider extends ContentProvider {
12: private PhotoDBHelper mPhotoDbHelper;
13: private static final String AUTHORITY = "com.bffmedia.content.PhotoProvider";
14: private static final String PHOTOS_BASE_PATH = "photos";
15: public static final Uri CONTENT_URI =
16:              Uri.parse("content://" + AUTHORITY+ "/" + PHOTOS_BASE_PATH);
17: //content://com.bffmedia.content.PhotoProvider/photos
18: public static final Uri PHOTOS_URI =
19:              Uri.parse(CONTENT_URI +"/page");
20: //content://com.bffmedia.content.PhotoProvider/page
21: public static final String CONTENT_ITEM_TYPE =
22:              ContentResolver.CURSOR_ITEM_BASE_TYPE + "/com.bffmedia.photo";
23: public static final String CONTENT_TYPE =
24:              ContentResolver.CURSOR_DIR_BASE_TYPE + "/ com.bffmedia.photo ";
25: public static final int PHOTOS = 10;
26: public static final int PHOTO_ID = 20;
27: private static final UriMatcher sURIMatcher =
28:              new UriMatcher(UriMatcher.NO_MATCH);
29: static {
30:   sURIMatcher.addURI(AUTHORITY, PHOTOS_BASE_PATH + "/page/#", PHOTOS);
31:   sURIMatcher.addURI(AUTHORITY, PHOTOS_BASE_PATH + "/#", PHOTO_ID);
32: }
```

In lines 13 to 19 of Listing 16.2, we define Strings and URIs that support the URI scheme that we defined previously. Lines 17 and 20 are comments that show what the URI will look like as a readable String.

We define Strings called CONTENT_ITEM_TYPE and CONTENT_TYPE on lines 21 to 24. These Strings represent the type of data we will return in the getType method. We can either return a list of photos or a single photo. The prefix to the list of Photos String is the ContentResolver constant field CURSOR_DIR_TYPE.

Lines 25 and 26 define constants called PHOTOS and PHOTO_ID. These will be used as codes for the type of URI we are passed. They are used by a UriMatcher.

Lines 27 to 32 define and add values to a field of type UriMatcher named sURIMatcher. Given a URI, the UriMatcher returns the integer code associated with the URI. In our case, we have URIs for getting a single photo based on id, and a URI for getting a list of photos based on page id. Lines 30 and 31 add these URIs to the UriMatcher and specify the integer values to return when a match is found.

We'll use the UriMatcher for two of the methods that we are required to implement when creating a ContentProvider. The getType method returns a String representing the type of data we are returning. In that case, we'll use the UriMatcher to determine if the request is for a single photo based on photo id or for a list of photos based on page id. We'll also use the UriMatcher for the query method. The URI passed will determine what query to perform.

ContentProvider Query Method

Our plan is to support two URIs in the PhotoProvider Content provider. When requested from PhotoProvider, these URIs will be fulfilled from the *query* method. We will implement the specific response required by these URIs. We will then cover the parameters that are passed to this method and consider alternative implementations.

Listing 16.3 implements the query method for PhotoProvider. It checks the URI that was passed and fulfills the request based on the URI. If the URI is not recognized, an exception is thrown.

LISTING 16.3 PhotoProvider Query Method

```
1:  @Override
2:  public Cursor query(Uri uri, String[] projection, String selection,
3:    String[] selectionArgs, String sortOrder) {
4:    Cursor cursor;
5:    int uriType = sURIMatcher.match(uri);
6:    switch (uriType) {
7:      case PHOTO_ID:
8:        cursor = mPhotoDbHelper.fetchByPhotoId(uri.getLastPathSegment());
9:        cursor.setNotificationUri(getContext().getContentResolver(), uri);
10:       break;
11:     case PHOTOS:
12:       cursor = mPhotoDbHelper.fetchByPageId(uri.getLastPathSegment());
13:       cursor.setNotificationUri(getContext().getContentResolver(), uri);
14:       break;
15:     default:
16:       throw new IllegalArgumentException("Unknown URI");
17:   }
18:   return cursor;
19: }
```

There are three things being handled in Listing 16.3:

▶ Identify the URI to handle using `UriMatcher`.

▶ Create a Cursor that fulfills the request for data.

▶ Set a Notification URI for the cursor.

Lines 9 and 13 set the notification URI for the cursor. The URI will be watched for changes. The ContentResolver associated with the context will be notified when a change occurs. That means that the ContentResolver associated with the Activity is observing this URI and will be notified of changes.

This implementation of PhotoProvider handles two URIs based on the last path segment of the URI. The `uriType` specifies whether we should return a single photo or a list pf photos. The call to `uri.getLastPathSegment` returns the value of a specific `photo_id` for retrieving a single photo or a `page_id` for retrieving a list of photos. The cursor for returning a single photo based on `photo_id` is on line 8.The cursor for fulfilling a list of photos based on `page_id` occurs on line 12.

By examining the parameters passed to the query method, we can see that an alternative solution based on a direct database query can be done. Lines 2 and 3 of Listing 16.3 show these parameters. We'll define each one.

```
String[] projection, String selection, String[] selectionArgs, String sortOrder
```

The `projection` parameter identifies the columns in a database table that should be returned. A null projection means to return all columns. To create a SQL query, we would use `selection` and optionally `selectionArgs` parameters. The `sortOrder` parameter defines the order of the data being returned.

These are the parameters that we would pass to a SQLDatabase `query` method. See Listing 15.7 in Hour 15 to see how we used a query in the `PhotoDBHelper` class. Alternative solutions can be done in several ways.

The `SQLiteDatabase` object is directly available to us in the `PhotoDBHelper` class, so we can use it to perform a direct database query based on the parameters passed to the ContentProvider query.

We can simplify this to say that the parameters from the query method in the ContentProvider will be passed to a SQLiteDatabase query method. That method is available to use because the SQLiteDatabase is available through `PhotoDBHelper`. The parameters will be used to form a query and return a Cursor. See Listing 16.4.

This allows us to support a third URI in our scheme. We can support the following URI:

```
content://com.bffmedia.content/photos/
```

Note that there is no page id appended to the end of this query. When we call it, we'll pass parameters to the PhotoProvider query method to specify the data to return.

We'll add a new declaration to PhotoProvider as a code for this query:

```
public static final int PHOTO_QUERY = 30;
```

We'll then add a new URI to the UriMatcher:

```
sURIMatcher.addURI(AUTHORITY, PHOTOS_BASE_PATH, PHOTO_QUERY); // QUERY Only
```

With those in place, we can update the ContentProvider query method to support the new URI by adding a new case to the switch statement.

LISTING 16.4   **Supporting Another URI in Query**

```
1: case PHOTO_QUERY:
2:    cursor =   mPhotoDbHelper.mDb.query(true, PhotoDBHelper.DATABASE_TABLE,
3:            projection, selection, selectionArgs, null,null,sortOrder, null);
4:    cursor.setNotificationUri(getContext().getContentResolver(), uri);
5:    break;
```

Using the PhotoProvider Query

As a review, we have implemented support for three URIs in the ContentProvider query method. The URIs are to get a page of photos, get an individual photo, and to get a group of photos via a query. We'll examine the two URIs that retrieve multiple photos in detail. The first way to create a cursor with a list of photos is by using the `PhotoProvider.PHOTOS_URI` and a page id as follows:

```
Cursor photoCursor = managedQuery (Uri.withAppendedPath (
    PhotoProvider.PHOTOS_URI ,"99394368305"), null, null, null, null);
```

When called from an Activity, we use the ContentProvider via a `managedQuery`. This calls the ContentProvider's query method with the parameters we have discussed. We create a URI with an appended path of the `page_id`. The URI is

```
content://com.bffmedia.content/photos/page/99394368305
```

That matches the `PHOTOS` code identified and initiates a call to `fetchByPageId`. See Listing 16.3, lines 11 and 12.

The second way to create a cursor to retrieve multiple photos for a page is by creating a query as follows:

```
Cursor photoCursor = managedQuery(PhotoProvider.CONTENT_URI, null,   "page_
id='99394368305'", null, null);
```

This uses the alternative solution using the CONTENT_URI we defined. It looks like this:

`content://com.bffmedia.content/photos/`

To get the photos associated with a particular page using this URI, we add a selection parameter in the call to manageQuery. We explicitly set the selection parameter to retrieve photos where page id is equal to 99394368305. We are performing a query and setting the where Clause with the page id set to a specific value.

Specifying the GetType Method

The purpose of the getType method is to return the type of data that will be returned. This will be a single photo or list of photos in PhotoProvider. Based on the URI passed, we will either return a CONTENT_TYPE or CONTENT_ITEM_TYPE. A complete getType method is shown in Listing 16.5

See lines 21 to 24 of Listing 16.2 to see where the values for PHOTOS, PHOTO_QUERY, and PHOTO_ID are declared.

LISTING 16.5   Return Type of Data in GetType

```
1:  public String getType(Uri uri) {
2:     int uriType = sURIMatcher.match(uri);
3:     switch (uriType) {
4:       case PHOTOS:
5:         return CONTENT_TYPE;
6:       case PHOTO_QUERY:
7:         return CONTENT_TYPE;
8:       case PHOTO_ID:
9:         return CONTENT_ITEM_TYPE;
10:     default:
11:       return null;
12:    }
13: }
```

Implement Insert, Update, and Delete Methods

To create a ContentProvider, we must implement insert, update, and delete methods. This provides a consistent way to keep the app in sync and aware of updates as they happen.

These methods must exist in the ContentProvider, but it is possible to make a read-only ContentProvider as well. To create a read-only ContentProvider, the query methods would be fully implemented to return results. The insert, update, and delete methods would exist, but would not actually change the underlying data.

Listing 16.6 shows a complete `insert` method.

In Listing 16.6 we insert the passed `ContentValues` into the database by accessing the `mDB` field in the `PhotoDBHelper` class directly.

LISTING 16.6   Insert Method

```
1: @Override
2: public Uri insert(Uri uri, ContentValues values) {
3:    long newID = mPhotoDbHelper.mDb.insert(PhotoDBHelper.DATABASE_TABLE, null,
values);
4:    if (newID > 0) {
5:      Uri newUri = ContentUris.withAppendedId(uri, newID);
6:      getContext().getContentResolver().notifyChange(uri, null);
7:      return newUri;
8:    } else {
9:      throw new SQLException("Failed to insert row into " + uri);
10:   }
11: }
```

Listing 16.7 shows the database update. With an update, the selection criteria is passed to the argument so that the rows to be updated can be identified.

LISTING 16.7   Update Method

```
1: @Override
2: public int update(Uri uri, ContentValues values, String selection,
3:                    String[] selectionArgs) {
4: return mPhotoDbHelper.mDb.update(PhotoDBHelper.DATABASE_TABLE,
5:         values, selection, selectionArgs);
6: }
```

Listing 16.8 shows the `delete` method. Like the `update` method it takes `selection` and `selectionArgs` parameters. When updating or deleting, we must specify the rows to act upon, which is done with these parameters.

LISTING 16.8   Delete Method

```
1: @Override
2: public int delete(Uri uri, String selection, String[] selectionArgs) {
3:    return mPhotoDbHelper.mDb.delete(PhotoDBHelper.DATABASE_TABLE,
4:         selection, selectionArgs);
5: }
```

Using PhotoProvider in Our App

We use a Cursor in two places in the app. One is in the preexecute method to determine if there are any entries in the database; the other is on the button click to get a Cursor so that we can select a random photo.

In this case, we can use either the URI with an appended page_id or a query with the page_id as a parameter. Both URIs are shown with the alternative commented out. Listing 16.9 and 16.10 both create a cursor from a URI and the content provider.

Listing 16.9 is the preExecute method of an AsyncTask. We create a Cursor on line 5. Then, on line 7, we check to see if there are results by calling the getCount method to check the number of results. If there are results, we enable mButton2. This checks to see if there are already results in the database. If there are, we allow the random image button to be shown. Note that lines 3 and 4 are commented out and show an alternative for creating an equivalent Cursor.

LISTING 16.9   OnPreExecute

```
1: @Override
2: protected void onPreExecute() {
3: //Cursor photoCursor = managedQuery(Uri.withAppendedPath(PhotoProvider.PHOTOS_URI
4:             ,"99394368305"), null, null, null, null);
5:    Cursor photoCursor = managedQuery(PhotoProvider.CONTENT_URI, null,
6:                    "page_id='99394368305'", null, null);
7:    if (photoCursor.getCount() >0){
8:        mButton2.setEnabled(true);
9:    }
10:}
```

Listing 16.10 retrieves a random photo from the ContentProvider. On line 3, the Cursor is created. On line 5 a random number is generated and used in line 6 to position the Cursor. That is, we generate a random number and point the Cursor at the row associated with that random number. In line 7, we retrieve the value and populate a Photo object named randomPhoto.

LISTING 16.10   Random Result from Cursor

```
1: //Cursor photoCursor = managedQuery(Uri.withAppendedPath(PhotoProvider.PHOTOS_URI,
2:            "99394368305"), null, null, null, null);
3: Cursor photoCursor = managedQuery(PhotoProvider.CONTENT_URI, null,
4:                    "page_id='99394368305'", null, null);
5: int random = (int)(Math.random() * photoCursor.getCount()-1);
6: photoCursor.moveToPosition(random);
7: Photo randomPhoto =  PhotoDBHelper.getPhotoFromCursor(photoCursor);1:
8: mButton2.setEnabled(true);
```

In Listing 16.11 we revise the portion of the `doInBackground` method where we currently insert or update photo objects with `PhotoDBHelper`. We use the PhotoProvider insert and `update` methods. We take an available Photo object and populate a `ContentValues` object with name/value pairs as required by the `insert` and `update` methods.

LISTING 16.11 Inserting and Updating Using ContentProvider

```
1:   mPagePhotos = Photo.makePhotoList(photoData);
2:   for (Photo currentPhoto : mPagePhotos) {
3:    currentPhoto.pageId = mPageId;
4:    ContentValues newValues = new ContentValues();
5:    if (currentPhoto.id!=null)
6:      newValues.put("photo_id", currentPhoto.id);
7:    if (currentPhoto.pageId!=null)
8:      newValues.put("page_id", currentPhoto.pageId);
9:    if (currentPhoto.name!=null)
10:     newValues.put("name", currentPhoto.name);
11:   if (currentPhoto.source!=null)
12:     newValues.put("source", currentPhoto.source);
13:   if (currentPhoto.picture!=null)
14:     newValues.put("picture", currentPhoto.picture);
15:   if (currentPhoto.createdDate!=0)
16:     newValues.put("createdDate", currentPhoto.createdDate);
17:   if (currentPhoto.modifiedDate!=0)
18:     newValues.put("modifiedDate", currentPhoto.modifiedDate);
19:   Photo exists = photoDbHelper.fetchPhotoById(currentPhoto.id);
20:   if (exists==null){
21:    Uri mNewUri = getContentResolver().insert(
22:               PhotoProvider.CONTENT_URI,
23:               newValues);
24:   } else{
25:    getContentResolver().update(
26:          PhotoProvider.CONTENT_URI,
27:          newValues, "photo_id" + "=" + exists.id, null);
28:   }
29: }
```

Requesting a File from a ContentProvider

We have updated our app to retrieve and display a random image from a page on Facebook. We can take an additional step and incorporate the retrieval of the random image file into the PhotoProvider class. That will cleanly separate all content retrieval in the app from presentation and logic. That means that the job of the ContentProvider is to retrieve content. That content may be data returned in a Cursor or a File returned to the app. The logic of the app and the visual presentation of the app is completely independent from the ContentProvider.

Currently, the code to retrieve the image is in the `ImageViewFragment` class. The source field in the Photo is a URL, and we retrieve the image contents from that URL. The result is written to the cache file system for faster retrieval on subsequent calls. We will still retrieve the image using the source field, but we'll add that functionality to the PhotoProvider class. The URI with the request for the file will specify a `photo_id` to retrieve.

We'll introduce the concept of a content observer. The class `ContentObserver` watches for changes in a given URI. This is important because we may request an image that has not yet been written as a file. In that case, we'll set a content observer to display the image file when it becomes available.

Listings 16.12 to 16.15 show the process of retrieving data from a file and using a `ContentObserver` to track whether the file has been written.

How to Return a File from a ContentProvider

We'll start with the changes to the PhotoProvider class. We will implement the `openFile` method. The PhotoProvider's `openFile` method is called when we request an `inputStream` from the provider. That is, a request in our app to open an `inputStream` from PhotoProvider like the following results in a call to the `openFile` method in our PhotoProvider class:

```
InputStream is=getActivity().getContentResolver(.
openInputStream(Uri.withAppendedPath(PhotoProvider.CONTENT_URI ,mPhotoId));
```

The URI that we'll use to grab the file is the CONTENT_URI with an appended photo id:

```
content://com.bffmedia.content/photos/12345
```

Listing 16.12 shows the implementation of the `openFile` method within the PhotoProvider class.

LISTING 16.12   Implementing File Support in PhotoProvider

```
1: @Override
2: public ParcelFileDescriptor openFile(Uri uri, String mode)
3:                                   throws FileNotFoundException {
4:    File root = new File(getContext().getApplicationContext().getCacheDir(),
5:    uri.getEncodedPath());
6:    root.mkdirs();
7:    File imageFile = new File(root,  "image.jpg");
8:    final OutputStream imageOS;
9:    final int imode = ParcelFileDescriptor.MODE_READ_ONLY;
10:   if (imageFile.exists()) {
```

```
11:     return ParcelFileDescriptor.open(imageFile, imode);
12:   }
13:   Cursor photoCursor = query(uri, null, null, null, null);
14:   if (photoCursor == null) return null;
15:   if (photoCursor.getCount()==0) return null;
16:   Photo currentPhoto = PhotoDBHelper.getPhotoFromCursor(photoCursor);
17:   final String imageString = currentPhoto.source;
18:   imageOS = new BufferedOutputStream(new FileOutputStream(imageFile));
19:   RetrieveImage ri = new RetrieveImage (uri, imageString, imageOS);
20:   ri.execute();
21:   throw ( new FileNotFoundException());
22: }
```

Listing 16.12 does two things. If the requested file exists, it is returned as a
ParcelFileDescriptor. If it does not exist, the code retrieves the image contents and throws a
FileNotFoundException. In the code requesting the file, we will need to handle the exception.

Lines 4 to 7 of Listing 16.12 create a directory for the file based on the URI and then
access a file called image.jpg on that directory. If the file exists, it is used to create a
ParcelFileDescriptor that is returned. ParcelFileDescriptors provide a way to work on
the original file. We use the file and set this to be read-only when we return it.

Retrieving an Image from a File or Remotely

If the file is not found, the code gets a Photo object based on the photo id. We use the query
method of the provider to get the Photo object. With the Photo object, we can get the source
field and retrieve the contents using AsyncTask RetrieveImage shown in Listing 16.13.

LISTING 16.13   Retrieving an Image in PhotoProvider

```
1:private class RetrieveImage extends AsyncTask<String , String , Long > {
2:   String  mImageString;
3:   OutputStream mImageOS;
4:   Uri mUri;
5:   public RetrieveImage ( Uri uri, String imageString, OutputStream imageOS){
6:     mImageString = imageString;
7:     mImageOS = imageOS;
8:     mUri = uri;
9:   }
10: @Override
11:   protected Long doInBackground(String... params) {
12:   try {
13:     URL imageUrl = new URL(mImageString);
14:     URLConnection connection = imageUrl.openConnection();
15:     connection.connect();
16:     InputStream is = connection.getInputStream();
```

```
17:     Bitmap mBitmap = BitmapFactory.decodeStream(is);
18:     mBitmap.compress(Bitmap.CompressFormat.JPEG, 100, mImageOS);
19:     mImageOS.flush();
20:     mImageOS.close();
21:     getContext().getContentResolver().notifyChange(mUri, null);
22:     return (01);
23:   } catch (MalformedURLException e) {
24:     e.printStackTrace();
25:     return (11);
26:   }
27:   catch (IOException e) {
28:     e.printStackTrace();
29:     return (11);
30:   }
31: }
32:}
```

The image is retrieved from the URL as we have done previously, but instead of creating a bitmap to return, we write the URL to the file that we created in the openFile method. We pass the RetrieveImage class a URI, a String containing the Photo's source field, and the OutputStream for writing the file.

In line 21, we call the notifyChange method of ContentResolver. A notification is sent to observers of the URI that a change has occurred. We'll set up an observer in the ImageViewFragment class to act on this notification.

Let's review the logic for the case where the file does not exist. Our ImageViewFragment will request the file. Because the file does not exist at that moment, the PhotoProvider will throw a FileNotFoundException. On getting that exception, the ImageViewFragment will set an observer to wait for the URI associated with the file to change. From the perspective of the ImageViewFragment, there is no file, but if it becomes available, there will be a notification.

Meanwhile, in addition to throwing the FileNotFoundException, the PhotoProvider is retrieving the image from Facebook. After the image is received and it is written to file, a notification is given. The ImageViewFragment receives that notification, opens the file, and creates a Bitmap.

Listing 16.14 is the onActivityCreated method of ImageViewFragment.

LISTING 16.14 Creating a Bitmap Using the ContentProvider

```
1:   @Override
2:   public void onActivityCreated(Bundle savedInstanceState) {
3:     super.onActivityCreated(savedInstanceState);
4:     Bundle b = this.getArguments();
5:     if (b!=null){
```

```
6:        mPhotoId=b.getString("PHOTO_ID");
7:     }
8:     Handler handler = new Handler();
9:     InputStream is;
10:    try {
11:       is = getActivity().getContentResolver().openInputStream
12:                    (Uri.withAppendedPath(PhotoProvider.CONTENT_URI ,mPhotoId));
13:       mBitmap =  BitmapFactory.decodeStream(is);
14:       mImageView.setImageBitmap(mBitmap);
15:    } catch (FileNotFoundException e) {
16:       getActivity().getContentResolver().registerContentObserver(
17:                    Uri.withAppendedPath(PhotoProvider.CONTENT_URI ,mPhotoId),
18:                    false, new PhotoContentObserver(handler));
19:    }
20: }
```

Instead of passing the contents of the source field in the Bundle, we are now passing the id of the photo. We use that id to form a URI and use that URI on lines 11 and 12 when we call open-InputStream. The call to openInputStream will call the PhotoProvider's openFile method. If no exception is thrown, lines 13 and 14 will execute, creating a Bitmap and displaying that Bitmap in an ImageView.

If an exception is thrown, we'll register a content observer called PhotoContentObserver to watch the specified URI for changes.

Using a ContentObserver When Content Changes

Listing 16.15 defines a class called PhotoContentObserver of type ContentObserver. The purpose of this class is to perform an action when the content being observed changes. In this case, the content being observed is the file we are trying to use.

LISTING 16.15   ContentObserver Defined in ImageViewFragment

```
1:  class PhotoContentObserver extends ContentObserver {
2:     public PhotoContentObserver(Handler handler) {
3:        super(handler);
4:     }
5:     @Override
6:     public void onChange(boolean selfChange) {
7:        InputStream is;
8:        try {
9:          if (ImageViewFragment.this.isAdded()){
10:            is = getActivity().getContentResolver().openInputStream
11:               Uri.withAppendedPath(PhotoProvider.CONTENT_URI ,mPhotoId));
12:            mBitmap =  BitmapFactory.decodeStream(is);
13:            mImageView.setImageBitmap(mBitmap);
```

```
14:        }
15:      } catch (FileNotFoundException e) {
16:      }
17:    }
18: }
```

The PhotoContentObserver is notified when a new file created in line 21 of Listing 16.13 sends that notification. When that occurs, the onChange method of the ContentObserver is called. Line 9 of Listing 16.15 checks to see if the Fragment is still attached to the Activity. It is possible that the notification of file availability will occur at a point when the ImageViewFragment is no longer in the current Activity. In that case, a call to getActivity() will return null. This check prevents that issue. Lines 10 to 12 get the inputStream for the file, create a Bitmap, and display it.

We have now created and used a ContentProvider for both data retrieval for a Cursor representing a database and to get an image represented by a file.

Summary

In this hour, we created our own ContentProvider by implementing `insert`, `query`, `update`, and `delete` methods. We saw how a UriMatcher is used to examine a URI and direct us to an action. After our PhotoProvider was in place, we used it on our random photo app for both data and file retrieval.

Q&A

Q. What kinds of content can be returned from a ContentProvider?

A. A ContentProvider can return data from a database in a Cursor, and it can return a file via the openFile method.

Q. How do ContentProviders use URIs?

A. In ContentProviders, URIs are used to identify the data to return. In this hour, we used URIs to get data based on a `page_id` and URIs that supported queries.

Q. What is the purpose of a Read-Only ContentProvider?

A. ContentProviders must include `insert`, `update`, and `delete` methods, but those methods are not required to change the underlying data. The purpose of a read-only ContentProvider is to make data from an app available to third-party apps, but to restrict those apps from changing the underlying data.

Workshop

Quiz

1. What method is used to call a ContentProvider query from an app?
2. What is a ContentObserver?
3. What method is called from an app to trigger a call to a ContentProvider's `openFile` method?

Answers

1. An Activity contains a `managedQuery` method.
2. A ContentObserver is a class that responds to changes in a given URI. When the URI changes, the `onChange` method of the ContentObserver fires.
3. A call to `openInputStream` does this:

   ```
   getActivity().getContentResolver().openInputStream
   ```

Exercises

1. Implement a new URI and query in the PhotoProvider class. The example in this hour uses the `page_id` to retrieve a list of photos. To implement a new URI and query, you would decide on the query criteria, create the query, and add the ContentProvider infrastructure by defining a new URI and using the UriMatcher to assure that the URI results in the query being performed.

2. Create a Gallery of Images using the ContentProvider created in this hour. Note that we will be doing this in Hour 18.

HOUR 17
Using Loaders and CursorLoaders

What You'll Learn in This Hour:

▶ How Loaders work
▶ What Loader classes are available
▶ How to initialize, create, and reset a Loader
▶ How to add loaders to ImageViewFragment

In Hour 16, "Creating a Content Provider," we created our own ContentProvider. PhotoProvider provides content about photos on Facebook pages and returns an image file when requested. One reason we developed our own ContentProvider was to take advantage of how well ContentProviders work with CursorLoaders.

In this hour, we change our app to take advantage of a CursorLoader. CursorLoaders are an implementation of the Loader class.

How Loaders Work

Loaders were introduced in Android 3.0. We are assured that they can be used in all of our Google TV apps. Loaders help to asynchronously load data in a Fragment or Activity. That is something we have been working on since Hour 14, "Accessing Remote Content for a Google TV App." We've covered downloading data, writing to a SQLite database, and creating a ContentProvider. We'll use all that work to create and use a CursorLoader in our ImageViewFragment.

Loaders provide the functionality of a ContentObserver by monitoring the source of their data and providing updates when the data changes. Much of the work that is commonly done in a data-driven app is done in a streamlined way using Loaders.

Loaders retain their data after being stopped. That means that if an Activity or Fragment that uses a Loader is stopped, the data in the Loader is retained. When the Fragment starts again, the data is available and the Fragment does not need to wait for the data to reload.

Loader Classes

When implementing Loaders, you'll use a number of classes and interfaces:

▶ Loader—A Loader is an abstract class to asynchronously load data.

▶ AsyncTaskLoader—An AsyncTaskLoader is an abstract class that is a subclass of Loader. It uses an AsyncTask to do the work of loading data.

▶ CursorLoader—A CursorLoader is a subclass of AsyncTaskLoader. Typically, you'll use a CursorLoader when implementing a Loader. A CursorLoader queries a ContentResolver and returns a Cursor that can be used in the Activity or Fragment. CursorLoaders and ContentProviders work very well together.

▶ LoaderManager—A LoaderManager is associated with each Activity or Fragment. There is a single LoaderManager for each Activity or Fragment, but a LoaderManager can manage more than one Loader.

▶ LoaderManagerCallbacks—LoaderManagerCallbacks is an interface for an Activity or Fragment to interact with the LoaderManager. A Fragment will implement a LoaderCallbacks interface:

```
public class ImageViewFragment extends Fragment implements
LoaderCallbacks<Cursor>
```

To implement LoaderManagerCallbacks, you must use the methods onCreateLoader, onLoadFinished, and onLoaderReset.

We will use a CursorLoader in our app and can think of it as our Loader.

To manage the connection between the Loader and a Fragment or Activity, the class LoaderManager is used. A LoaderManager includes the interface LoaderManager.LoaderCallbacks to communicate between the LoaderManager and the Fragment or Activity.

Loader States and LoaderManager.Callbacks

Loaders can be used in an Activity or in a Fragment. Loaders must be initialized. In an Activity, a Loader is initialized in the `onCreate` method. In a Fragment, a Loader is initialized in the `onActivityCreated` method. For the rest of our examples, we will assume that a Fragment is using the Loader.

After initialization, a Loader will be created if it does not already exist. If it does exist, it will be used immediately. When data is available from a Loader, the Fragment will be notified via the LoaderManager.Callback method, `onLoadFinished`. If `initLoader` is called and data is available, `onLoadFinished` is called immediately.

Initializing a Loader

A Loader is initialized with a call to the `initLoader` method of the LoaderManager. That will look something like this:

```
getLoaderManager().initLoader(LOADER_ID, null, this);
```

The `getLoaderManager` method gives us the LoaderManager for the current Fragment. `LOADER_ID` is a unique id integer value that identifies the Loader. That is important if there is more than one Loader. The id is passed to LoaderManager.Callbacks' methods to identify a particular loader. The last parameter is a class that implements LoaderManager.Callbacks. Because we will be implementing LoaderManager.Callbacks in our Fragment, we can use `this`. The second parameter is a Bundle for passing any optional parameters to the Loader constructor. In this case, that parameter is `null`.

Creating a Loader

When the `initLoader` method is called, if the Loader does not exist, a call to the LoaderManager.Callback's `onCreateLoader` method is called. The Loader is created within this method.

When creating a CursorLoader, we use the parameters of a query on a ContentProvider. Specifically, as we saw in Hour 16, the query requires a `uri`, `projection`, `selection`, `selectionArgs`, and `sortOrder`. The CursorLoader is created using these parameters and is returned in `onCreateLoader`.

When Data Is Available

The LoaderManager.Callback method `onLoadFinished` is called when data is available. In the case of CursorLoader implementation, this method is passed the Cursor to use. In the example we've been using, we'll pick a random photo using this Cursor and display it.

When working with a `CursorAdapter`, you use the `onLoadFinished` method to swap in new data with a call to the Adapter's `swapCursor` method. An example is shown later in this hour in Listing 17.3.

A simplified version of these relationships is shown in Figure 17.1.

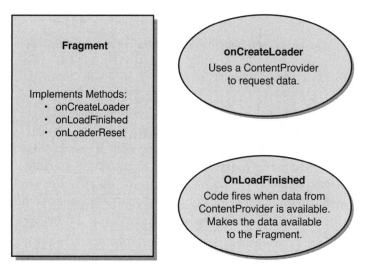

FIGURE 17.1
Relationship of a Fragment to LoaderManager.Callback methods.

Resetting a Loader

When the application determines that the Loader no longer has any associated data, the onLoaderReset method fires at that point. This is an opportunity to remove any references to the data.

With a CursorLoader, this is the point where the cursor associated with the Loader is about to be closed. If more than one cursor is associated with the Loader, the onLoaderReset method fires when the last cursor is about to be closed.

When using a CursorAdapter with the CursorLoader, this is the opportunity to reset the cursor to null with a call to the adapter's swapCursor method:

```
MyAdapter.swapCursor(null);
```

Adding Loaders to ImageViewFragment

We will add loaders to our implementation of our app to show a random image from a given Facebook page. In this case, the ImageViewFragment class does all the work and implements a CursorLoader. When the data becomes available to the Fragment, a random image is chosen and displayed.

In addition, we'll create a ListFragment that shows a photo id and the source of the photo. The purpose of that example is to show a typical implementation of a Loader with a CursorLoader and CursorAdapter. In this hour, we'll use a SimpleCursorAdapter. In Hour 18, "Developing a Complete App," we'll develop a complete example and create our own custom CursorAdapter.

Using a CursorLoader to Show a Random Image

We will continue with our Facebook page photo example. In this implementation using a CursorLoader, the ImageViewFragment will be passed the page id to use. The page id will be used to query the PhotoProvider ContentProvider to create a CursorLoader.

Listing 17.1 shows the ImageViewFragment code to create the Fragment and the Cursor. Note that the import statements for ImageViewFragment now include Loader and CursorLoader:

```
import android.content.CursorLoader;
import android.content.Loader;
```

LISTING 17.1 ImageViewFragment Loader Setup

```
1:  public class ImageViewFragment extends Fragment implements LoaderCallbacks<Cursor>{
2:      ImageView mImageView;
3:      String mPageId;
4:      Bitmap mBitmap;
5:      String mPhotoId;
6:      @Override
7:      public void onActivityCreated(Bundle savedInstanceState) {
8:        super.onActivityCreated(savedInstanceState);
9:        Bundle b = this.getArguments();;
10:       mPageId=b.getString("PAGE_ID");
11:       getLoaderManager().initLoader(0, null, this);
12:     }
13:     @Override
14:     public View onCreateView(LayoutInflater inflater,
15:               ViewGroup container, Bundle savedInstanceState) {
16:       mImageView  = (ImageView) inflater.inflate(R.layout.image_fragment,
17:                   container, false);
18:       return mImageView;
19:     }
20:     @Override
21:     public Loader<Cursor> onCreateLoader(int id, Bundle arg1) {
22:       CursorLoader cursorLoader = new CursorLoader(getActivity(),
23:       Uri.withAppendedPath(PhotoProvider.PHOTOS_URI ,mPageId),
24:                               null, null, null, null);
25:       return cursorLoader;
26:     }
27:     @Override
28:     public void onLoaderReset(Loader<Cursor> arg0) {
29:     }
```

Listing 17.1 includes Fragment methods `onCreateView` and `onActivityCreated`. The `onCreateView` method returns an ImageView. The `onActivityCreated` method gets the page id parameter that was passed in the Bundle. On line 11, it initializes this loader. The id of the loader is 0. Because ImageViewFragment implements LoaderCallbacks, the last parameter to `initLoader` is this.

Listing 17.1 also includes the LoaderManager.Callbacks methods `onCreateLoader` and `onLoaderReset`. Because we are using one Loader, we do not check the id. When using more than one Loader, we check the id that was passed in the `initLoader` method. In the `onCreateLoader` method in lines 22 to 24, we create a CursorLoader using the PhotoProvider ContentProvider. In this case, we are doing that with the URI that specifies the page id. The alternative is to pass query parameters to create the CursorLoader as we did in Hour 16:

```
CursorLoader cursorLoader = new CursorLoader(getActivity(),
            PhotoProvider.CONTENT_URI, null, "page_id='99394368305'", null,
null);
```

In this example, we do not need to do anything in the `onLoaderReset` method. Had we associated the Cursor with a CursorAdapter, the `onLoaderReset` method is where we would break the connection. We will cover that later in Listing 17.3. Listing 17.2 shows what happens after the data is loaded.

LISTING 17.2 ImageViewFragment Using the Data

```
1:  @Override
2:  public void onLoadFinished(Loader<Cursor> loader, Cursor cursor) {
3:      int random = (int)(Math.random() * cursor.getCount()-1);
4:      cursor.moveToPosition(random);
5:      Photo randomPhoto = PhotoDBHelper.getPhotoFromCursor(cursor);
6:      mPhotoId = randomPhoto.id;
7:      Handler handler = new Handler();
8:      InputStream is;
9:      try {
10:        if (ImageViewFragment.this.isAdded()){
11:          is = getActivity().getContentResolver(). openInputStream
12:             (Uri.withAppendedPath(PhotoProvider.CONTENT_URI ,mPhotoId));
13:          mBitmap = BitmapFactory.decodeStream(is);
14:          mImageView.setImageBitmap(mBitmap);
15:        }
16:      } catch (FileNotFoundException e) {
17:        getActivity().getContentResolver(). registerContentObserver(
18:        Uri.withAppendedPath(PhotoProvider.CONTENT_URI ,mPhotoId), false,
19:        new PhotoContentObserver(handler));
20:      }
21: }
```

```
22: class PhotoContentObserver extends ContentObserver {
23:   public PhotoContentObserver(Handler handler) {
24:     super(handler);
25:
26:     @Override
27:     public void onChange(boolean selfChange) {
28:       InputStream is;
29:       try {
30:         if (ImageViewFragment.this.isAdded()){
31:           is = getActivity().getContentResolver().
32:           openInputStream(Uri.withAppendedPath(
33:                 PhotoProvider.CONTENT_URI,mPhotoId));
34:           mBitmap = BitmapFactory.decodeStream(is);
35:           mImageView.setImageBitmap(mBitmap);
36:         }
37:       } catch (FileNotFoundException e) {
38:     }
39:   }
40: }
```

In Listing 17.2, we use the onLoadFinished method to acquire a Cursor and show a random photo. In line 2, the cursor is passed as a parameter. By creating a CursorLoader, we get to use the cursor directly when the data becomes available.

In lines 3 to 6, we create a random number and grab a photo object from the cursor. The remainder of the code in Listing 17.2 acquires the photo and displays it. The CursorLoader retrieved the photo data, but we must still do the work to retrieve an image from the ContentProvider.

Listing 17.2 illustrates how a CursorLoader can be used in our sample application. Listing 17.3 shows how a CursorLoader and a CursorAdapter can work together.

Using a CursorLoader with a CursorAdapter

Using a CursorLoader with a CursorAdapter is very powerful. The CursorAdapter uses the data from the Loader to show the data. The CursorLoader keeps the data up to date. As the data changes, the display changes. As shown in Listing 17.3, when we use a CursorLoader this can be done with very little code. Listing 17.3 uses a SimpleCursorAdapter to display a photo's id and source in a ListFragment. It contains the entire code for that new Fragment.

LISTING 17.3 Showing Photo Data in a List with PhotoListFragment.java

```
1:  public class PhotoListFragment extends ListFragment
2:              implements LoaderCallbacks<Cursor>  {
3:    SimpleCursorAdapter mAdapter;
4:    String mPageId;
```

```
 5:    @Override
 6:    public void onActivityCreated(Bundle savedInstanceState) {
 7:      super.onActivityCreated(savedInstanceState);
 8:      Bundle b = this.getArguments();;
 9:      mPageId=b.getString("PAGE_ID");
10:      getLoaderManager().initLoader(0, null, this);
11:      mAdapter = new SimpleCursorAdapter(getActivity(),
12:        android.R.layout.simple_list_item_2,
13:        null, //Cursor
14:        new String[] {"photo_id", "source"},
15:        new int[] { android.R.id.text1, android.R.id.text2 }, 0);
16:      setListAdapter(mAdapter);
17:    }
18:    @Override
19:    public Loader<Cursor> onCreateLoader(int id, Bundle args) {
20:      CursorLoader cursorLoader = new CursorLoader(getActivity(),
21:      Uri.withAppendedPath(PhotoProvider.PHOTOS_URI ,mPageId),
22:                        null, null, null, null);
23:      return cursorLoader;
24:    }
25:    @Override
26:    public void onLoadFinished(Loader<Cursor> Loader, Cursor cursor) {
27:      mAdapter.swapCursor(cursor);
28:    }
29:    @Override
30:    public void onLoaderReset(Loader<Cursor> arg0) {
31:      mAdapter.swapCursor(null);
32:    }
33: }
```

The PhotoListFragment class defined in Listing 17.3 is a ListFragment that implements LoaderCallbacks. A SimpleCursorAdapter is used to show the data from the Loader. The app is a simple list showing the photo's id and source field. The app is shown in Figure 17.2.

The Loader is initialized on Line 10. Lines 11 to 15 define the adapter. We are using values defined in the Android platform to specify the adapter details. Line 12 indicates a two-line layout, and line 15 shows the two TextViews where the data will be loaded. When creating a SimpleCursorAdapter, we need a Layout and target views for the data. Line 13 is the cursor to use for the adapter. Initially, this is null. Line 14 indicates the fields from the database that should be used. The database fields are the "from" fields and the TextViews are the "to" views.

Line 16 associates the Fragment's ListView with the Adapter just defined.

With that setup complete, we can see the power of the LoaderCallbacks. Lines 18 to 24 implement the onCreateLoader method.

FIGURE 17.2
PhotoListFragment showing results.

The `onLoadFinished` method on lines 26 to 28 uses the passed cursor parameter to swap cursors. The newly available cursor data is now used by the adapter. The adapter that was initially defined with a null cursor on line 13 now has the cursor provided in `onLoadFinished`.

Similarly, the `onLoaderReset` method swaps in a new null cursor.

Figure 17.3 shows a simplified diagram of how a Fragment uses a CursorLoader and CursorAdapter.

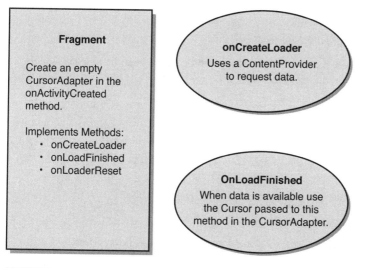

FIGURE 17.3
Fragment using a CursorLoader and CursorAdapter.

Summary

In this hour, we covered Loaders at a conceptual level and implemented two examples using a CursorLoader. To accomplish this, we used the PhotoProvider ContentProvider that we developed in Hour 16. We saw how a CursorLoader and CursorAdapter can work together in a Fragment that implements LoaderManager.LoaderCallbacks.

Q&A

Q. How do *onCreateLoader* **and** *onLoadFinished* **work together?**

A. The onCreateLoader method requests data using a ContentProvider and returns a CursorLoader. The onLoadFinished method fires when the data from the ContentProvider is available, so the onCreateLoader creates the ContentProvider and the onLoadFinished uses the data.

Q. What is the advantage of using a CursorAdapter with Loaders?

A. A CursorAdapter maps data from a Cursor to a display. Because onLoadFinished returns a Cursor, a CursorAdapter can be used in the onLoadFinished method to display the data that is available from the loader. The CursorAdapter is created in the onActivityCreated method and in the onLoadFinished method a new Cursor is swapped in.

Q. What is the relationship between an AsyncTaskLoader and a CursorLoader?

A. A CursorLoader is a subclass of AsyncTaskLoader. AsyncTaskLoader is a subclass of Loader.

Q. Can Loaders be used on Android 2.x devices?

A. No, Loaders were introduced in Android 3.0 (HoneyComb). We can use Loaders in Google TV apps because Google TVs run Honeycomb.

Workshop

Quiz

1. What methods would typically call an Adapter's swapCursor method?

2. What method fires when data is available?

3. What is the first parameter of the initLoader method and why is it important?

Answers

1. The `onLoadFinished` and `onLoaderReset` methods use `swapCursor`.

2. `onLoadFinished` fires when data is available.

3. The first parameter to `initLoader` is an id. It is important because it identifies the Loader if more than one Loader exists in the Fragment or Activity. It is passed to the LoaderManager.Callbacks methods.

Exercises

1. Rewrite the examples using the PhotoProvider and the `PHOTOS_URI`. The examples in this hour use the PhotoProvider and a query to request data with the `CONTENTS_URI`. In Hour 16 we implement support for these two URIs in the PhotoProvider class.

2. Implement a GalleryView to show the ids of the Photos. Base this on the PhotoListFragment class. A GalleryView shows data in a way that is very similar to a ListView. Review Hour 12 for the implementation of a Fragment that displays data in a GalleryView. The exercise requires implementing a CursorLoader with a Fragment that uses a GalleryView.

HOUR 18
Developing a Complete App

What You'll Learn in This Hour:

▶ What the app will do
▶ How to develop the GridFragment
▶ How to enhance the Activity Class
▶ How to add the ActionBar

In Hours 7 through 17, we covered many aspects of developing an Android app for Google TV. You learned about Layouts, the ActionBar, and Fragments. In the past four hours you learned about retrieving remote data, using ContentProviders, Cursors, and CursorLoaders.

In this hour, we will create a complete app that takes advantage of these features. We'll use the Facebook page photo app as a starting point, but we'll make it more useful by adding the capability to select a page. When the page is selected, the photos for that page will be displayed.

Determining What the App Will Do

For phone app development, one philosophy is that an app should do one thing and do it very well. No one knows if the same concept applies to TV apps. It seems safe to say that a TV app is more like a phone app or tablet app than a full-blown program on a personal computer. Users don't expect to do word processing or desktop publishing on their TVs.

For this hour, the first goal is to decide what the app will do. Deciding what the app does and what features to keep in and which features to take out may be the most important decisions made in any app project.

Facebook Page Photos as a Starting Point

We've worked with Facebook page photos, so that is a good place to start. We've been using the Coca-Cola page for our sample code. It is one of the examples that Facebook uses, and it works well to demonstrate concepts such as retrieving data.

Right now, we're hard-coding the Coca-Cola page id into the app. Imagine that we've been given an assignment to create an app that displays photos from a set of related pages. Given that scope, we can use the same model and specifically select the pages to use. An example of this kind of app might be a TV network that wants to show off some featured shows. We'll select a small number of specific pages to use in this app.

In this sample app, users would pick the page to show. If we do this for our app, what will the first page of the app look like? We'll pick a default page to show when the app starts. To change pages, the user will select alternatives from the ActionBar.

But, because this is TV, should we consider showing videos from Facebook for these pages? It would be great to do that, but we would have to dive deeper into working with Facebook and Facebook libraries. The Facebook API for getting pages' videos requires a logged in user. That is not something this book will cover, but with VideoViews and the work we've done on the Photo and PhotoProvider classes, it is something that should be within reach of everyone reading this book.

We've decided to keep the app to photos and to allow users to select the pages to use. We will use a default page for the initial experience. For each page, the app will show a GridView of photos. When a photo in the Grid is selected, a full-page view of the photo will be displayed. After a few seconds, the next photo in the set will be shown.

Creating a Wireframe for the App

Figures 18.1 through 18.3 show three very simple wireframe diagrams used to describe the app. Wireframes help when considering the layout and data required for our app.

They show we will need an ActionBar, GridView, and dialog window. We will need a way to update the GridView based on the selected page. When an image is selected, we need to know which one it is and display it.

We will use a widget called the AdapterViewFlipper to display the image and begin flipping through the images on the page. An AdapterViewFlipper provides the equivalent of a slideshow for Android views. In this case, we'll use it as a slideshow for images.

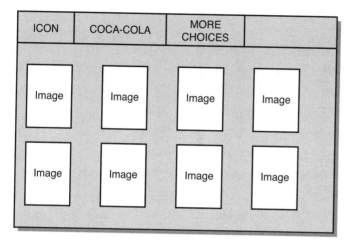

FIGURE 18.1
Wireframe entry screen showing the default page first.

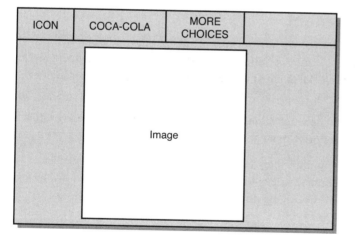

FIGURE 18.2
Wireframe showing selected image (images change automatically).

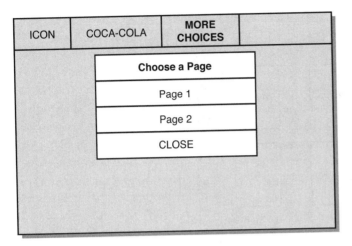

FIGURE 18.3
Wireframe showing dialog for selecting an alternative page.

Planning App Development

We need to create a GridView for this app. We'll create a GridFragment that is similar to the ListFragment we created in Hour 12, "Using Specialized Fragments." We will need a layout for displaying items within the grid. The GridFragment will use a CursorAdapter. A CursorAdapter ties cursor data to a display.

We'll use a similar CursorAdapter to show individual images in the full view. The display will be a new Fragment that uses an AdapterViewFlipper.

We want to display the images from multiple pages in this app. We'll add the Pepsi Facebook page and several others. To change from the Coca-Cola page to the Pepsi page, we'll use direct ActionBar Tabs. To switch between the Coca-Cola and Pepsi pages, the user will choose the proper tab.

For additional pages, we'll use a tab that creates a DialogFragment. That DialogFragment will list the other available pages. When those pages are selected from the list, their images will be displayed.

Throughout this process, we'll be checking whether we have the data required to display the page as required.

Figure 18.4 shows the DialogFragment.

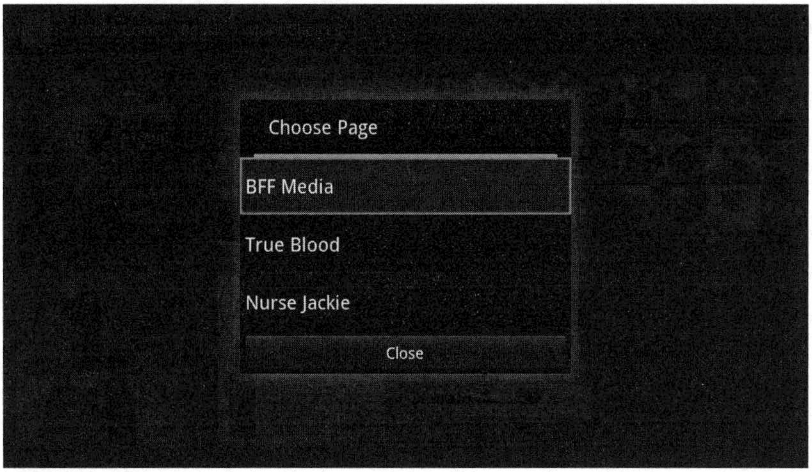

FIGURE 18.4
ListDialogFragment display.

Figure 18.5 shows photo results when the page for BFF Media is selected.

FIGURE 18.5
GridFragment display.

Developing the GridFragment

The GridFragment is very similar to the ListFragment from Hour 12. The Activity does the work of downloading all the required data. The relationship between the Fragment and Activity will be covered in detail. A CursorAdapter will be needed for the GridFragment.

In Hour 12, we used a GridView and an ArrayList to create a GridFragment. In that case, we used an ArrayAdapter and Android default views to display the data. Now we will use a CursorLoader and create a custom CursorAdapter for displaying the data.

Listing 18.1 shows the GridFragment's `onCreateView` method and the methods required to implement LoaderCallbacks. In line 4, a GridView is used.

LISTING 18.1   Creating the GridView

```
1:  @Override
2:  public View onCreateView(LayoutInflater inflater, ViewGroup container,
3:              Bundle savedInstanceState) {
4:    grid = (GridView) inflater.inflate(R.layout.grid_fragment, container, false);
5:    return grid;
6:  }
7:  @Override
8:  public Loader<Cursor> onCreateLoader(int id, Bundle args) {
9:    CursorLoader cursorLoader = new CursorLoader(getActivity(),
10:   Uri.withAppendedPath(PhotoProvider.PHOTOS_URI ,mPageId),
11:             null, null, null, null);
12:   return cursorLoader;
13: }
14: @Override
15: public void onLoadFinished(Loader<Cursor> loader, Cursor cursor) {
16:   gridAdapter.swapCursor(cursor);
17: }
18: @Override
19: public void onLoaderReset(Loader<Cursor> loader) {
20:   gridAdapter.changeCursor(null);
21: }
```

Listing 18.2 shows the layout used for the GridView. It is a simple GridView set to show four columns.

LISTING 18.2   GridView Layout

```
1:  <?xml version="1.0" encoding="utf-8"?>
2:  <GridView
3:      xmlns:android="http://schemas.android.com/apk/res/android"
4:      android:layout_width="fill_parent"
```

```
5:        android:layout_height="fill_parent"
6:        android:numColumns="4">
7:    </GridView>
```

Listing 18.3 shows onActivityCreated method for GridFragment. Several new things are introduced. GridFragment uses a CursorAdapter called PhotoCursorAdapter. An setOnItem-ClickListener is also used.

LISTING 18.3   Adding an Adapter in onActivityCreated

```
1:  public void onActivityCreated(Bundle savedInstanceState) {
2:      super.onActivityCreated(savedInstanceState);
3:      Bundle b = this.getArguments();;
4:      mPageId=b.getString("PAGE_ID");
5:      currentActivity = this.getActivity();
6:      getLoaderManager().initLoader(2, null, this);
7:      gridAdapter = new PhotoGridCursorAdapter(currentActivity, null, grid);
8:      grid.setAdapter(gridAdapter);
9:      grid.setOnItemClickListener(new OnItemClickListener() {
10:       public void onItemClick(AdapterView<?> parent, View view,int position,long id) {
11:         Bundle args = new Bundle();
12:         args.putString("PAGE_ID", mPageId);
13:         args.putInt("PHOTO_POSITION", position);
14:         PhotoAdapterViewFragment pgFragment = new PhotoAdapterViewFragment();
15:         pgFragment.setArguments(args);
16:         FragmentTransaction ft = getFragmentManager().beginTransaction();
17:         ft.replace(R.id.linearLayout1, pgFragment, "Image Viewer");
18:         ft.commit();
19:       }
20:     });
21: }
```

Line 6 of Listing 18.3 initialized the Loader. In line 7, a new PhotoGridCursorAdapter is created and assigned to the field gridAdapter. This is a custom CursorAdapter class that we will cover in detail. Lines 10 to 20 add an OnItemClickListener to the GridView. When an item in the grid is clicked, this will fire. Line 14 shows that a new fragment is created. That Fragment is passed the page id in a Bundle and displayed.

From the new classes introduced in Listing 18.3, we will examine the new PhotoCursorGridAdapter and the PhotoAdapterViewFragment.

The PhotoCursorGridAdapter

The `PhotoGridCursorAdapter` extends the CursorAdapter class. The job of a CursorAdapter is to tie the data that the Cursor provides to a new View. The `PhotoGridCursorAdapter` creates a view for each item in the Grid and specifies how to display data in that view.

To get data to display, the `PhotoGridCursorAdapter` uses the cursor supplied in line 16 of Listing 18.1. Specifically, the GridFragment class implements LoaderCallbacks. The `onLoadFinished` method of the LoaderCallbacks interface swaps in a new Cursor for this adapter.

A CursorAdapter creates a new view and binds data to that view. Listing 18.4 defines a new CursorAdapter.

LISTING 18.4   Creating the PhotoCursorGridAdapter

```
1:   public class PhotoGridCursorAdapter extends android.widget.CursorAdapter  {
2:       Context context;
3:       Activity mActivity;
4:       Cursor c;
5:       Bitmap mBitmap;
6:       GridView mGrid;
7:       private LayoutInflater inflater;
8:       public PhotoGridCursorAdapter(Context context, Cursor c, GridView g) {
9:           super(context, c);
10:          this.context = context;
11:          this.inflater = LayoutInflater.from(context);
12:          this.c = c;
13:          this.mGrid=g;
14:          this.mActivity = (Activity) context;
15:      }
16:      @Override
17:      public View newView(Context context, Cursor cursor, ViewGroup parent) {
18:          View v = inflater.inflate(R.layout.photo_grid_item, parent, false);
19:          return (v);
20:      }
```

The GridView is passed as a parameter to the constructor in line 8. Lines 17 to 20 override the `newView` method and inflate a layout called `photo_grid_item`. It is shown in Listing 18.5.

LISTING 18.5   Grid Item Layout

```
1:   <?xml version="1.0" encoding="utf-8"?>
2:   <RelativeLayout xmlns:android="http://schemas.android.com/apk/res/android"
3:       android:id="@+id/relativeLayout1"
4:       android:layout_width="wrap_content" android:layout_height="wrap_content"
5:       android:cacheColorHint="#00000000"  android:padding="12dp" >
6:       <ImageView
```

```
 7:              android:id="@+id/photoImage"
 8:              android:layout_width="200dp"
 9:              android:layout_height="200dp"
10:              android:layout_centerHorizontal="true"
11:              android:adjustViewBounds="true"
12:              android:paddingBottom="2dp"
13:              android:paddingLeft="4dp"
14:              android:paddingRight="4dp"
15:              android:paddingTop="8dp"
16:              android:scaleType="centerCrop"
17:       </ImageView>
18:   </RelativeLayout>
```

The photo_grid_item.xml layout shown in Listing 18.5 defines an ImageView within a RelativeLayout. A more complex layout could be used for an example where we wanted to display more data. We could add TextViews to display other info about the photos, for example.

In this case, we use an ImageView with the goal of showing a single photo in each grid view item. The ImageView has width and height set to 200dp on lines 8 and 9. That is 200 device pixels and will be sized appropriately for the target device. By specifying the width and height and a scaleType of "centerCrop" on line 16, we have specified that all images displayed in the grid will be shown with the same dimensions. The scaleType will show the center of the image and large images will be cropped.

Listing 18.6 shows the bindView method of the CursorAdapter and the PhotoViewHolder class. The bindView method is passed a Cursor that is used to supply data for the view. It is also passed the View to populate with data.

LISTING 18.6   PhotoCursorGridAdapter BindView

```
 1:   @Override
 2:   public void bindView(View v, Context context, Cursor c) {
 3:     PhotoViewHolder vh = (PhotoViewHolder) v.getTag();
 4:     if(vh==null){
 5:       vh = new PhotoViewHolder();
 6:       vh.imageView = (ImageView) v.findViewById(R.id.photoImage);
 7:       v.setTag(vh);
 8:     }
 9:     int idCol = c.getColumnIndex("photo_id");
10:     String id = c.getString(idCol);
11:     vh.imageView.setTag(id);
12:     Handler handler = new Handler();
13:     InputStream is;
14:     try {
15:       is =  mActivity.getContentResolver().openInputStream
16:           (Uri.withAppendedPath(PhotoProvider.CONTENT_URI ,id));
```

```
17:        mBitmap = BitmapFactory.decodeStream(is);
18:        vh.imageView.setImageBitmap(mBitmap);
19:      } catch (FileNotFoundException e) {
20:        mActivity.getContentResolver().registerContentObserver
21:        (Uri.withAppendedPath(PhotoProvider.CONTENT_URI ,id), false,
22:        new PhotoGridContentObserver(handler, id));
23:      }
24:    }
25:  public static class PhotoViewHolder{
26:    public long imageId;
27:    public ImageView imageView;
28:  }
```

Lines 3 to 8 assure that we have a PhotoViewHolder to use. In line 3, we try to get a
PhotoViewHolder by calling v.getTag(). If a PhotoViewHolder object is tied to the View v, it
will be returned by this call. If there is not an object associated with the View, lines 5 to 7 are
executed. A new PhotoViewHolder object is declared, the ImageView in the PhotoViewHolder is
populated, and the PhotoViewHolder is set as a tag on the view.

This is known as the View Holder pattern. It is used to minimize the creation of new View
objects. Creating a new ImageView is a relatively costly operation. If we can reuse an existing
view, we save that operation.

After we have a View and a Cursor, we tie the two together. Lines 9 and 10 use the cursor to
get an id for the photo. That is then used to retrieve the Bitmap associated with the photo. The
PhotoContentProvider is used. This is very similar to how we displayed a random image in
Listing 14.2 of Hour 14, "Accessing Remote Content for a Google TV App," but there is an important difference. In Hour 14, we displayed a single random image in a single ImageView. In the
case of the CursorAdapter, we have multiple images in multiple ImageViews. Listing 18.7 shows
our new PhotoContentObserver and how this issue is resolved.

LISTING 18.7 PhotoCursorGridAdapter BindView

```
1: class PhotoGridContentObserver extends ContentObserver {
2:   String mId;
3:   public PhotoGridContentObserver(Handler handler, String id) {
4:     super(handler);
5:     mId = id;
6:   }
7:   @Override
8:   public void onChange(boolean selfChange) {
9:     InputStream is;
10:    try {
11:        is = mActivity.getContentResolver().openInputStream
```

```
12:                (Uri.withAppendedPath(PhotoProvider.CONTENT_URI ,mId));
13:         mBitmap =  BitmapFactory.decodeStream(is);
14:         ImageView imageViewByTag = (ImageView) mGrid.findViewWithTag(mId);
15:         if (imageViewByTag != null) {
16:             imageViewByTag.setImageBitmap(mBitmap);
17:         }
18:     } catch (FileNotFoundException e) {
19:     }
20:  }
21:}
```

In lines 14 to 18 of Listing 18.6, we attempt to get a Bitmap from a file and display it in an ImageView. If the file is not found, a ContentObserver is initialized. The PhotoContentObserver defined in Listing 18.7 is passed the id of the image to retrieve. The id of the image provides us with enough information to retrieve the image.

We still need to tie that image to a particular ImageView. We do that in two steps. The first step is to set a tag on the ImageView with the id of the associated Image. That is done on line 11 of Listing 18.6. The second step is to retrieve that particular ImageView from the Grid. That is done on line 14 of Listing 18.7. The method findViewWithTag will give us the ImageView. Having the image id and the ImageView to display the image in, gives us what we need to retrieve the image using the PhotoContentProvider and to display it.

The PhotoAdapterViewFragment

In the GridFragment, we specified what should happen when an item in the Grid was clicked. In Listing 18.3 on lines 9 to 20, we specified that a PhotoAdapterViewFragment should be displayed when an item within the Grid is clicked.

The PhotoAdapterViewFragment follows our now familiar pattern of creating a Fragment and implementing LoaderCallbacks. We continue to work with the same set of data, so the URI for the ContentProvider is the same. There are two small differences to consider with the PhotoAdapterViewFragment. First, when an image in the GridView is selected, that image should be displayed. Second, a feature of the AdapterViewFlipper widget is that it can flip through views. Both features are handled in the onLoadFinished method shown in Listing 18.8.

LISTING 18.8   PhotoAdapterViewFragment onLoadFinished

```
1: @Override
2: public void onLoadFinished(Loader<Cursor> loader, Cursor cursor) {
3:     adapter.swapCursor(cursor);
4:     mAdapterView.setSelection(photoPosition);
5:     mAdapterView.setAutoStart(true);
6:     mAdapterView.startFlipping();
7: }
```

The PhotoAdapterViewFragment uses a custom CursorAdapter similar to PhotoCursorGridAdapter. The difference is in the layout used and the fact that an AdapterViewFlipper view is passed. In this case, the example uses a Fragment and a matching CursorAdapter. In some cases, it may make sense to have several Fragments that use the same Adapter.

For example, we might have a list of books to display. In one part of the app, we would want to display all the books in a vertical list. We could use a ListView and a CursorAdapter to do that. In another part of the app, we might want to display a handful of books that were selected by an editor. In that section, we could use a GalleryView and the same CursorAdapter. The contents for each book will display in the same way, but the container would be different

The layout for the AdapterViewFlipper used in the PhotoAdapterViewFragment is shown in Listing 18.9. The AdapterViewFlipper is set as the same size as the parent container.

LISTING 18.9   Layout view_fragment.xml

```
1: <?xml version="1.0" encoding="utf-8"?>
2: <AdapterViewFlipper
3: xmlns:android="http://schemas.android.com/apk/res/android"
4: android:layout_width="fill_parent"
5: android:layout_height="fill_parent" >
6: </AdapterViewFlipper>
```

The entire layout consists of an AdapterViewFlipper with width and height set to fill the parent.

The layout to show a single item is very similar to Listing 18.5, where the display of an item in the GridView was defined. In that case, the width and height were set to 200dp. For displaying an individual image, each dimension is set to match_parent and the scaleType is set to fit-Center. That assures that the entire image is displayed.

Figure 18.6 shows a single image being displayed. The AdapterViewFlipper will continue to display images, making this user interface like a slideshow.

FIGURE 18.6
Single image display.

Enhancing the Activity Class

When our goal was to get the data for a single page and display a random image, we used an AsyncTask in the Activity to load the data. Because we are adding the capability to dynamically pick a page and display the images, we need to reconsider that strategy.

We'll still use a LoadPhoto class that extends AsyncTask and takes the page id that we want to retrieve as a parameter. The change is that in the onPostExecute method, we will set a notification that the data has been updated. Any Fragments using LoaderCallbacks will then be notified to update their data. That is shown in Listing 18.10.

LISTING 18.10   Layout view_fragment.xml

```
1: @Override
2: protected void onPostExecute(Long result) {
3: getContentResolver().notifyChange
4:                (Uri.withAppendedPath(PhotoProvider.PHOTOS_URI ,mPageId), null);
5: }
```

Any Fragments that implemented LoaderCallbacks with the URI specified in line 4 of Listing 18.10 will be notified when the data is updated.

The ShowPagePhoto method shown in Listing 18.11 was added to the Activity. It loads data based on a page id passed as a parameter and displays a GridFragment. Because the GridFragment is passed the page id in a Bundle, it is waiting for the same data that is being retrieved.

LISTING 18.11 ShowPagePhoto Method

```
1:  public void showPagePhoto(String id){
2:      LoadPhotos lp = new LoadPhotos(id );
3:      lp.execute();
4:      GridFragment plFragment = new GridFragment();
5:      Bundle args = new Bundle();
6:      args.putString("PAGE_ID", id);
7:      plFragment.setArguments(args);
8:      FragmentTransaction ft = getFragmentManager().beginTransaction();
9:      ft.addToBackStack(id);
10:     ft.replace(R.id.linearLayout1, plFragment, "page "+ id);
11:     ft.commit();
12: }
```

Lines 2 and 3 of Listing 18.11 begin loading data for the passed page id with a call to the AsyncTask LoadPhotos. Lines 4 to 11 then display a GridFragment. The GridFragment is passed the same page id.

Looking back at Listing 18.1, we see that the GridFragment loads a Uri defined by

`Uri.withAppendedPath(PhotoProvider.PHOTOS_URI ,mPageId)`

The LoadPhotos AsyncTask retrieves data for the same Uri. As we see in Listing 18.10, when this data is available, a change notification is broadcast. That will trigger the `onLoadFinished` method in the GridFragment, and an update will occur if needed.

This sequence assures that as data is retrieved and the local database is updated, the display will be shown properly. We will initially navigate to a blank screen and then an update will occur. After the image data and corresponding images are downloaded the first time, we will not see the blank screen.

Adding the ActionBar

We introduced the ActionBar in Hour 10, "Organizing Google TV Apps Using the ActionBar." For this app, we will define three tabs. The first two tabs show Facebook page names that can be selected directly. When these tabs are selected, a GridFragment is displayed and populated with the appropriate data. The third tab opens a DialogFragment where the user can choose a Facebook page from a list. The `showPagePhoto` method is called directly from the first two tabs.

Defining the ActionBar

Listing 18.12 shows the Activity onCreate method that defines the ActionBar and the tabs. It shows a portion of the TabListener to illustrate how the showPagePhoto method is used.

The third tab shows a ListDialogFragment. We cover the ListDialogFragment implementation in the next section.

LISTING 18.12 Defining the ActionBar

```
1:    @Override
2:    public void onCreate(Bundle savedInstanceState) {
3:      super.onCreate(savedInstanceState);
4:      setContentView(R.layout.main);
5:      mActionBar = getActionBar();
6:      mTab1= mActionBar.newTab().setText("Coca Cola").
7:            setTabListener(new PagePhotoTabListener());
8:      mTab2= mActionBar.newTab().setText("Pepsi").
9:            setTabListener(new PagePhotoTabListener());
10:     mTab3= mActionBar.newTab().setText("More Choices").
11:           setTabListener(new PagePhotoTabListener());
12:     mActionBar.setDisplayShowTitleEnabled(false);
13:     mActionBar.setNavigationMode(ActionBar.NAVIGATION_MODE_TABS);
14:     mActionBar.addTab(mTab1);
15:     mActionBar.addTab(mTab2);
16:     mActionBar.addTab(mTab3);
17:   }
18:   private class PagePhotoTabListener implements ActionBar.TabListener {
19:   @Override
20:     public void onTabSelected(Tab tab, FragmentTransaction ft) {
21:       if (tab ==mTab1){
22:         showPagePhoto("99394368305");
23:       }
24:       if (tab ==mTab2){
25:         showPagePhoto("123490744049");
26:       }
27:       if (tab==mTab3){
28:         ListDialogFragment listDialog = new ListDialogFragment();
29:         listDialog.show(getFragmentManager(), "list_dialog");
30:       }
31:   }
```

Lines 5 to 16 of Listing 18.12 defined the ActionBar and associated tabs. Lines 18 to 31 show a portion of the PagePhotoTabListener class that implements an ActionBar.TabListener that listens for and acts on tab events like onTabSelected. Line 22 shows a call to the showPagePhoto method for the Coca-Cola page. Lines 28 and 29 declare and show a ListDialogFragment.

The ListDialogFragment

The goal of the ListDialogFragment is to show a list of Facebook pages that the user can select and to display a GridFragment containing the results. We'll use a HashMap consisting of Facebook page names and page ids to define the list to display. To show the GridFragment, we'll call the Activity showPagePhoto method. Listing 18.13 shows the onCreateView method for the ListDialogFragment.

LISTING 18.13   ListDialogFragment onCreateView

```
1:   @Override
2:   public View onCreateView(LayoutInflater inflater, ViewGroup
3:              container, Bundle savedInstanceState) {
4:     View v = inflater.inflate(R.layout.list_dialog_fragment, container, false);
5:     mListView = (ListView)v.findViewById(R.id.listView1);
6:     Button button = (Button)v.findViewById(R.id.button1);
7:     button.setOnClickListener(new OnClickListener() {
8:       public void onClick(View v) {
9:         ListDialogFragment.this.dismiss();
10:      }
11:    });
12:    return v;
13: }
```

A ListView and Button are defined. The Button closes the window. The ListView is populated in the onActivityCreated method shown in Listing 18.14.

LISTING 18.14   ListDialogFragment onActivityCreated

```
1:   public class ListDialogFragment extends DialogFragment    {
2:     ListView mListView;
3:     HashMap mValues = new HashMap();
4:     @Override
5:     public void onActivityCreated(Bundle savedInstanceState) {
6:       super.onActivityCreated(savedInstanceState);
7:       mValues.put("BFF Media","304703469573709");
8:       mValues.put("Nurse Jackie","183648859772");
9:       mValues.put("True Blood","81916858562");
10:      getDialog().setTitle("Choose Page");
11:      final Object[] values = mValues.keySet().toArray();
12:      ArrayAdapter adapter = new ArrayAdapter(
13:        getActivity(),
14:        android.R.layout.simple_list_item_1,
15:        values);
16:      mListView.setAdapter(adapter);
```

```
17:        mListView.setOnItemClickListener(new OnItemClickListener() {
18:          public void onItemClick(AdapterView<?> parent, View v, int position, long
id){
19:            Hour18Activity activity = (Hour18Activity)getActivity();
20:            activity.showPagePhoto((String)mValues.get(values[position]));
21:            ListDialogFragment.this.dismiss();
22:          }
23:        });
24:  }
```

In Listing 18.14, the goal is to show a list of Facebook page names in a ListView. When the page name is selected, we use the associated page id to retrieve and display the proper information. A HashMap is used to store the Facebook page name and ids. A HashMap consists of a key and a value. In our case, we use the page name for the key and the page id for the value. The HashMap is declared on line 3 and populated on lines 7 to 9.

An ArrayAdapter is used to display the list of names in the ListView. On line 11, we get an Array from the HashMap keys. We use that Array in line 15 when the ArrayAdapter is defined.

Lines 17 to 23 show what happens when an item in the list is clicked. On line 20, we use the key returned from the Array to look up the page id in the HashMap. The page id is used in a call to the Activity's showPagePhoto method, and in line 21 the ListFragmentDialog window is closed.

This allows us to display a potentially long list of Facebook page names in a relatively small area.

TRY IT YOURSELF ▼

Putting It All Together

As a challenge, modify the photo_grid_item.xml layout file and the PhotoGridCursorAdapter to display an additional field for each item in the GridFragment. We are assured that each photo will have an id, so add a TextView under the ImageView and display the photo id.

1. Add a TextView to the photo_grid_item.xml layout file.

2. Modify the PhotoGridCursorAdapter bindView method and PhotoViewHolder to refer to the new TextView. See Listing 18.6 for guidance.

3. Populate the TextView with the photo id. The id is associated with a row in the database. We are already getting the value for photo_id in lines 9 and 10 of Listing 18.6.

Summary

In this hour, we implemented a full app using topics we covered from Hour 7 through Hour 17. That includes using Fragments, DialogFragments, and a GridView. We introduced a custom CursorAdapter and the AdapterViewFlipper widget. By using Content Providers, Cursors, CursorLoaders, and CursorAdapters, we demonstrated the capability to easily show the same data in different views.

Q&A

Q. What is the purpose of a CursorAdapter?

A. A CursorAdapter populates a View from data provided in a Cursor. It maps the data to specific UI components.

Q. Why are two layout XML files needed to show images in the GridFragment?

A. One defines the `GridView` for the GridFragment. Another defines the items displayed in the `GridView`. We can think of one view defining the container and another view defining the contents of the container. The GridView is used for the container. A CursorAdapter maps data from the Cursor to the content items within the container.

Q. What was accomplished by using tabs in the ActionBar and a DialogFragment?

A. By using tabs in the ActionBar, we allow the user to switch between Coca-Cola, Pepsi, and a list of other pages. The `DialogFragment` provides the list of other pages. Taken together, the user can get to primary content very easily and still have access to all other content.

Workshop

Quiz

1. How was the LoadPhoto AsyncTask changed to better support this app?

2. What method is called to close the ListDialogFragment window?

3. Given a HashMap defined as `mValues`, what does `mValues.keySet().toArray();` do?

Answers

1. A change notification was added to the LoadPhoto's `onPostExecute` method. The notification indicates the content has changed.

2. Windows are closed with a call to dismiss. In this case, we would use `ListDialogFragment.this.dismiss()`.

3. HashMaps are defined as a set of keys and values. Using `keySet().toArray()` returns the set of keys from the HashMap as an Array. We used this to populate the ArrayAdapter in the ListFragmentDialog.

Exercises

1. Change the layout for items in the GridFragment to display a full image with no cropping. Experiment with dimensions and `scaleType`.

2. Implement a Gallery instead of a GridView to display the set of images. We saw in Hour 12 that we can switch between a Gallery and GridView with minor changes to the Fragments that are defined. The Fragment's onCreateView method would need to return a Gallery, and other changes would be required throughout the Fragment definition.

Mastering the Android Manifest File

What You'll Learn in This Hour:

▶ How the Android Manifest file works

▶ Understanding Intents and Categories

▶ How the Manifest files work with Google TV

▶ How to publish your app with the Manifest file

An Android manifest file with the name `AndroidManifest.xml` is part of every Android application. The manifest file defines many attributes and permissions required for an app. In this hour, we'll dissect the manifest file for the app we created in Hour 18, "Developing a Complete App," and then examine other aspects of the manifest file. In particular, we'll spend time on the options for making an app available in Google Play for Google TV and include additional information on publishing apps for Google TV.

Android Manifest Basics

First we'll examine the XML file, `AndroidManifest.xml`, for the sample app from Hour 18. Listing 19.1 shows the entire file.

LISTING 19.1   AndroidManifest.xml

```
1: <?xml version="1.0" encoding="utf-8"?>
2: <manifest xmlns:android="http://schemas.android.com/apk/res/android"
3:     package="com.bffmedia.content"
4:     android:versionCode="1"
5:     android:versionName="1.0" >
6:     <application
7:         android:icon="@drawable/icon"
8:         android:label="@string/app_name" >
9:         <activity
10:            android:name=".Hour18Activity"
11:            android:label="@string/app_name" >
12:            <intent-filter>
13:                <action android:name="android.intent.action.MAIN" />
```

```
14:                    <category android:name="android.intent.category.LAUNCHER" />
15:                </intent-filter>
16:            </activity>
17:            <provider
18:                android:name="com.bffmedia.content.PhotoProvider"
19:                android:authorities="com.bffmedia.content.PhotoProvider"
20:                android:multiprocess="true" >
21:            </provider>
22:        </application>
23:        <uses-sdk android:minSdkVersion="12" />
24:        <uses-permission android:name="android.permission.INTERNET" >
25:        </uses-permission>
26: </manifest>
```

Breaking Down the Manifest File

When we use Eclipse to create a project, a manifest file is created. The manifest file from Hour 18 uses many of the defaults created by Eclipse. We'll examine the Hour 18 manifest to gain a working understanding of the Android Manifest file, and then we'll examine more general aspects of the file.

The name of the Activity is Hour18Activity and it is defined in the package com.bffmedia.content. Both the package and Activity name are used in the manifest file to specify the Activity to launch for this app.

Line 3 of Listing 19.1 defines the package for the application. This is very important. The package name specifies a unique application to an Android device like a Google TV. The convention is to use a URL in reverse. In this case, that becomes com.bffmedia. We then append content to give the full package name, com.bffmedia.content. The package name uniquely identifies the app on the Android market and on an Android device.

Lines 4 and 5 are the version code and version name. The version code is used by developers for internal tracking and is used by the Android market to know if a new version of code is available. The version name is displayed in the market. These two are unlikely to be the same.

Lines 6 to 22 specify the details of the application. We'll look at these separately.

Lines 7 and 8 specify the icon and label to be used for the application. The icon is used as the launch icon for the app. In this case, we are using the Android image. It is displayed in the ActionBar in the screenshots in Hour 18.

An Activity may also have a label. Line 11 defines the label as a value that is defined in a String resource. Eclipse uses the name of the app and generates this value.

Lines 9 to 16 define the Activity. The name in line 10 begins with a dot, which means that the name should be prepended with the package name. So `.Hour18Activity` is interpreted as the class `com.bffmedia.content.Hour18Activity`.

Lines 12 to 15 define the intent filter for the Activity and include an action and a category. The job of an intent filter is to help the system decide which Activity to run. We have been explicitly making that decision for our apps.

Intents may have multiple actions. The intent `android.intent.action.MAIN` indicates that `Hour18Activity` should start as the initial Activity. The category for the Activity is `android.intent.category.LAUNCHER`. This indicates that the Activity is launched when the app starts. The `MAIN` action and `LAUNCHER` category are used to start the app. Other activities within the app can use `android.intent.category.DEFAULT` or other actions. Note that in our apps, we launched an Activity and then used Fragments for all subsequent display and navigation.

Lines 17 to 21 define the ContentProvider. In this case, we use the full name, but we could have started the name with a dot, as we did with the Activity name.

In Line 23, the minimum SDK version for the app is set to 12. SDK level 12 is the Android 3.1 platform known as HoneyComb. HoneyComb runs on Android tablets and Google TV. It will also run on phones running Ice Cream Sandwich.

Setting permissions is an important part of the `AndroidManifest.xml` file. On lines 24 and 25, we indicate that the app uses permission `android.permission.INTERNET`. By setting that permission we allow the app to access remote data.

Including Services and Receivers to the Manifest

By examining the details of the manifest file for Hour 18, we have been able to cover key components of the file. The Hour 18 file included defining an Activity, a ContentProvider, and included setting permissions.

Some additional basic pieces may be included in a manifest file. Services and receivers are defined similarly to Activities. Both services and receivers are fired based on intent filters that are included in the manifest file.

A service is an Android class like an Activity that has no user interface component. We could have used the `LoadPhotos` AsyncTask class from Hour 18 as the basis for a data retrieval service. Services can be started and stopped within an Activity. The Android manifest must know about the service to make it available. A service can be defined on the manifest as

```
<service android:enabled="true" android:name=".ExampleService" />
```

A receiver fires when an Activity within our app should fire based on something that happens in the system. A receiver is also known as a broadcast receiver. An event in the system is broadcast, and a receiver reacts to it. Broadcast receivers will respond to system actions that include `ACTION_BOOT_COMPLETED`, which fires once when the system has finished booting, and `ACTION_PACKAGE_ADDED`, which fires when a new application package has been added to the device.

In this example, the class `MyReceiver` will fire when the action `ACTION_BOOT_COMPLETED` occurs:

```
<receiver android:name=".MyReceiver" android:enabled="true">
<intent-filter>
<action android:name="android.intent.action.ACTION_BOOT_COMPLETED "></action>
</intent-filter>
</receiver>
```

Several other sets of elements may be defined in the manifest file: in particular, `<uses-feature>` and `<uses-library>`. When we use a library, it must be specified in the manifest. The `<uses-feature>` element specifies features for the application. This is very helpful when considering Google TV specifics.

Understanding Intents

An *Intent* represents an operation to be performed. That is a very broad definition. In practice, an Intent is used with `startActivity` to launch an Activity. Intents are also used with broadcast receivers and services to determine how to handle actions within the Android system.

An Intent includes the action to perform and any other information required to complete the action. If the goal of the intent is to view a URL, the action is `Intent.ACTION_VIEW` and the data is the URL to view. The Intent to show http://www.google.com can be created as follows:

```
Intent browseIntent = new Intent(Intent.ACTION_VIEW, Uri.parse("http://www.google.
com"));
startActivity(browseIntent);
```

The Intent to make a phone call will open the dialer with the phone number displayed. It can be created by specifying the action as `Intent.ACTION_CALL`, as follows:

```
Intent dialIntent = new Intent(Intent.ACTION_CALL);
dialIntent.setData(Uri.parse("tel:5551111234"));
```

Line 13 of Listing 19.1 specified the action as `android.intent.action.MAIN`. The action was included in the XML section that defined an `intent-filter`. The `<intent-filter>` begins on line 12 and ends in line 15. An Action and a category are defined within the `<intent-filter>` tags. The action MAIN means that the specified Activity should be the initial Activity with no input and no returned data. It is the start of the app.

Following are common Intent actions:

- ACTION_MAIN: Main entry point to app.

- ACTION_VIEW: Display data to user. Data is included in Intent.

- ACTION_ATTACH_DATA: Data should be attached. Data is part of the Intent.

- ACTION_EDIT: Access is given to edit the included data.

- ACTION_PICK: Pick an item from the data.

- ACTION_CHOOSER: User picks an Activity to act on the content.

- ACTION_GET_CONTENT: User selects a type of content like an Image.

- ACTION_DIAL: Dial a phone number.

- ACTION_CALL: Call a number.

- ACTION_SEND: Deliver data to someone. Could be email or other app.

- ACTION_SENDTO: Deliver data to user specified in the Intent data.

- ACTION_ANSWER: Handle an incoming call.

- ACTION_INSERT: Insert new data.

- ACTION_DELETE: Delete specified data.

- ACTION_RUN: Run the data. Result is specific to data.

- ACTION_SYNC: Synchronize data.

- ACTION_PICK_ACTIVITY: Pick an Activity for the Intent.

- ACTION_SEARCH: Perform a search.

- ACTION_WEB_SEARCH: Perform a web search.

- ACTION_FACTORY_TEST: Entry point for Factory tests.

Line 14 of Listing 19.1 shows that category is of type LAUNCHER. It means that this Activity can be the initial Activity. MAIN and LAUNCHER go together to say that this Activity really starts the app. A category is a part of an Intent.

The following are some common categories:

▶ CATEGORY_DEFAULT: The default action that is used in Intent filters.

▶ CATEGORY_BROWSABLE: The Activity can show data in a browser.

▶ CATEGORY_LAUNCHER: The Activity can be the initial Activity of an app.

Actions and Categories work together to specify when the Intent should fire. When we use explicit Intents, such as the name of the Activity, we can indicate one Activity with the action set to ACTION_MAIN and the category set to CATEGORY_LAUNCHER. For other explicit intents for Activities defined in the Android manifest file, we could set action to ACTION_MAIN and category to CATEGORY_DEFAULT.

It is also possible to use actions like ACTION_VIEW and ACTION_EDIT as implicit intents. That means that if we defined an Activity to view images, our Activity will be presented as an option to handle any image viewing on the system. We would need to be prepared to accept any data passed in the Intent.

Adding Google TV Specifics to the Manifest File

The basics for an AndroidManifest.xml file apply to all Android apps. A package name and Activities must be defined. Permissions are set, and Content Providers may be defined.

For Google TV apps, we must handle all the basic parts of the manifest. There are some things that we must do to assure that the app we've worked on will really be available to Google TV users.

Market Filters

Developers generally create apps to be available in the Google Play app market. To assure that happens for Google TV apps, we must assure that the Google Play app on the TV does not filter out the app. The Google Play Marketplace filters applications based on settings in the AndroidManifest.xml file. We'll look at options for those settings and in the last section of this hour, we'll look at the steps to publish an app on Google Play.

Google TVs do not have touchscreens, and Google Play checks for this. We must specifically set touchscreen required to false in the manifest file for our app to be available on Google TV. The manifest must include the following:

```
<uses-feature android:name="android.hardware.touchscreen" android:required="false"/>
```

That does not mean that the touchscreen will not be used if this app runs on a phone. It means that a touchscreen is not required to run the app. Running the Hour 18 code on an Ice Cream Sandwich phone device works well and supports the touchscreen.

The Google TV SDK version is at level 12, so that is how the minimum SDK version must be set:

```
<uses-sdk android:minSdkVersion="12" />
```

In other cases, Google Play may filter out an app. If you expect your Google TV app to appear in the market and it is not, you can check several things. If you are using a library that is not available for Google TV, your app will not show in the market. If you are using a feature or setting that implies that a touchscreen is required, the app will not show.

In general, the AndroidManifest.xml file is the place to start for any issue with an app not showing in Google Play.

Universal Apps

It's possible to create an app that runs on phones, tablets, and on Google TV. For that app, we might define a minimum SDK. In addition to the minimum SDK, there is a target SDK and a max SDK:

```
<uses-sdk android:targetSdkVersion="12" />
```

By using the target SDK and minimum SDK versions, we can specify a range of devices that will be supported with one app. One potential problem is that not all features may be available to our app. For example, CursorLoaders were introduced in API Level 11 on Android 3.0.

One solution is to consider the compatibility library that Google has provided. It allows new features to be incorporated into old apps. There is a version of CursorLoaders and Fragments in the compatibility library.

For a particular app, it might make sense to create two versions. One version would be built for Android 3.0 and later. That version of the app would support tablets, Google TV, and new phones running Ice Cream Sandwich. We would define a min SDK of 12 and make sure we set touchscreen required to false.

Specifying Google TV Only Apps

For an app that would run only on Google TV, the minimum SDK would be set to 12 and touchscreen required is set to false. To assure a Google TV only app, use

```
<uses-feature android:name="com.google.android.tv" android:required="true"/>
```

Running Multiple Versions of the App

It is possible in code to check both for a specific system feature in an app and to check the minimum SDK. Using a PackageManager, we can check for a particular feature:

```
if (getPackageManager().hasSystemFeature("com.google.android.tv")) {
  // do something
}
```

There is a `Build.VERSION` class that will tell the app what level api is running. So, if the goal is one code base for all devices, then that is possible. Depending on the app, it may be an easy or difficult thing to accomplish. For a simple app, it should be possible to create one version to run on all devices. Factors that make this more complicated include screen size and screen density, which affect how images display on various devices. Features included in various Android versions are another consideration. To create an app that runs on all versions, you must not use an API feature from a subsequent version.

A reasonable option is having multiple versions of the app for phones running API Level 11 and lower and for tablets running API Level 12 and higher. There would be two sets of code. Android provides a compatibility library for earlier versions of Android. The library includes Fragments and CursorLoaders, so the code can be made to be very similar to later versions. It would be possible to se the compatibility library for one set of code and devices and use native Android 3.0 and later features for devices with newer versions.

There is another reason for multiple versions. It may make sense from a user experience and even marketing perspective to have several versions of the same app. That is more work because you are creating and maintaining multiple versions of the app on different code bases. The advantage is that it allows a developer to create one app specifically for Google TV, another specific to phones, and another specific to tablets. It is possible to break that down further and target 7" tablets and 10" tablets. It is even possible to target specific devices like the Nexus 7 or Kindle Fire.

The choice on how to approach handling multiple devices depends on your app and the requirements for UI and display on various devices. If you are creating a Google TV only app, the approach is more direct.

Publishing Your App

In this hour, we've covered what is required to make your TV app available in the Google Play store. Now we'll cover how to publish your app.

To make your app available on Google Play, you must register for a Google Play publisher account. Go to the Google Play publish URL at https://play.google.com/apps/publish/ and enter your basic information about your developer identity, and agree to the Developer Distribution

Agreement. The cost to become a developer is $25 USD. You must pay via Google Checkout. If you do not have a Google Checkout account you can set one up.

If you want to sell your apps, you will need to set up a Google Checkout Merchant Account. Go to the same Google Play publish URL and choose Edit Profile. You can then follow the instructions to set up your merchant account.

Android apps are compiled into APK files. So a compiled app would create the file `myapp.apk`. You would load `myapp.apk` to the Google Play market to make it available to users. You can also upload certain marketing materials, such as name, description, and screenshots, with your app. After your app is uploaded and the material is correct, you will publish your app to make it available in the market.

The Google Play Developer Console shows your apps, including the number of downloads, active installs, and comments, as shown in Figure 19.1. Detailed app stats and error reports are available from the console.

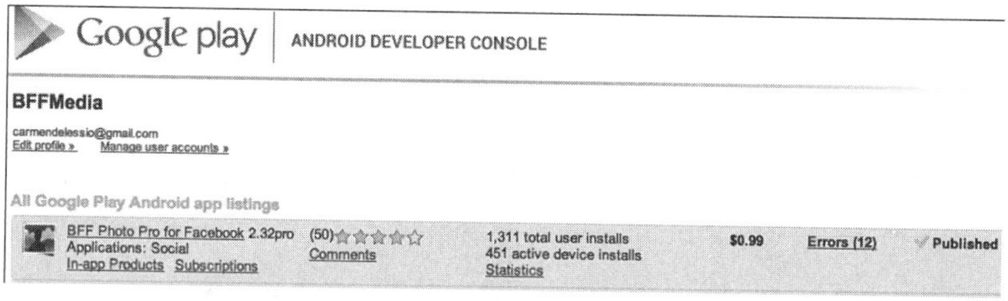

FIGURE 19.1
A phone app in the Google Play Developer Console.

Summary

In this hour, we covered the `AndroidManifest.xml` file in detail by examining the file used in Hour 18. The importance of the `AndroidManifest.xml` file to our app being available in Google Play was covered, along with the importance of Intents and how they work based on Actions and Categories. The system considers intent-filters to determine what Activity to display.

Google TV-specific requirements for the Android Manifest file were covered. These are important for assuring that a Google TV app shows up in the Google Play store on TVs. We discussed the options for apps that run on all devices and apps that run only on specific devices. It is possible to create a universal app that runs on all devices, but an option is to create multiple versions of apps and to target specific devices.

The reason for many of the Google TV specific entries in the Android Manifest file is to assure that these apps show up on the Google Play store. The steps to becoming a Google Play publisher were included.

Q&A

Q. What is the minimum SDK version to use for Google TV?

A. The Google TV SDK version is at level 12, so that is how the minimum SDK version must be set.

Q. What does the AndroidManifest.xml file have to do with my app retrieving data from the Internet ?

A. The `AndroidManifest.xml` file specifies app permissions. A permission must be set to retrieve data from the Internet.

Q. What is the difference between versionCode and versionName?

A. The versionName is displayed in the Google Play Marketplace. The versionCode is used to determine if an update has been made to the app.

Workshop

Quiz

1. What must be set in the Android Manifest file for a Google TV app to show up in Google Play?

2. What is the compatibility package?

3. Besides an Activity, what user-created classes might be specified in the `AndroidManifest.xml` file?

Answers

1. Touchscreen must be set to `false`.

2. The compatibility package brings some newer Android platform features to older versions. It is not needed for Google TV apps.

3. ContentProviders, Services, and Receivers.

Exercises

1. Use `ACTION_VIEW` in an app to show a URL. You will use the example in this hour that displayed the Google home page and include it in an Activity or Fragment. Note that displaying URLs can be a good way to add help or additional info sections to an app. The advantage is that you can update the content of those pages without updating the app.

2. Change the label and icon for a previous sample app by updating the manifest file. Look at Listing 19.1 and the related discussion to see how to do this.

Using the Channel Listing Provider

What You'll Learn in This Hour:

▶ How to get data from the Channel Listing provider

▶ How to list all the channels

▶ How to change the channel

▶ How to handle audio focus

In Hour 16, "Creating a Content Provider," you learned how to create and use a `ContentProvider`. Google TV includes a Channel Listing provider to provide information about available TV channels. When you use an existing `ContentProvider`, it is important to understand the data that is being made available and how to use it. In this hour, we will access data from the Channel Listing provider and use it to create an app for changing channels. We will also use what we learn from the channel changing app to examine how audio focus should be handled in apps.

Getting Data from the Channel Listing Provider

The Channel Listing provider is a `ContentProvider` that is specific to Google TV. It provides a listing of available TV channels. In Hour 16, we created a SQLite database for photo information. The columns in that database were mapped to the `ContentProvider` for returning photo data.

For publicly available content providers like the Channel Listing provider, column names and the data they contain must be documented for third-party users (that's us). The information needed to make the required URI must also be provided.

Data Available from the Channel Listing Provider

The columns available in the Channel Listing provider are documented here: https://developers. google.com/tv/android/docs/gtv_provider#CLProvider. The columns are as follows:

- ▶ Row identifier, `_id`—An integer that uniquely identifies the row.

- ▶ URI as a String, `channel_uri`—A String that represents a URI for the channel. This value is used to change channels.

- ▶ Channel's callsign, `callsign`—A String containing the callsign of the channel. For example MSNBC or CNN.

- ▶ Channel's name, `channel_name`—A String with a long channel name.

- ▶ Channel's number, `channel_number`—A String with the channel number. This value may not be unique within the provider.

Forming a URI to Access Data

To use the content provider we need the `authority` and `path` information. In Hour 16, we created these ourselves and used them when we wanted to access data. For the Channel Listing provider they are as follows:

- ▶ Authority—`com.google.android.tv.provider`

- ▶ Path—`channel_listing`

A `ContentResolver` uses the information from a `ContentProvider` to create a query and return data in a `Cursor`. The information in the `ContentProvider` is accessed using a URI that is created from the authority and path information. For the Channel Listing provider, the URI is created using the following:

```
Uri channelUri = Uri.parse("content://" +
"com.google.android.tv.provider" + "/" + "channel_listing");
```

That produces the String

```
content://com.google.android.tv.provider/channel_listing.
```

A `ContentResolver` queries the `ContentProvider`, and the available columns for the Channel Listing provider provide the information needed to create a simple app for accessing the Channel Listing Provider.

Using the Channel Listing Provider in an Activity

We'll create an `Activity` that provides available information on CNN. To do that, we'll create a query that looks for CNN for the callsign column.

Note that that Android manifest must be updated with a permission to use the Channel Listing provider:

```
<uses-permission android:name="com.google.android.tv.permission.READ_CHANNELS" />
```

CAUTION

Remember to Update the Manifest File

When we created our own Content Provider, we updated the Android manifest XML file. When we used the Channel Listing provider, we set the permission to READ_CHANNELS.

Listing 20.1 shows the entire Activity for retrieving the CNN data and displaying it in a `Toast` message.

LISTING 20.1   Accessing Data in the Channel Provider

```
1:   package com.bffmedia.channel;
2:   import android.app.Activity;
3:   import android.database.Cursor;
4:   import android.net.Uri;
5:   import android.os.Bundle;
6:   import android.widget.Toast;
7:   public class Hour20ChannelActivity extends Activity {
8:   @Override
9:   public void onCreate(Bundle savedInstanceState) {
10:    super.onCreate(savedInstanceState);
11:    setContentView(R.layout.main);
12:    Uri channelUri = Uri.parse("content://"
13:                              + "com.google.android.tv.provider"
14:                              + "/" + "channel_listing");
15:    String mWhere = "callsign = 'CNN'";
16:    Cursor mCursor = getContentResolver().query(channelUri,
17:                null,  mWhere, null, null
18:    );
19:    if (null == mCursor) {
20:        Toast.makeText(this,"Empty cursor",Toast.LENGTH_LONG).show();
21:        return;
22:    }
23:    if (mCursor.getCount() == 0 ) {
24:        Toast.makeText(this,"Callsign Not Found",Toast.LENGTH_LONG).show();
25:        return;
26:    }
```

```
27:    mCursor.moveToFirst();
28:    Toast.makeText(this,
29:        mCursor.getString(mCursor.getColumnIndex("callsign"))
30:        + "\n Channel " + mCursor.getString(mCursor.getColumnIndex("channel_number"))
31:        + "\n" + mCursor.getString(mCursor.getColumnIndex("channel_name")),
32:        Toast.LENGTH_LONG).show();
33: }     // end OnCreate
34:}      // end Activity
```

Lines 12 to 14 of Listing 20.1 create the URI for the Channel Listing provider. A query is created in Line 15. We want to retrieve data where the callsign has a value of CNN. Lines 16 and 17 use the Activity's getContentResolver method to query the Channel Listing provider. A query is done using the URI and where clause that was created. The result of the query is returned as a Cursor.

Line 17 moves the Cursor to the first position. This is important so that a value can be read from the Cursor.

Lines 19 to 26 do two types of error checking on the returned Cursor. A check is done for a null cursor and for a Cursor in which no values are returned.

Lines 28 to 32 display a Toast message on the TV screen with the returned information. The result is shown in Figure 20.1.

FIGURE 20.1
CNN information from Channel Listing provider.

Listing All Channels

We'll retrieve all the available channels and show them in a `ListFragment`. To do that, we use a `SimpleCursorAdapter` and take advantage of `CursorLoaders`.

A `SimpleCursorAdapter` maps the columns from a `ContentProvider` to a specific layout for display. Android defines a number of layouts, including one called `android.R.layout.simple_list_item_2`. That layout displays two `TextViews`. We will use it with the `SimpleCursorAdapter` and provide the columns for callsign and channel_name to be displayed. The channels will be ordered by callsign. We will not specify a `where` clause for the query. That will result in all the channel listings being returned.

The app consists of an Activity that loads the `ChannelListFragment`. The `ChannelListFragment` is shown in Listing 20.2.

LISTING 20.2   Channels in a ListFragment

```
1:   public class ChannelListFragment extends ListFragment
2:                 implements LoaderCallbacks<Cursor>  {
3:     SimpleCursorAdapter mAdapter;
4:     @Override
5:     public void onActivityCreated(Bundle savedInstanceState) {
6:       super.onActivityCreated(savedInstanceState);
7:       getLoaderManager().initLoader(0, null, this);
8:       mAdapter = new SimpleCursorAdapter(getActivity(),
9:           android.R.layout.simple_list_item_2,
10:          null,
11:          new String[] {"callsign", "channel_name"},
12:          new int[] { android.R.id.text1, android.R.id.text2 }, 0);
13:      setListAdapter(mAdapter);
14:    }
15:    @Override
16:    public Loader<Cursor> onCreateLoader(int id, Bundle args) {
17:      Uri channelProviderUri = Uri.parse("content://"
18:                          + "com.google.android.tv.provider"
19:                          + "/" + "channel_listing");
20:      CursorLoader cursorLoader = new CursorLoader(getActivity(),
21:      channelProviderUri ,
22:          null, null, null, "callsign ASC");
23:      return cursorLoader;
24:    }
25:    @Override
26:    public void onLoadFinished(Loader<Cursor> Loader, Cursor cursor) {
27:      mAdapter.swapCursor(cursor);
28:    }
29:    @Override
30:    public void onLoaderReset(Loader<Cursor> arg0) {
```

```
31:        mAdapter.swapCursor(null);
32:      }
33:  }
```

The `ChannelListFragment` shown in Listing 20.2 is an instance of a `ListFragment`. ListFragments have an inherent `ListView` available. Lines 8 to 12 define a `SimpleCursorAdapter` called mAdapter. Line 13 sets mAdapter as the Adapter for the ListFragment using the setListAdapter method.

As we saw in Hour 17, we do the work of the `CursorLoader` in the `onCreateLoader` method. Lines 17 to 19 create the URI for the Channel Listing provider. Lines 20 to 22 create the `CursorLoader`. In this case, in line 22, we use the URI created and add the `orderBy` field to sort in ascending order by callsign.

Because we implemented `LoaderCallbacks` in line 2, we must implement the methods `onCreateLoader`, `OnLoadFinished`, and `onLoaderReset`. Those methods complete the `ChannelListFragment` class.

The result of listing the channels is shown in Figure 20.2.

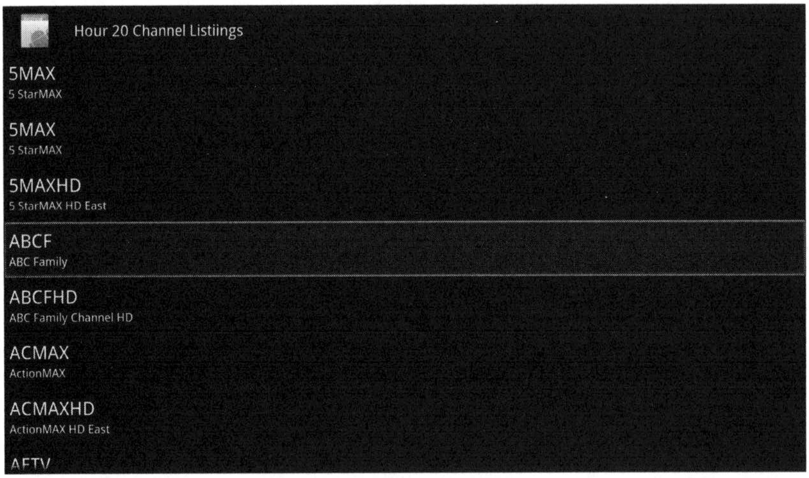

FIGURE 20.2
Channel Listings displayed using a ListFragment.

Changing the Channel

The Channel Listing provider gives us a callsign, channel number, channel name, and channel URI. The channel_uri is used to change the channel on a TV.

To show the additional data available from the Channel Listing provider, we will use a GridView within a Fragment. Each child within the GridView will display all the information for one channel. In this example, we will change channels using Intents.

Examples of a channel_uri can be seen by logging or printing it and checking LogCat. The following is the channel_uri for Animal Planet. We see the callsign APL and the channel 57. The other piece of data is the deviceId.

```
tv://channel/APL?deviceId=irb_0&channelNumber=57
```

The channel_uri is a URI known to the Google TV system. URIs can be parsed and made into Intents, and Intents are used to start Activities. We want to view the TV channel associated with the channel_uri.

We would not normally refer to the value of the channel_uri directly, but the following shows how to create a URI for Animal Planet and change the channel. Starting the Activity that is associated with the ACTION_VIEW intent changes the channel:

```
Uri channelUri = Uri.parse("tv://channel/APL?deviceId=irb_0&channelNumber=57");
startActivity(new Intent(Intent.ACTION_VIEW, channelUri));
```

The GridFragment code shown in Listing 20.3 is very similar to the ChannelListFragment code, but we create our own View and use a custom Adapter instead of a SimpleCursorAdapter.

LISTING 20.3   GridView Fragment for Changing Channels

```
1:public class GridFragment extends Fragment implements LoaderCallbacks<Cursor> {
2:   GridView grid;
3:   Activity currentActivity;
4:   ChannelGridCursorAdapter gridAdapter;
5:   @Override
6:   public void onActivityCreated(Bundle savedInstanceState) {
7:     super.onActivityCreated(savedInstanceState);
8:     currentActivity = this.getActivity();
9:     getLoaderManager().initLoader(0, null, this);
10:    gridAdapter = new ChannelGridCursorAdapter(currentActivity, null, grid);
11:    grid.setAdapter(gridAdapter);
12:    grid.setOnItemClickListener(new OnItemClickListener() {
13:     public void onItemClick(AdapterView<?> parent,View view,int position,long
id) {
14:       ChannelViewHolder channelInfo = (ChannelViewHolder) view.getTag();
```

```
15:        System.out.println(channelInfo.channelUri);
16:        Uri channelUri = Uri.parse(channelInfo.channelUri);
17:        startActivity(new Intent(Intent.ACTION_VIEW, channelUri));
18:     }
19:   });
20:  }
21:  @Override
22:  public View onCreateView(LayoutInflater inflater, ViewGroup container,
23:              Bundle savedInstanceState) {
24:     grid = (GridView) inflater.inflate(R.layout.grid_fragment, container,
false);
25:     return grid;
26:  }
27:  @Override
28:  public Loader<Cursor> onCreateLoader(int id, Bundle args) {
29:     Uri channelProviderUri = Uri.parse("content://"
30:        + "com.google.android.tv.provider" + "/" + "channel_listing");
31:     CursorLoader cursorLoader = new CursorLoader(getActivity(),
32:     channelProviderUri ,
32:     null, null, null, "callsign ASC");
34:     return cursorLoader;
35:  }
```

Listing 20.3 retrieves the data in precisely the same way as does the ChannelListFragment. The work is done in onCreateLoader in lines 28 to 35. The methods onLoadFinished and onLoaderReset are not shown.

For the GridFragment class, we create the view in the onCreateView method on line 22. We inflate a GridView from an XML layout file.

Lines 12 to 17 define the action that occurs when an item on the GridView is clicked. On line 14, the tag associated with the clicked view is retrieved and cast to a ChannelViewHolder. The ChannelViewHolder contains a String called channelUri that is used on lines 16 and 17 to change the channel. We will see how those values are populated when we review Listing 20.4.

A custom adapter called the ChannelGridCursorAdapter is used to display the data. It is used in line 10 of Listing 20.3.

The code for the ChannelGridCursorAdapter is shown in Listing 20.4.

LISTING 20.4   ChannelGridCursorAdapter Snippet

```
1: @Override
2:  public void bindView(View v, Context context, Cursor c) {
3:     ChannelViewHolder vh = (ChannelViewHolder) v.getTag();
4:     if(vh==null){
5:        vh = new ChannelViewHolder();
6:        vh.callsignView = (TextView) v.findViewById(R.id.callsign);
7:        vh.channelNumberView = (TextView) v.findViewById(R.id.channel);
8:        vh.channelNameView = (TextView) v.findViewById(R.id.name);
9:        v.setTag(vh);
10:    }
11:    int callsignCol = c.getColumnIndex("callsign");
12:    String callsign = c.getString(callsignCol);
13:    vh.callsignView.setText(callsign);
14:    int channelNumberCol = c.getColumnIndex("channel_number");
15:    String channelNumber = c.getString(channelNumberCol);
16:    vh.channelNumberView.setText(channelNumber);
17:    int channelNameCol = c.getColumnIndex("channel_name");
18:    String channelName = c.getString(channelNameCol);
19:    vh.channelNameView.setText(channelName);
20:    int channelUriCol = c.getColumnIndex("channel_uri");
21:    vh.channelUri = c.getString(channelUriCol);
22:    v.setTag(vh);
23: }
24: public static class ChannelViewHolder{
25:    public TextView callsignView;
26:    public TextView channelNumberView;
27:    public TextView channelNameView;
28:    public String channelUri;
29: }
```

Listing 20.4 shows the ChannelViewHolder class and the bindView method for the custom Adapter ChannelGridCursorAdapter. Typically we use the view holder pattern for efficiency. When using the view holder pattern, the TextViews are reused in the display and do not need to be created as new values. In this case, we also use the ChannelViewHolder to store the value for the channel URI. That allows us to retrieve it when the user clicks an item on the grid. Line 14 of Listing 20.3 reads the ChannelViewHolder from the tag. Lines 20 to 22 of Listing 20.4 retrieve the value from the Cursor, assign it in the view holder, and set the tag on the View to contain this ChannelViewHolder.

In lines 11 to 19 of Listing 20.4, we retrieve the callsign, channel_number, and channel_name and populate the associated TextViews.

The result is shown in Figure 20.3. Using the D-Pad, the user can select the channel. When the user chooses the channel displayed, the TV begins to play and switches to that station.

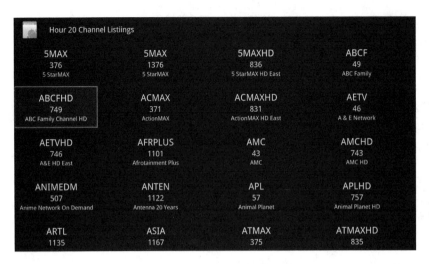

FIGURE 20.3
Channel Listings in a Grid with capability to change channels.

Understanding Audio Focus

When looking at the Logcat while switching channels, you will notice a call to start the TV intent. Soon after that, there is a call to the `AudioManager` to request focus. We referred to Logcat previously as part of the Eclipse and Android environment. Logcat is a valuable tool for debugging our own apps, but it can also be used to understand what is happening on the system.

When we called the `Intent` to change the channel, Logcat shows the following:

```
I/ActivityManager(331): Starting: Intent { act=android.intent.action.VIEW
dat=tv://channel/APL?deviceId=irb_0&channelNumber=57
cmp=com.google.tv.player/.PlayerActivity } from pid 4439
```

We can see that there is a `VIEW` Intent and the information being passed is the Animal Planet URI. It looks like the `Activity` that will handle this is the `PlayerActivity` in package `com.google.tv.player`.

About a tenth of a second later, this appears in Logcat:

```
I/AudioService(331): AudioFocus requestAudioFocus() from android.media.
AudioManager@6724d398com.google.tv.player.PlayerActivity$7@66dace20
```

The TV app has made a call to `requestAudioFocus`.

The AudioFocus API was introduced in Android 2.2, so it is available for use in all Google TV apps. Android is a multitasking environment. It is possible that several applications may produce audio and end up competing for the audio output.

The AudioFocus API was created to address that issue. The AudioFocus API has two key concepts:

▶ Request AudioFocus when needed.

▶ List changes to AudioFocus and adjust accordingly.

An Activity that requests AudioFocus must implement `AudioManager.OnAudioFocusChangeListener`. For an Activity it would look like this:

```
public class AudioFocus extends Activity implements AudioManager.
OnAudioFocusChangeListener{
```

AudioFocus is requested within the Activity, which is shown in Listing 20.5.

LISTING 20.5   Requesting AudioFocus

```
1: AudioManager audioManager = (AudioManager) getSystemService(Context.AUDIO_
SERVICE);
2: int result = audioManager.requestAudioFocus(this, AudioManager.STREAM_MUSIC,
3:     AudioManager.AUDIOFOCUS_GAIN);
4: if (result != AudioManager.AUDIOFOCUS_REQUEST_GRANTED) {
5: }
```

To implement the `AudioManager.OnAudioFocusChangeListener`, the method `onAudioChange` must be implemented. The `onAudioChange` method takes a parameter called `focusChange`. The value of `focusChange` indicates what you should do in your app.

AudioFocus is made to work in a cooperative environment between apps. In general, if you have focus you can play media and control the audio. If you lose audio focus to another app, you should stop playing media and perhaps release media resources. There are two other cases where you have temporarily lost audio focus. Those are covered next in the list of possible values for `focusChange`.

The parameter `focusChange` is passed to the `onAudioFocusChange` method. These are all possible values and that specify how your app should respond:

▶ `AUDIOFOCUS_GAIN`—You have gained the audio focus.

▶ `AUDIOFOCUS_LOSS`—You have lost the audio focus. Stop all audio playback. This is a good time to clean up media resources.

▶ AUDIOFOCUS_LOSS_TRANSIENT—You have temporarily lost audio focus. Stop audio play-back, but do not clean up resources.

▶ AUDIOFOCUS_LOSS_TRANSIENT_CAN_DUCK—You have temporarily lost audio focus. In this case, the focusChange indicates that it is acceptable to lower the volume. The audio playback is not required to stop.

Listing 20.6 shows a shell for using the onAudioFocusChange method. Listing 20.6 show the options for the possible values returned by focusChange.

LISTING 20.6   **Handling a Change in AudioFocus**

```
1: public void onAudioFocusChange(int focusChange) {
2:     switch (focusChange) {
3:         case AudioManager.AUDIOFOCUS_GAIN:
4:             // gained focus
5:             break;
6:         case AudioManager.AUDIOFOCUS_LOSS:
7:             // Lost focus
8:             break;
9:         case AudioManager.AUDIOFOCUS_LOSS_TRANSIENT:
10:             // Lost focus temporarily.  Stop playback
11:             break;
12:         case AudioManager.AUDIOFOCUS_LOSS_TRANSIENT_CAN_DUCK:
13:             // Lost focus temporarily. Lower volume.
14:             break;
15:     }
16:}
```

Summary

In this hour, the focus was on the Channel Listing provider. We identified the data available in the Channel Listing provider and learned that it is possible to change channels on the TV using that information. The Channel Listing provider is a ContentProvider that can be queried and used directly in Fragments that implement CursorLoaders. After observing how the TV app handles receiving audio focus, we examined the audio focus implementation.

Q&A

Q. When using an existing ContentProvider like the Channel Listing provider, how can you learn what data is available and how to access the data?

A. When using an existing ContentProvider, the only way to understand what data is available and how to use it is by reading the documentation provided. You should expect a list of columns in the database and information on how to create a URI to access that data.

Q. What needs to be done to change a TV channel programmatically?

A. A channel_uri is required. A channel_uri is part of the Channel Listing provider data. It contains channel number and call letter information in a URI format that specifically identifies a channel. After a channel_uri is available, the channel can be changed by using an ACTION_VIEW intent with the channel_uri included as the data for the intent.

Q. What exactly is AudioFocus?

A. AudioFocus describes the point in which a running app gains or loses AudioFocus. That means that the app has control of the audio for the TV. To implement AudioFocus, apps must implement the onAudioFocusChange method. Apps work cooperatively to handle AudioFocus. When an app loses AudioFocus, it should decrease the audio level.

Workshop

Quiz

1. What data is included in the Channel Listing provider?

2. How do you create a URI for the Channel Listing provider?

3. When an app is notified of a change in AudioFocus, there are four possible states to be handled. What are those states?

Answers

1. Channel Listing data includes id, channel uri, callsign, channel name, and channel number.

2. The URI is formed from the authority and the path information. The authority is `com.google.android.tv.provider` and the path is `channel_listing`.

3. The four possible states an app will be notified of when there is a change in AudioFocus are AUDIOFOCUS_GAIN, AUDIOFOCUS_LOSS, AUDIOFOCUS_LOSS_TRANSIENT, and AUDIOFOCUS_LOSS_TRANSIENT_CAN_DUCK.

Exercises

1. Listing 20.1 uses the CNN callsign to form a query to get additional information from the Channel Listing provider about CNN. First, modify this code to use a different callsign to get the data. Second, modify the query to use a channel number to get the same data.

2. Listing 20.2 shows channel data in a list. Listing 20.3 and 20.4 show channel data in a grid and change channels when the user selects a channel from the grid. Modify and expand on Listing 20.2 to allow channels to be selected and changed from the list. This requires detecting when an item on the list has been clicked and getting the channel uri for the selected item. One direct way to do this is to display the `channel_uri` in the list so that it is available for use. The alternative may require building a custom CursorAdapter.

Using Second Screen Apps with Google TV

What You'll Learn in This Hour:

▶ How second screen apps are in use today

▶ What types of second screen apps are available

▶ How users interact with second screen apps

▶ How to discover and pair a second screen with a TV

A *second screen app* is any app that a user uses on a second device, such as a smart phone or tablet, while also using a TV. Second screen apps provide a unique development opportunity for Google TV. Second screen apps are not a new phenomenon, but they are gaining in popularity and sophistication. There are many exciting possibilities for creating apps that tie a Google TV to a second screen.

How Second Screen Apps Are Used

For many apps, using a TV means the same as watching a TV, but second screen apps can be created that interact with apps that run on the TV. In that case, the user is not watching TV. The user is actively interacting with the TV.

Second screen apps can run on computers, tablets, or smartphones. Second screen apps are not new, but as people buy smart TVs and have smartphones and tablets, they are becoming more and more popular. New types of second screen apps are likely to be invented.

In 2009, Turner Sports introduced two-second screen apps for NBA basketball and NASCAR racing. On NBA.com and Racebuddy on NASCAR.com, Overtime provided web and mobile web users with additional high-definition camera views of live action, timely scores, and interviews. At the time, Racebuddy averaged 492,000 unique visitors per race and streamed over two million videos.

GetGlue is a popular mobile app on both Android and iPhone. With GetGlue, users check in to their favorite TV shows to interact with each other and to earn badges.

Popular TV shows like *Breaking Bad* and others have viewers sync their viewing with their second screen to provide additional features.

A remote control app on a phone is also a second screen app; one example is using an Android phone to change channels on a Google TV.

Second screen apps may not have anything to do with traditional TV viewing. In Hour 22, "Examining an Example Second Screen App," we will run and install a Blackjack sample app. In that app, the screen shows the cards played, and the remote device shows the options for the player.

Types of Second Screen Apps

When designing a second screen app, it is helpful to consider the goal of the app and what type of app it is. There are several types of second screen apps:

- ▶ **Enhanced Viewing app**—An enhanced viewing app supplements a broadcast TV show. These apps sync with a specific show and provide additional content. The *Breaking Bad* app and GetGlue are enhanced viewing apps.

- ▶ **Remote Control app**—Remote control apps control the TV. They can provide the functionality of a traditional remote with changing channels and setting volume. They can also provide enhanced capabilities, such as finding TV shows or launching Google TV apps.

- ▶ **Content Selection app**—In a content selection app, the user finds content using the remote device, such as the phone or tablet, and then displays the content on the TV. It is easier to use gestures and commands on a phone than to navigate on a TV. Using a content selection app makes finding content easier, leaving the TV only for display. The YouTube Remote app is a good example of a content selection app.

- ▶ **Interactive app**—In an interactive app there is a phone app and a Google TV app working together. The Blackjack app, where the cards are displayed on the TV and the players' decisions are made on the phone, is a good example of an interactive app.

User Interaction with Second Screen Apps

User perspective refers to how the user experiences these apps. We should consider where the user is looking and what the relationship is to what is being viewed. Is the user looking exclusively at the TV, at the phone, or a little bit of both? If the user is using the phone as a steering wheel on a car, then both the phone and the TV are experienced as moving in a forward direction. If the user is interacting with the phone to select cards, and the TV shows the results, the experience is like that of a Blackjack table where the user makes decisions and the dealer is facing the user.

Considering the User Perspective

For an enhanced TV app or content selection app, the view on the TV and on the second screen are related, but the user perspective is clear. For an enhanced viewing app, the user is viewing additional information on the second screen and perhaps interacting with other users based on the contents of the TV show. For a content selection app, the selection occurs on the remote app, and the display occurs on the TV. In both of those cases, the perspective of the user is clear.

The perspective of the user is less clear in an interactive app. In the case of the simple Blackjack app, users make decisions about their cards, and the cards are displayed on the TV. In that case, the app is acting like a remote for what happens on the screen, and perspective is not important.

It is easy to envision a second screen app where a phone acts as a game controller. In that case, the user is interacting with the phone to make things happen on TV. It is likely the user is looking at the TV the entire time after the user understands the controls.

With a phone or a tablet, the level of visual interaction can be much greater than that of a game controller. We can see what is happening on the phone. What might a first-person-shooter game look like on Google TV when the user is using a phone to control the action? There are at least two choices for this example. One is to use the phone as a simple game controller and have the gun and all action shown on the TV. The other is to have the action occur on the TV screen and have the phone or tablet show the gun and other game specifics. In the first case, the gun is shown on the TV screen; in the second case, the gun is shown on the phone.

Let's consider the simple archery target practice game shown in Figure 21.1. The goal is to shoot the center of the target. The phone controls the flight of the arrow. The plus sign (+) represents where the arrow is pointing. The person designing this game has the option to put a visual representation of the arrow on the phone or on the TV.

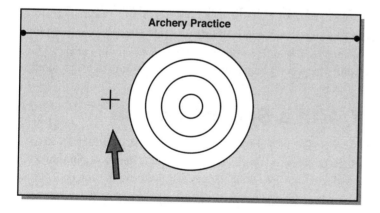

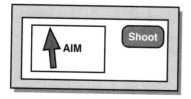

FIGURE 21.1
User perspective for a second-screen app. Where should the arrow be displayed?

Incorporating a Phone's Accelerometer

For Android and other smartphones, the Accelerometer can be incorporated into the design. The Accelerometer is a sensor on a phone that detects location and motions. If you shake your phone to make something happen in an app, the accelerometer is being used. The accelerometer knows if the phone is level, turned, or moving quickly. The accelerometer provides the opportunity to use gestures and motion to interact with the TV.

There is also an opportunity to create second screen apps for groups of people who are all watching one TV. That can lead to some interesting scenarios. Each user will have a remote device, so private information can be presented to each user. Common information can be presented on the TV. For first-person shooters, an individual experience could be presented on a tablet, and a common experience could be presented on the TV. Two people could race cars against each other, with the race being shown on the screen and the driver's perspective being shown on the tablet.

Second Screen Apps as a Social Experience

There is also the possibility of a social gaming experience where only one person uses the remote, but everyone plays the game. For example, consider a drawing game in which the remote device says what to draw to the person holding the tablet. That user draws the item on the tablet and it appears on the TV. The other guests in the room guess what it is. Other games can be considered in this type of scenario. You could play a strategic game like *Risk*, with the board shown on the screen and the player's decisions and turns made on remote devices.

Beyond games, second screen apps could turn a Google TV into a family message center or bulletin board. There may even be someone who makes interactive second screen apps relevant for specific business uses. The possibilities for second screen apps are just beginning to be explored.

Connecting a TV with a Second Screen

All second screen apps will have a remote device and a TV. The remote device and the TV need to discover and pair with each other. *Discovery* is the process of the remote device finding the TV. *Pairing* is the process of the remote device and TV establishing a communication protocol.

The YouTube Remote app requires users to sign in on their devices and on their YouTube accounts on a computer or connected TV. The discovery and pairing process is handled manually by the user by signing into the two devices. Communication is not directly between the TV and the remote device; the apps communicate over the Internet based on the common login.

Enhanced viewing apps also require some level of discovery and pairing. For an app like GetGlue, this is in the users' control as they check in to a TV show. For other apps, like the *Breaking Bad* second screen, the user pairs the app with the TV manually at a specific point in the beginning of the show. In that case, timing is important. Quick Response codes, known as QR codes, can be displayed on a TV and scanned by an app to help with pairing a device and a TV. Other apps recognize audio or other cues to sync TV shows and apps.

Interactive apps and content apps that are developed with both a remote app and an app running directly on Google TV have a specific discovery and pairing protocol called Anymote, but there are other methods. We'll consider second screen apps where we write the code for both the TV app and the Android device that controls that app.

Discovery

When a Google TV starts, it sends messages over the local network to say that is available to communicate with second screen apps. Specifically, the Anymote service sends an mDNS broadcast containing information such as the following:

```
"My IP address is xxx.xxx.x.x, I offer service _anymote._tcp on port xxxx"
```

DNS stands for domain name server. It is a communication protocol for connecting a website address like http://www.google.com to a specific IP address. Google TV uses mDNS which stands for multicast DNS. It allows us to use the DNS protocol on a small local network and to discover the IP addresses of the devices on the network. So instead of tying IP addresses to URLs, we are tying IP addresses to devices over the network.

The responsibility of the remote is to detect the mDNS messages sent by the TV and to acquire the necessary information to begin communication with the TV. The remote app checks for mDNS messages looking for a string like `_anymote._tcp`. When an mDNS message is found, it is parsed to extract the relevant TV information. The information is the device name, IP address, and port number.

At that point the remote has discovered the TV. The remote must pair with the TV.

Figure 21.2 shows the phone screen for an app that has discovered a TV.

FIGURE 21.2
A remote device discovering a TV.

Pairing

Pairing is the process of the remote identifying itself and authenticating with the TV. The Pairing service runs on the TV. The remote and TV communicate via the Google TV Pairing Protocol.

In the discovery phase, we said that a port number was included in the mDNS message. The Anymote service sends that message including the port number. The Pairing service runs on the next consecutive port. So if the mDNS message broadcast by the Anymote service indicates port number 9551, the Pairing service is running on port 9552. The remote should connect to port 9552 to set up the pairing session.

The Pairing service displays information for the user to provide to authenticate. The Pairing service on the TV will display a pin to enter or a QR code to scan to authenticate the user, as shown in Figure 21.3. This process of authentication is known as a *challenge*. The response is supplied by the user in the remote app.

If the pin is entered correctly or the QR code is scanned, the pairing has succeeded and the remote application will be issued a secure certificate. That certificate can be used in subsequent connections to show that the app is already authenticated, as shown in Figure 21.4.

FIGURE 21.3
TV displaying user authentication info for pairing.

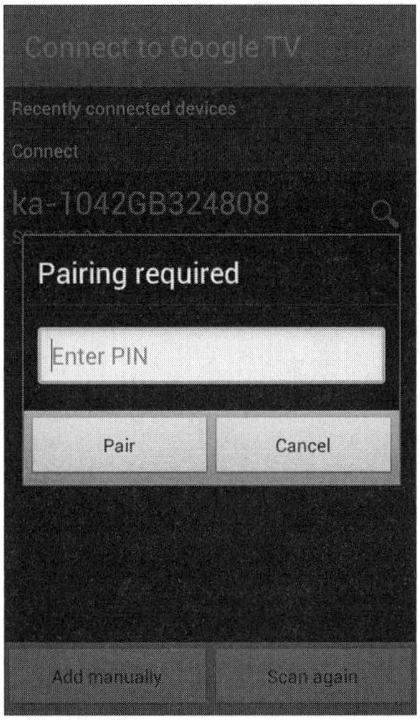

FIGURE 21.4
Enter PIN or authentication.

Commands from Remote to TV

After the Anymote and Pairing services run and the user has authenticated the remote, we are ready for the remote app to send commands to the TV.

The Anymote protocol uses requests and responses for communication between the remote and the TV. The remote sends one of the following requests, and the Anymote service running on the TV sends a response:

- ▶ Key events
- ▶ Mouse events
- ▶ Connection events
- ▶ Intents

Key events include keys like Volume Up and Volume Down. Mouse events include an event that is initiated by a mouse. A connection event includes things like the remote's initial connection to the TV.

Intent is an Android concept for launching apps or events within apps; for example, launching an app, showing a web page, or showing a YouTube video. By having the remote launch Intents on the TV, the Anymote protocol provides a powerful capability to completely control Google TV apps from a second screen device.

Summary

In this hour, we examined the types of second screen apps and how user perspective is a consideration when designing these apps. For most second screen apps, the developer and designer are creating designs for two screens. The steps involved in running a second screen app include creating a trusted connection between the TV and the remote device. Those processes are called Discovery and Pairing. Google TV uses the Anymote and Pairing protocols to communicate between a TV and a remote device and to pair the TV with the device.

Q&A

Q. What is the difference between Discovery and Pairing?

A. Discovery is the process of an app on a remote device discovering whether a TV is available to connect to. Pairing is the process of creating a trusted connection between the remote device and the TV.

Q. The Anymote protocol includes the capability for an app running on a phone to send an Intent to the TV. What does that mean and what can it be used for?

A. An Intent can start an Activity. That means that the Anymote protocol provides a way for a second screen app to start Activities on the TV. Because an Intent can be to start a browser or play a YouTube video, those actions can be selected on the phone and shown on the TV.

Q. When referring to the Pairing protocol, what is a challenge?

A. A challenge is a question or action to be taken to allow the device to pair with the TV. The TV issues the challenge. Sample challenges are to enter a specific 4-digit code or to scan a QR code. The user must answer the challenge on the remote device to establish a trusted connection.

Workshop

Quiz

1. What does "Pairing" mean?

2. What are some commands that can be sent from a remote to a TV using the Anymote protocol?

3. Is the following statement true or false? For security reasons, a remote app on a phone can never launch an app on Google TV. The remote provided with the TV must be used.

Answers

1. Pairing is the process of a Google TV and remote device recognizing each other so that communication via the Anymote protocol can begin.

2. Key and Mouse commands can be sent from a remote to the TV. Intents such as launching an app, showing a YouTube Video, or opening a web page in a browser are supported.

3. This is false. Authentication happens during pairing. That provides security.

Exercises

1. If you have a Google TV and an Android device, download and try the YouTube second screen app. Try the Google Remote app and the Able Remote app. Search Google Play for other second screen apps. Note the types of apps and how they implement Discovery and Pairing.

2. Check whether any of your favorite shows implement second screen apps. Many shows provide second screen apps that do not require Discovery or Pairing as described. The connection to the TV show is the time at which the show is broadcast.

HOUR 22
Examining an Example Second Screen App

What You'll Learn in This Hour:

▶ How to set up a second screen app
▶ How to run the example app
▶ How the code in the example app works
▶ What is included in the Anymote Library code

Hour 21, "Using Second Screen Apps with Google TV," covered how a device discovers a Google TV and pairs with it. Discovery pairing and communication from remote to TV are done using the Anymote Library. This hour starts with instructions to install and run the sample Blackjack second screen example app created by Google. The sample app demonstrates the structure of a second screen app. By examining the app we'll see how the Anymote Library works and learn how to develop second screen apps. We will cover the relationship between Anymote Protocol, Pairing Protocol, and the Anymote Library.

Preparing the Blackjack Second Screen App

Second screen apps usually have two separate apps, one for the TV and one for the phone. The Blackjack second screen app is an example app provided by Google. It allows the user to play a very primitive game of Blackjack. One fun part is that the cards are displayed on the TV screen while the choice about how to play the cards is done remotely using a phone, as shown in Figure 22.1.

All cards are shown on the TV screen. The player's hand in this image is the ace and the deuce. The dealer's hand shows one card facing down and a four of spades. On the phone app are buttons for hit, stand, and start over. The cards on the phone app just represent the logo for the game.

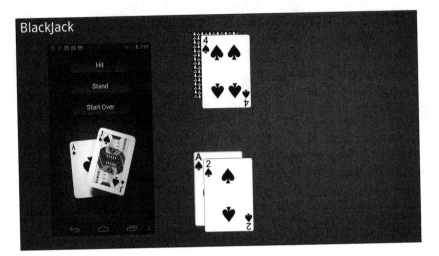

FIGURE 22.1
Phone Black-jack app shown over TV app.

Downloading and Installing the Blackjack App Files

A complete set of Android examples for Google TV can be found here: http://code.google.com/p/googletv-android-samples/.

Go to that page and choose Source; you will be provided with instructions on how to download the contents. The source is in a Git repository. If you use Git, to create a local copy you would use:

```
git clone https://code.google.com/p/googletv-android-samples/
```

If you browse the code, you will see a list of files like those in Figure 22.2.

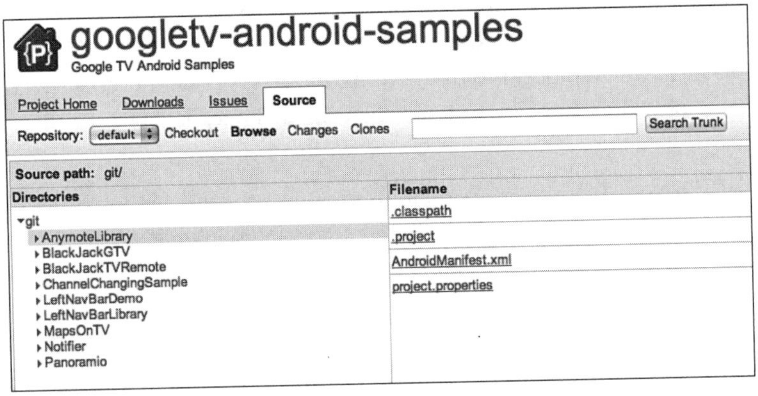

FIGURE 22.2
Android Samples for Google TV.

The code for the Blackjack second screen app uses the first three files from Figure 22.2. We need the AnymoteLibrary, BlackJackGTV, and BlackJackTVRemote files. These should be installed as three separate projects in Eclipse.

Setting Up the Eclipse Projects

The Blackjack app and other apps that we will create are based on using the Anymote library. That means that there are three Android projects required in Eclipse to run a second screen app:

▶ Anymote Library (AnymoteLibrary)

▶ Google TV App (BlackJackGTV)

▶ Remote App (BlackJackTVRemote)

These projects can be added to Eclipse by importing the projects or by adding a new Android project and using the **Create It from Existing Source Code** option. Figure 22.3 shows the Eclipse window for adding a project from an existing source. Your version of Eclipse may be different, but you should see a similar window for adding a project. You can name these projects appropriately when you add them.

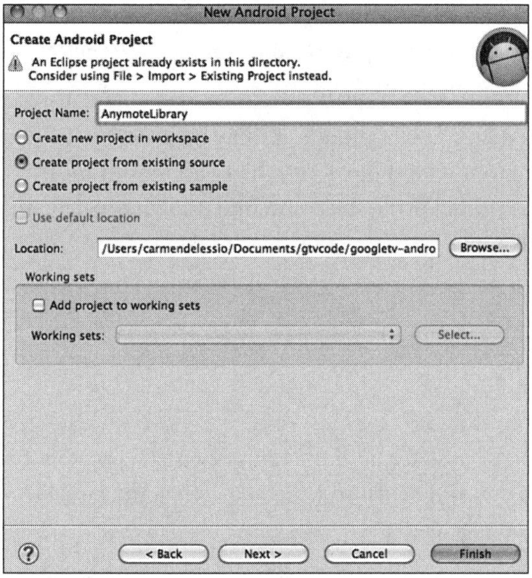

FIGURE 22.3
Adding projects to Eclipse.

There is a chance that the projects will not compile. You should make sure these projects do compile. It is good to start by using the Eclipse *clean* command. The clean command removes all existing compiled files and sets up a clean rebuild of the entire project. To use the command, highlight the project and choose **Project**, **Clean** from the menu.

The TV and remote projects both require the Anymote Library. If the Anymote Library compiles, make sure the other projects refer to it properly. When you choose **Properties**, **Android** for a project, you will see the Android version and all library references. The library should point to the Anymote project that you created. If it is pointing to the wrong place, delete the wrong library and choose **Add** to add a new one.

The correct version of Android for the project must be available in your development environment. That can be checked the same way. It may make sense to change the Android version on these projects. Google TV runs on version 3.1 (HoneyComb). After installing the code, the development version for the project was set to 4.1 (Ice Cream Sandwich). This was changed in the Android properties screen in Eclipse. Check the version of Android running on your phone and build for it. The Blackjack remote app will compile and run with version 2.2 and later.

Running the Blackjack App

After the three Android projects are set up and compiled in Eclipse, you are ready to run the Blackjack app. That means running two programs. The TV app is installed and run on the TV, and the remote app is installed and run on a phone (or an Android Tablet).

In Hour 7, "Android and Google TV," you learned how to run an app directly on a device. It requires configuring the TV by setting debugging to true and providing the IP address of the computer running the debugger. The debugger is started using the command line and specifying the IP address of the TV. That command looks like this:

```
adb connect 192.168.1.101
```

The response looks like this:

```
connected to 192.168.1.101:5555
```

In Eclipse, you can set run configurations. It makes sense for both the remote and TV app to set the run configuration to "manual." That means you will be asked which device should be used to run the app. That way, the phone or TV can be specified.

When both apps are started, the remote app discovers the TV and displays them, as shown in Figure 22.4.

FIGURE 22.4
Blackjack remote discovers TVs.

After devices are discovered, pairing occurs. Figure 22.5 shows both the TV and phone screen for pairing. After pairing occurs, the app begins.

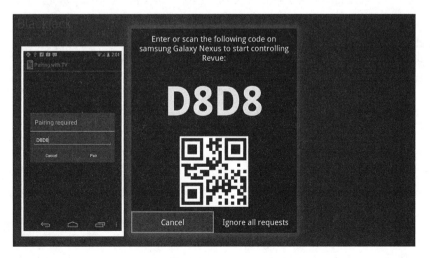

FIGURE 22.5
Blackjack pairing with TV and Remote app shown.

Exploring the Blackjack App Code

The Blackjack remote consists of one Activity called `BlackJackRemoteActivity`. It implements the Anymote `ClientListener`. It is declared as follows:

```
public class BlackJackRemoteActivity extends Activity implements ClientListener
```

`ClientListener` is an interface that is defined in the Anymote library. It requires three methods to be implemented:

```
public void onConnected(AnymoteSender anymoteSender);
public void onDisconnected();
public void onConnectionFailed();
```

In `BlackJackRemoteActivity`, the `onConnected` method uses the `anymoteSender` parameter that is passed and sets it as a class variable:

```
@Override
    public void onConnected(final AnymoteSender anymoteSender) {
        this.anymoteSender = anymoteSender;
```

Then it defines an Intent called `blackJackTVLaunchIntent` and starts the app on the TV using the `sendIntent` method:

```
anymoteSender.sendIntent(blackJackTVLaunchIntent);
```

After the TV app has started, choices made on the remote app are sent to the TV app as events. In `BlackJackRemoteActivity`, that is done in several steps. A button is clicked and the private method `sendKeyEvent` is called. The `sendKeyEvent` method uses the Anymote protocol to send a keystroke to the TV app.

Listings 22.1 and 22.2 are part of BlackJackRemoteActivity. `BlackJackRemoteActivity` runs in the remote. Together these two methods send `KeyEvent.KEYCODE_H` to the TV app. Listing 22.1 shows the `onClick` method to send the letter H.

LISTING 22.1 The Blackjack "Hit" Button Code

```
1: hit.setOnClickListener(new OnClickListener() {
2:    @Override
3:    public void onClick(View v) {
4:    // Sends Keycode H for 'Hit'.
5:        sendKeyEvent(KeyEvent.KEYCODE_H);
6:    }
7: });
```

Listing 22.2 shows the `sendKeyEvent` method that was used in line 5 of Listing 22.1. If the `anymoteSender` is `null`, an error message is displayed. If it is not `null`, the `anymoteSender` sends the `keyEvent`.

LISTING 22.2   Sending a Key to TV App

```
1:  private void sendKeyEvent(final int keyEvent) {
2:     if (anymoteSender == null) {
3:        Toast.makeText(BlackJackRemoteActivity.this, "Waiting for connection",
4:                           Toast.LENGTH_LONG).show();
5:        return;
6:     }
7:     anymoteSender.sendKeyPress(keyEvent);
8:  }
```

The TV app responds to the key by acting on it. Specifically, the `BlackJackTableActivity` receives the key and takes an action based on the value. To do that, the `BlackJackTableActivity` implements the `onKeyDown` method. Listing 22.3 shows how the `onKeyDown` method handles receiving the "H" key. We don't care about how the app plays Blackjack, but we are interested to see how keys sent from the remote to the TV are handled.

LISTING 22.3   Handling a Key Sent from the Remote App

```
1:  @Override
2:     public boolean onKeyDown(int keyCode, KeyEvent event) {
3:        if (keyCode == KeyEvent.KEYCODE_H) {
4:           mBoundService.hitPlayer();
5:        }
```

The Android manifest file for the remote app requires two elements so that the app can work with the Anymote. One is a reference to the Anymote service. The second is the definition of an Activity within the Anymote library. Both are shown in Listing 22.4. Lines 1 to 3 define the service. Lines 4 to 9 define the Activity.

LISTING 22.4   Android Manifest for Remote App

```
1:  <service android:name=
2:     "com.example.google.tv.anymotelibrary.client.AnymoteClientService">
3:  </service>
4:  <activity
5:     android:name=
6:     "com.example.google.tv.anymotelibrary.connection.PairingActivity"
7:     android:configChanges="orientation"
8:     android:label="Pairing with TV"
9:     android:screenOrientation="portrait" />
```

For most second screen apps, it will make sense to use the Anymote library as is. The library includes the `PairingActivity` referred to in line 6 of Listing 22.4. The `PairingActivity` is an actual Activity that includes the display to pair the TV with the device. It is possible to customize the functionality of the `PairingActivity` if that is required. The code is available and can be extended for different needs.

Exploring the Anymote Library Code

The Blackjack app relies on the Anymote library project. The Anymote library uses other libraries by including Jar files, such as `anymote.jar` and `polo.jar`.

By examining the code for AnymoteSender, we can understand the relationships in the code. AnymoteSender.java is in package `com.example.google.tv.anymotelibrary.client`. The import statements used in AnymoteSender.java include the following:

```
import com.google.anymote.common.AnymoteFactory;
import com.google.anymote.common.ConnectInfo;
import com.google.anymote.common.ErrorListener;
import com.google.anymote.device.DeviceAdapter;
import com.google.anymote.device.MessageReceiver;
```

These import statements refer to packages that are included in the `anymote.jar` file. The `anymote.jar` file is the library for the actual Anymote protocol. The Anymote protocol is the messaging protocol that applications on remote device use to communicate with Google TV. The Anymote Library that we imported wraps this protocol and makes it easier to use. The source code for the Anymote protocol can be found at http://code.google.com/p/anymote-protocol/.

The Anymote Library project also includes `polo.jar`. That is the library for the Pairing protocol that handles the pairing of the second screen app. The Google TV Pairing protocol pairs a client and server over a local network. The client contacts the server, and the server issues a challenge for the client to complete. We saw this in Figure 22.5. The server is the TV and issues the challenge to enter code D8D8. The client is the remote where that code is entered. The source code for the Pairing protocol can be found at: http://code.google.com/p/google-tv-pairing-protocol/.

▶ Pairing protocol connects the TV and remote over a local network.

▶ Anymote protocol sends messages from the remote to the TV.

▶ Anymote Library uses both of these to provide an easy-to-use development library for second screen apps.

To get a sense of the code for making connections between the TV and the device, we'll examine a snippet of code from the Pairing protocol. Listing 22.5 shows the `doInitializationPhase()`

method from the class ClientPairingSession. ClientPairingSession extends the class PairingSession.

The doInitializePhase() method shows a sequence of methods being sent and received. Thee messages are familiar to us from understanding the sequence of events when pairing occurs.

LISTING 22.5   **Android Manifest for Remote App**

```
1:   @Override
2:     protected void doInitializationPhase()
3:         throws PoloException, IOException {
4:       logDebug("Sending PairingRequest... " + mServiceName);
5:       PairingRequestMessage msg = new PairingRequestMessage(mServiceName);
6:       sendMessage(msg);
7:       logDebug("Waiting for PairingRequestAck ...");
8:       PairingRequestAckMessage ack = (PairingRequestAckMessage) getNextMessage(
9:           PoloMessageType.PAIRING_REQUEST_ACK);
10:      if (ack.hasServerName()) {
11:        mPeerName = ack.getServerName();
12:        logDebug("Got PairingRequestAck with server name = " + mPeerName);
13:     } else {
14:       mPeerName = null;
15:     }
16:     logDebug("Sending Options ...");
17:     sendMessage(mLocalOptions);
18:     logDebug("Waiting for Options...");
19:     OptionsMessage serverOptions = (OptionsMessage) getNextMessage(
20:         PoloMessageType.OPTIONS);
21:    // Compare compatibility with server options, and save config.
22:     System.out.println("Local config = " + mLocalOptions);
23:     System.out.println("Server options = " + serverOptions);
24:     setConfiguration(mLocalOptions.getBestConfiguration(serverOptions));
25:     }
```

Summary

In this hour, we installed the Blackjack sample second screen app and examined how it uses the Anymote Library. The app accepts input entered on the phone and changes the results of the game on the TV. For you to use the Anymote Library, this hour covered the steps to include a library project using Eclipse. The Anymote and Pairing protocols were explained. As second screen app developers, we will generally use the Anymote Library within our apps to connect and communicate from a remote to a TV.

Q&A

Q. Which device issues a challenge?

A. As part of the Pairing protocol, a Google TV issues a challenge.

Q. On what device will code for a ClientListener run?

A. A ClientListener will run on a remote device. The `BlackJackRemoteActivity` implements a ClientListener.

Q. What protocol is being used when a challenge is issued?

A. The Pairing protocol.

Workshop

Quiz

1. What does `KeyEvent.KEYCODE_H` mean?

2. What two things must be in the Android manifest file for a remote app?

3. What method is implemented in the Google TV activity to handle key events sent from the remote?

4. How does a remote app start an app on Google TV?

Answers

1. It means the letter "H" on the keyboard. In the Blackjack app, an "H" is sent from the remote app to the TV app to indicate that the player wants to "HIT" or take a card.

2. The Android manifest file will refer to the Anymote service and include an Activity for Pairing from the Anymote Library.

3. The `onKeyDown` method handles key events sent from the remote.

4. The remote app uses the Anymote protocol and sends an Intent to the TV. The Intent contains info on which app to start.

Exercises

1. Download and run the Blackjack app. You will need to use Eclipse and properly set up the Anymote library files.

2. Modify the Blackjack app to accept the keycode "X" to indicate the user has surrendered his or her hand. The game logic for handling this is not important. You will add a button for Surrender to the phone app. When that button is pressed, send "X" to the TV app. The TV app should recognize this and show a Toast message saying, "You surrendered!"

Developing Second Screen Apps

What You'll Learn in This Hour:

▶ How to fling a URL

▶ How to send KeyEvents to the TV

▶ How to send mouse events to the TV

In Hour 22, "Examining an Example Second Screen App," you installed the example Blackjack second screen app. In doing so, you downloaded and installed the Anymote Library and set up three Eclipse projects. Those projects were the Anymote Library, the remote control app, and the TV app.

In this hour, we will develop several second screen apps. The first app takes a URL entered on the remote device and opens the corresponding web page in the Chrome browser on Google TV. That represents a simple content app that pairs with the TV, but runs only on the remote. It provides an example of a basic remote app and uses the ability to fling an Android Intent to the TV. Apps for keyboard input and mouse events will also be developed. We'll use the phone's Accelerometer as the input device for sending mouse events to the TV. These example apps provide a foundation for creating more sophisticated second screen apps.

Flinging a URL

By installing and running the Blackjack second screen app in Hour 22, you added the Anymote Library to your Eclipse projects. We'll use the Anymote Library and develop a remote app that takes a URL as input on an Android phone and opens the website on the Chrome browser on a Google TV. Because we can use an Android Intent to show the website on the TV, there is no need to create a separate TV app.

An App for Displaying Websites on a Google TV

We'll start with an Android app that includes an `EditText` field for input and a button to initiate an action. We'll make it a Google TV remote app by doing the following:

▶ Adding the Anymote Library

▶ Implementing the Activity as an `AnymoteClientService ClientListener`

▶ Binding to the Anymote Service

▶ Modifying the Android manifest to support the Anymote Library

All these things were done in the code for the Blackjack remote app, and we will use that as our model.

The input field for this app will accept a URL. The button in the activity reads the URL and attempts to send it to the TV. Figure 23.1 shows the remote user interface.

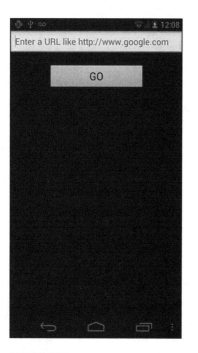

FIGURE 23.1
Send a URL to the Chrome Browser remotely.

The Anymote Library is added to the working Eclipse project, as it was in Hour 22.

For this app, we need only the remote app, and it will consist of a single Activity. Each remote app in this hour has a similar code structure:

▶ An Activity that implements the AnymoteClientService ClientListener

▶ A declaration of a ServiceConnection to bind to the Anymote Service

▶ The Activity's onCreate method that includes the binding to the Anymote Service

▶ The implementation of the three methods required for ClientListener

Our Activity is called ExampleOneActivity. Similar to the BlackJackRemoteActivity, it is declared as follows:

```
public class ExampleOneActivity extends Activity implements ClientListener
```

Listing 23.1 shows the declaration of the Anymote sender and the service connection. A ServiceConnection is an Interface for monitoring the state of an application service. In our case, the service is the AnymoteClientService.

LISTING 23.1   ServiceConnection Declaration

```
1: private AnymoteSender anymoteSender;
2: private ServiceConnection mConnection = new ServiceConnection() {
3:    public void onServiceConnected(ComponentName name, IBinder service) {
4:       mAnymoteClientService=((AnymoteClientService.AnymoteClientServiceBinder)
5:       service).getService();
6:       mAnymoteClientService.attachClientListener(ExampleOneActivity.this);
7:    }
8:    public void onServiceDisconnected(ComponentName name) {
9:       mAnymoteClientService.detachClientListener(ExampleOneActivity.this);
10:       mAnymoteClientService = null;
11:    }
12:};
```

In the onCreate method, we bind the AnymoteClientService to the Activity. The code to do that is shown next. An Intent is created using the activity and the AnymoteClientService class. A call to bindService binds the intent to the ServiceConnecton mService that we declared earlier. The flag BIND_AUTO_CREATE indicates that the service should be created.

```
Intent intent = new Intent(ExampleOneActivity.this,
                  AnymoteClientService.class);
bindService(intent, mConnection, Context.BIND_AUTO_CREATE);
```

Listing 23.2 shows the complete onCreate method for the Activity.

LISTING 23.2   **Remote Activity onCreate Method**

```
1:  @Override
2:  public void onCreate(Bundle savedInstanceState) {
3:    super.onCreate(savedInstanceState);
4:    mContext = this;
5:    setContentView(R.layout.main);
6:    progressBar = (ProgressBar) findViewById(R.id.a_progressbar);
7:    progressBar.setVisibility(View.VISIBLE);
8:    Button go = (Button) findViewById(R.id.go);
9:    final EditText destination = (EditText) findViewById(R.id.destination);
10:   go.setOnClickListener(new OnClickListener() {
11:     @Override
12:     public void onClick(View v) {
13:       String url = destination.getText().toString();
14:       final Intent intent = new Intent(Intent.ACTION_VIEW, Uri.parse(url));
15:       anymoteSender.sendUrl (intent.toUri(Intent.URI_INTENT_SCHEME));
16:     }
17:   });
18:   handler = new Handler();
19:   Intent intent = new Intent(ExampleOneActivity.this, AnymoteClientService.
class);
20:   bindService(intent, mConnection, Context.BIND_AUTO_CREATE);
21: }
```

Lines 19 and 20 in Listing 23.2 show the binding of the AnymoteClientService to the Activity.

Lines 5 to 9 define the UI components. A ProgressBar is shown while pairing occurs. An EditText and Button are defined. A URL can be entered into the EditText. The Go Button initiates the action of displaying the URL on the TV. Figure 23.1 showed what these look like on the remote.

Lines 10 to 17 define the action that occurs when the Button is pressed. The value in the EditText field is read in line 13. In line 14, that value is used to create an Intent. Line 15 sends the Intent to the Google TV using the anymoteSender. The TV will launch the Chrome browser and display the page associated with the URL.

The work of the app is done in the onCreate method, but the setup of the AnymoteService and library is required to make it happen. Finally, the three methods required for the ClientListener must be implemented. Those are the onConnected, onDisconnected, and onConnectionFailed methods. They are shown in Listing 23.3. Because the Activity implements ClientListener, we can say that it is a ClientListener.

We are relying on the Anymote Library for the user interface for pairing. Our app controls the ProgressBar and provides the UI for navigating to a URL. Listing 23.3 shows that we hide the ProgressBar when the connection is made. The field anymoteSender is populated in the onConnected method on line 3.

LISTING 23.3 Required Methods for ClientListener

```
1:   @Override
2:   public void onConnected(final AnymoteSender anymoteSender) {
3:     this.anymoteSender = anymoteSender;
4:     handler.post(new Runnable() {
5:       public void run() {
6:         progressBar.setVisibility(View.INVISIBLE);
7:       }
8:     });
9:   }
10:  @Override
11:  public void onDisconnected() {
12:    this.anymoteSender = null;
13:  }
14:  @Override
15:  public void onConnectionFailed() {
16:    System.out.println("connection failed");
17:  }
```

The onDestroy method for the Activity is used to clean up any outstanding resources when the Activity is destroyed. In Listing 23.4, we use the onDestroy method to detach and unbind the Anymote services from the current Activity.

LISTING 23.4 Cleaning Up in the onDestroy Method

```
1:   @Override
2:   protected void onDestroy() {
3:     if (mAnymoteClientService != null) {
4:       mAnymoteClientService.detachClientListener(this);
5:     }
6:     unbindService(mConnection);
7:     super.onDestroy();
8:   }
```

The Anymote Library handles the UI for discovery and pairing. For this remote app, no companion TV app is required. The native functionality of flinging an Intent to the TV provides the functionality required.

An App for Showing a Facebook Image on a Google TV

We will create another second content app that flings a URL to the TV that is based on the work we did in Hour 18, "Developing a Complete App." In that hour, we created a Google TV app that showed random images from a Facebook page. We will turn that app into a remote content app using the Anymote protocol. The phone will show a random image when a button is pressed. The TV will show the same image.

The onCreate method for the app shows how we make this happen. It is shown in Listing 23.5. The basic infrastructure of a remote app is followed. The Activity extends ClientListener and binds to the AnymoteClientService.

In the app in Hour 17, "Using Cursors and CursorLoaders," we retrieved a list of photos from Facebook. We parsed the data and selected a random image to display. We select the random URL as a String in line 16 of Listing 23.5. We then use that URL for two things. We use an ImageViewFragment to display it on the phone and we use the Anymote Service to fling it to the TV as an Intent. The flinging occurs in lines 18 and 19.

LISTING 23.5 Facebook Random Image Remote App

```
1:  @Override
2:  public void onCreate(Bundle savedInstanceState) {
3:    super.onCreate(savedInstanceState);
4:    setContentView(R.layout.main);
5:    LoadPhotos lp = new LoadPhotos("99394368305" );
6:    lp.execute();
7:    progressBar = (ProgressBar) findViewById(R.id.progressBar1);
8:    progressBar.setVisibility(View.VISIBLE);
9:    mButton2= (Button)findViewById(R.id.button2);
10:   mButton2.setEnabled(false);
11:   mButton2.setOnClickListener(new OnClickListener() {
12:     public void onClick(View v) {
13:       ImageViewFragment fbImg = new ImageViewFragment();
14:       Bundle args = new Bundle();
15:       int random = (int)(Math.random() * mPagePhotos.size());
16:       String url = mPagePhotos.get(random).source;
17:       args.putString("URL", url);
18:       final Intent intent = new Intent(Intent.ACTION_VIEW, Uri.parse(url));
19:       anymoteSender.sendUrl (intent.toUri(Intent.URI_INTENT_SCHEME));
20:       fbImg.setArguments(args);
21:       FragmentTransaction ft = getFragmentManager().beginTransaction();
22:       ft.replace(R.id.linearLayout1, fbImg, "Image from Facebook");
23:       ft.commit();
24:     }
25:   });
26:   handler = new Handler();
```

```
27:    Intent intent = new Intent(ExampleTwoActivity.this, AnymoteClientService.class);
28:    bindService(intent, mConnection, Context.BIND_AUTO_CREATE);
29: }
```

Both of the examples used simple interfaces on the remote device and displayed the resulting content on the TV. They show the basic use of flinging a URL to the TV for display in a Chrome browser. It is easy to envision more complex user interfaces that also result in a URL being displayed on the TV. For example, an app could allow a user to enter complex search criteria into a phone and have the result displayed on the TV.

Sending KeyEvents to the TV

We'll continue to follow the basic structure of a remote app. The Anymote protocol can handle sending Android Intents, KeyEvents, and mouse events. Using KeyEvents, an app can send whatever keystrokes are entered on a remote device directly to the Google TV app that is being displayed. It can be used to enter search terms on YouTube or other apps, and it is a way to fill out a web form being displayed in the Google Chrome browser.

Handling onKeyDown and onKeyUp Methods

By implementing an Activity's onKeyDown and onKeyUp methods for the Activity, we can correctly send KeyEvents to the TV using the Anymote protocol. We'll do that in an Activity called Hour23EchoRemote. Listing 23.6 shows the onKeyDown and onKeyUp methods.

LISTING 23.6 onKeyDown and onKeyUp Methods

```
1:  @Override
2:     public boolean onKeyDown(int keyCode, KeyEvent event) {
3:        anymoteSender.sendKey(Code.valueOf(keyCode),Key.Action.DOWN);
4:        return true;
5:     }
6:     @Override
7:     public boolean onKeyUp(int keyCode, KeyEvent event) {
8:        anymoteSender.sendKey(Code.valueOf(keyCode),Key.Action.UP);
9:        return true;
10:    }
```

Listing 23.6 used the anymoteSender.sendKey method in lines 3 and 8. The sendKey method takes a Code and an Action as parameters. The keyCode parameter passed to the onKeyUp and onKeyDown events is an int. That int corresponds to the physical key pressed. The sendKey method requires a Code corresponding to that key. The Code class was defined in the keycodes. proto file. By using Code.valueOf(keyCode) in line 8, we get the desired result.

The `Action` represents either a key up or key down event.

By explicitly using these KeyEvents, we are sending the TV precisely what was entered by pressing a key on the remote device. If the user presses the special keys on the phone to shift to capital letters, numbers, or special characters, that is reflected in what is sent to the TV.

The Blackjack app used a different method. When the user chose Hit or Stand, the H or S key was sent using the `anymoteSender.sendKeyPress` method:

```
anymoteSender.sendKeyPress(keyEvent);
```

Where `keyEvent` is either `KeyEvent.KEYCODE_H` or `KeyEvent.KEYCODE_S`. The `sendKey-Press` method always sends the value of the physical key from the keyboard. It will send a capital H regardless of whether lowercase h or uppercase H was selected on the device.

For this example app, we implemented the `onKeyUp` and `onKeyDown` methods for the Activity itself. There was no UI with `EditText` fields to accept the input. If there had been, the Activity would never have received the keystrokes. The `EditText` would have consumed them.

To show the keyboard on the Activity, we use the following setting in the Android Manifest for this project:

```
android:windowSoftInputMode="stateVisible"
```

The method `setOnKeyListener (View.OnKeyListener l)` is available for all Views. An alternative to showing an empty Activity with an onscreen keyboard for input is to create a UI that uses Views like `EditText` fields to send keystrokes to the TV. To do that, the `EditText` field would use the `setOnKeyListener` method.

The `onKeyListener` requires the `onKey` method to be implemented. That method passes the `keyCode` and `KeyEvent`, so it would be straightforward to implement an input field for accepting keystrokes and sending them to the TV. The definition of the `onKey` method looks like this:

```
public abstract boolean onKey (View v, int keyCode, KeyEvent event)
```

Developing the TV App

We can use the `Hour23EchoRemote` app as the basis for creating an interactive app. We defined the remote app. Now we need to create the companion app that runs on the TV. Our remote app just sends keystrokes to the TV, so our companion app on the TV will be very simple. We'll show an `EditText` field that can be filled out.

Listing 23.7 shows the entire app that runs on the TV. The layout file contains an `EditText` field to display input. When a key is pressed in the remote app, it is sent to the companion app and displayed. Uppercase, lowercase, and special characters are sent properly from the remote to the TV. To tie these apps together, we must modify the remote code to launch this app on the TV when pairing is complete.

LISTING 23.7   Companion Activity on TV for Echoing Keystrokes

```
1:   public class Hour23Echo extends Activity {
2:      EditText echoText;
3:      @Override
4:        public void onCreate(Bundle savedInstanceState) {
5:           super.onCreate(savedInstanceState);
6:           setContentView(R.layout.main);
7:           echoText= (EditText)findViewById(R.id.echo);
8:      }
9:   }
```

Our goal is for the companion app to launch on the TV when the remote app successfully pairs with the TV. We can look to the Blackjack app as a model for how to do this. We need to fling the Intent we want to start on the TV. That is, we want to create an Intent that corresponds to the Activity on the TV and start that Activity.

Listing 23.8 shows the code to start the TV app from the remote app. The action occurs in the onConnected method.

The name of the Activity on the TV is Hour23Echo, but more specifically, we should refer to the package name and the class name to create the intent. The package name is com.bffmedia. hour23echo. In line 5 of Listing 23.8, we create a new Intent named echoIntent. Lines 6 to 8 set echoIntent to the values for the package and the class. Line 9 sends the Intent from the remote app to the TV. We are creating Android Intent and using the Anymote protocol to request that the TV launch the Intent.

LISTING 23.8   Starting the Companion App from the Remote App

```
1:   @Override
2:   public void onConnected(final AnymoteSender anymoteSender) {
3:      this.anymoteSender = anymoteSender;
4:      //Add this section to open the Companion App
5:      final Intent echoIntent = new Intent("android.intent.action.MAIN");
6:      echoIntent.setComponent(new ComponentName(
7:          "com.bffmedia.hour23echo",
8:          "com.bffmedia.hour23echo.Hour23Echo"));
9:      anymoteSender.sendIntent(echoIntent);
10:     handler.post(new Runnable() {
11:       public void run() {
12:         progressBar.setVisibility(View.INVISIBLE);
13:       }
14:     });
15:  }
```

Sending Mouse Events to the TV

Using the Anymote protocol we have the capability to send messages to the TV that appear to the TV as mouse events. That is, the messages are equivalent to using the mousepad or trackpad on the remote that comes with the TV. We do this using the Anymote Library `sendMoveRelative` method.

Using the Accelerometer

For this remote app, we will use the phone's `Accelerometer` to create the values to send to the TV. Android phones have sensors that can detect a number of values from the real world. The `Accelerometer` detects how the phone is accelerating through space. It detects three values as the phone moves. The x, y, and z values represent a three-dimensional coordinate system, as shown in Figure 23.2.

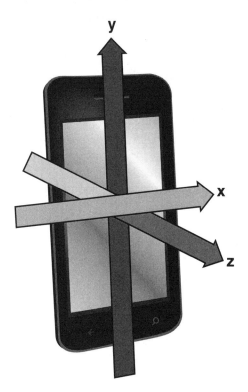

FIGURE 23.2
The coordinate system. Image from Google.

If you move the phone to the right, the x value increases. If you push the phone straight away from you, the y value increases. If you move the phone upward, the z value increases.

We will do a simple mapping of the returned x and y values to create mouselike movements to send to the TV. The effect is to use the phone as a mouse where tilting and moving results in the mouse cursor moving in a reasonable way on the TV.

We implement one `Button` in the app. It is a Click Button that sends the equivalent of a mouse click to the TV. This makes our remote useful as a mouse, but does not provide for D-Pad navigation, a back button, or any other keyboard input.

Listing 23.9 shows the `onCreate` method for the `Accelerometer` remote app. This handles the Click Button by sending mouse down and mouse up keys to the TV.

LISTING 23.9   Accelerometer App onCreate

```
1:  Button click = (Button) findViewById(R.id.button1);
2:  click.setOnClickListener(new OnClickListener() {
3:     @Override
4:     public void onClick(View v) {
5:        anymoteSender.sendKey (Code.BTN_MOUSE, Action.DOWN);
6:        anymoteSender.sendKey (Code.BTN_MOUSE, Action.UP);
7:     }
8:  });
```

Detecting Changes Using SensorEventListener

To use the Accelerometer, we must implement a `SensorEventListener` for the Activity:

```
public class Hour23AccelerometerRemote extends Activity implements ClientListener,
SensorEventListener{
```

A `SensorManager` field is defined for the class:

```
private SensorManager sensorManager;
```

The logic for the Accelerometer remote app is the following:

1. Pair with the TV.

2. Begin listening for Accelerometer events.

3. Send those events to the TV as mouse movements.

To accomplish this, we create the `SensorManager` after the connection is made between the TV and the remote, so we do it in the `onConnected` method. The `onConnected` method for the example is shown in Listing 23.10.

LISTING 23.10   Defining SensorManager in onConnected Method

```
1:  @Override
2:  public void onConnected(final AnymoteSender anymoteSender) {
3:    this.anymoteSender = anymoteSender;
4:    sensorManager=(SensorManager)getSystemService(SENSOR_SERVICE);
5:    sensorManager.registerListener(this,
6:    sensorManager.getDefaultSensor(Sensor.TYPE_ACCELEROMETER),
7:      SensorManager.SENSOR_DELAY_FASTEST);
8:    handler.post(new Runnable() {
9:      public void run() {
10:        progressBar.setVisibility(View.INVISIBLE);
11:      }
12:    });
13:  }
```

The `sensorManager` is defined in line 4 of Listing 23.10. In lines 5 to 8, the `sensorManager` is set up to listen for Accelerometer events. We use the flag `SensorManager.SENSOR_DELAY_FASTEST` to capture all values from the sensor.

For the `SensorEventListener` we must implement two methods: `onAccuracyChanged` and `onSensorChanged`. To demonstrate sending a mouse movement to the TV, the work will be done in the `onSensorChanged` method.

Listing 23.11 shows both methods. Line 6 checks to see if the sensor is an Accelerometer. If it is, the values for x, y, and z are populated. Line 10 sends the mouse movement to the TV. In this implementation, 1 is subtracted from y as a simple way to compensate for gravity. Each value is multiplied by -1 to set the proper direction on the TV screen.

This is a very simple movement detection and translation scheme that handles gravity and shows how to make the connection between a sensor on the phone and an action on the TV.

LISTING 23.11   Detecting Sensor Changes

```
1:  @Override
2:  public void onAccuracyChanged(Sensor Sensor, int accuracy) {
3:  }
4:  @Override
5:  public void onSensorChanged(SensorEvent event) {
6:    if(event.sensor.getType()==Sensor.TYPE_ACCELEROMETER){
7:      float x=event.values[0];
8:      float y=event.values[1];
9:      float z=event.values[2];
10:      anymoteSender.sendMoveRelative((int)x*-1,(int) ((y-1)*-1));
11:    }
12:  }
```

Using the Accelerometer, we can detect motion of a phone and successfully translate that motion into mouse events on a Google TV. There are a number of other sensors available in most Android phones. Sensors can detect things like temperature, light, and proximity. Using phone sensors and Google TV creates new opportunities for detecting information using a phone and displaying it on a TV.

Summary

In this hour, we created several remote apps using the Anymote library. The basic structure of a remote app was examined. A remote app will implement a `ClientListener` and bind to the `AnymoteClientService`. These apps started the Chrome browser and showed a specific URL by flinging an Intent to the TV. They sent both keystrokes and mouse movements to the TV. Together these example apps provide a basis for creating more sophisticated remote apps.

Q&A

Q. **What interface must be implemented by an Activity to use the Anymote protocol?**

A. `AnymoteClientService ClientListener` must be implemented. The Activity then acts as a ClientListener and detects when Anymote is connected and disconnected.

Q. **Two actions that can be sent from an Activity to a TV mimic what can be done on the TV remote keyboard. What are they?**

A. Sending a keystroke via `SendKey` mimics entering a keystroke on the remote control. It is used as follows:

```
anymoteSender.sendKey (Code.BTN_MOUSE, Action.DOWN);
```

Sending a move event mimics a mouse movement on the remote. It is used as follows:

```
anymoteSender.sendMoveRelative(x,y);
```

Q. **How can a sensor on a phone like the accelerometer be used in second screen apps ?**

A. At a high level, anything detected by the sensor can be communicated to the TV using the Anymote protocol and commands to fling, send keystrokes, and move the mouse. The sensor detects something and the app with the sensor translates the results to something that can be sent with the Anymote protocol to communicate the result to the TV.

Workshop

Quiz

1. What method must be implemented in an `onKeyListener`?

2. What interface includes the `onConnected` method?

3. What does fling mean when using the Anymote protocol?

4. How does the remote app start an Activity on the TV?

Answers

1. The `onKey` method must be implemented. That method accepts the `keyCode` and `KeyEvent`, so entered keystrokes can be detected.

2. ClientListeners must implement three methods, including `onConnected`. The others are `onDisconnected` and `onConnectionFailed`.

3. Fling refers to sending an Intent from the remote to the TV. The app can fling a URL to be displayed on the Chrome browser. The Intent is to view the URL.

4. The remote app starts an Activity on the TV by creating an Intent on the remote that refers to the Activity on the TV. The remote app then flings that Intent to the TV using the sendIntent method. For example:

```
anymoteSender.sendIntent(echoIntent);
```

Exercises

1. Try the Accelerometer app directly on a Google TV. You can try this at a department store if you don't have your own Google TV.

2. Modify the Accelerometer code to use the x and z values for changing mouse motion on the TV. See what happens.

Working with Anymote and Pairing Protocols

What You'll Learn in This Hour:

▶ How the Anymote protocol works

▶ How the Pairing protocol works

▶ How to use a Chrome extension with the Anymote and Pairing protocols

In Hours 21 through 23, we designed and developed second screen apps. These apps relied on the Anymote and Pairing Protocols. In this hour, we take a closer look at the protocols themselves and how they work. We consider what is required to implement second screen apps on devices besides Android phones or tablets by examining a Chrome browser extension that implements the protocols. The difference between this hour and previous hours is that we are moving the focus to how the underlying protocols work, not just how to use them.

The Anymote Protocol

The Anymote protocol is the messaging system between a TV and a remote device. Google TV runs an Anymote service that receives and responds to Anymote messages. Remote Applications running on phones, tablets, or other devices send Anymote messages to the Anymote service on the TV.

The Anymote Protocol uses messages that in are in the `protocol buffers` format. Protocol buffers are an efficient platform-independent way of encoding structured data. Protocol buffers end in a `.proto` extension and can be compiled into C++, Java, or Python using the `protoc` compiler. Anymote protocol reference versions are available in C++ and Java using common protocol buffers for the messaging format. Two protocol buffers are used. One is `keycodes.proto` and the other is `remote.proto`.

Defining Keycodes

The `keycodes.proto` file defines the keycodes for Anymote. Those keys includes any key on the remote, including DPAD keys such as `KEYCODE_DPAD_UP` and `KEYCODE_DPAD_DOWN`. It also defines the Action DOWN for pressing a key and the Action UP for releasing a key. The entire key-codes.proto file defines all keycodes and the action of pressing or releasing keys. Listing 24.1 shows a snippet of the file.

LISTING 24.1   Keycode Proto File Snippet

```
 1:    enum Code {
 2:        KEYCODE_UNKNOWN          = 0;
 3:        KEYCODE_SOFT_LEFT        = 1;
 4:        KEYCODE_SOFT_RIGHT       = 2;
 5:        KEYCODE_HOME             = 3;
 6:        KEYCODE_BACK             = 4;
 7:    ...
 8:        KEYCODE_DPAD_UP          = 19;
 9:        KEYCODE_DPAD_DOWN        = 20;
10:        KEYCODE_DPAD_LEFT        = 21;
11:        KEYCODE_DPAD_RIGHT       = 22;
12:        KEYCODE_DPAD_CENTER      = 23;
13:    ...
14:        BTN_BACK                 = 278;
15:        BTN_TASK                 = 279;
16:    }
17:    enum Action {
18:        // Key released
19:        UP      = 0;
20:        // Key pressed
21:        DOWN    = 1;
22:    }
```

Defining Request and Response Messages

The remote.proto file defines the messages used in the Anymote protocol. Request and response messages are defined. Request messages are sent from the remote or client, and response messages are returned from the Google TV or server.

Listing 24.2 shows the request messages defined in the proto file. The messages are

- ▶ Key Event—Sends a keycode
- ▶ MouseEvent—Sends a mouse event
- ▶ MouseWheel—Sends a mouse wheel event
- ▶ Data—Sends data
- ▶ Connect—Sends on connection
- ▶ Fling—Sends an Android Intent message

LISTING 24.2   Request Messages in the Remote Proto File

```
 1:    / Sends a key event to the server
 2:    message KeyEvent {
 3:      // Key code
 4:      required Code keycode = 1;
 5:      // Action (Up/Down)
 6:     required Action action = 2;
 7:    }
 8:    // Sends a mouse event to the server
 9:    message MouseEvent {
10:      // Relative movement of the cursor on the xAxis
11:      required int32 x_delta = 1;
12:      // Relative movement of the cursor on the yAxis
13:      required int32 y_delta = 2;
14:    }
15:    // Sends a mouse wheel to the server
16:    message MouseWheel {
17:      // Scrolling along the x-axis
18:      required int32 x_scroll = 1;
19:      // Scrolling along the y-axis
20:      required int32 y_scroll = 2;
21:    }
22:    message Connect {
23:      // Remote device name
24:      required string device_name = 1;
25:      // Version number for a given device software
26:      optional int32 version = 2;
27:    }
28:    message Fling {
29:      // Flinged URI
30:      required string uri = 1;
31:    }
```

KeyEvents sends the keycodes and actions defined on the keycodes.proto file. There is a key like KEYCODE_DPAD_LEFT and an action of UP or DOWN.

Although there are KeyEvents and MouseEvents, a mouse click is sent as a KeyEvent with a keycode that has BTN_ as a prefix, such as BTN_MOUSE. A mouse click-down event would be sent as

```
anymoteSender.sendKey (Code.BTN_MOUSE, Action.DOWN);
```

Mouse movement events are sent as MouseEvents. MouseEvents are defined in lines 9 to 12 of Listing 24.2. The values sent are the changes in x and y values of the position of the mouse.

MouseWheel events include scroll x and scroll y values. The application on the TV receiving the Mousewheel events decides how to interpret them.

A Data event sends a sequence of keystrokes to Google TV. Data events include a type and associated data. For the AnyMote implementation on Google TV, the type in the message must be "com.google.tv.string."

Fling events send an event to Google TV to start an Activity associated with the specified Intent that is sent as a String. Android Intents include an action and the data to act on. For example, suppose there is an Intent to view a URL or to play a YouTube Video. On receiving a `FlingEvent` message, Google TV will call `startActivity` on the Android system. The remote app converts the Intent object into a String by calling `Intent.toUri(int)`, then adds that String into a `FlingEvent` message. When Google TV receives the message, it creates an Intent from the message and passes it to the Android system by calling `startActivity()`.

The YouTube app on Google TV will play the specified video when it receives a `FlingEvent` from the remote app. The following snippet defines an Intent with the action of `Intent.ACTION_VIEW` and parses a URI that includes the YouTube Android schema. The Intent is converted to a Uri and sent via the anyMote Sender:

```
final Intent intent = new Intent(Intent.ACTION_VIEW, Uri.parse("vnd.
youtube://<video_id>");
anymoteSender.sendUrl (intent.toUri(Intent.URI_INTENT_SCHEME));
```

Similarly, the Chrome browser will launch when sent a URL. Notice that the Intent has the same action `Intent.ACTION_VIEW`:

```
final Intent intent = new Intent(Intent.ACTION_VIEW, Uri.parse("http://<webpage_
url>");
anymoteSender.sendUrl (intent.toUri(Intent.URI_INTENT_SCHEME));
```

A fling request may include a sequence number. The `responseMessage` to a `FlingEvent` indicates success or failure. The sequence number is included in the response so that requests and responses can be matched.

Anymote Protocol Reference Implementation

We used the Anymote Library in our apps in Hour 23, "Developing Second Screen Apps," and the Blackjack app in Hour 22, "Examining an Example Second Screen App." That library makes it convenient for application developers to use the Anymote protocol. In the Anymote library, the Anymote protocol is included as a jar file. The Anymote protocol reference implementation is available in Java and C++ as a code.google.com project at http://code.google.com/p/anymote-protocol/.

The project includes the required keycode and remote proto files and the associated proto jar file. The Anymote protocol source includes both device and server code. The `.proto` files are used to define the messages and keycodes used in this code.

Listing 24.3 is the method interpret message from `ServerMessageAdapter.java`. The message is defined as a response message. Response messages are defined in `remote.proto`.

LISTING 24.3   Interpreting a Request Message

```
1:    /*
2:     * Interprets a request message.
3:     * @param message the request message
4:     */
5:    private void interpretRequest(RequestMessage message, Integer sequenceNumber)
{
6:      ResponseMessage.Builder builder = ResponseMessage.newBuilder();
7:      boolean reply = sequenceNumber != null;
8:    if (message.hasKeyEventMessage()) {
9:        reply = false;
10:       onKeyEvent(message.getKeyEventMessage());
11:     }
12:     if (message.hasMouseEventMessage()) {
13:       reply = false;
14:       onMouseEvent(message.getMouseEventMessage());
15:     }
16:     if (message.hasMouseWheelMessage()) {
17:       reply = false;
18:       onMouseWheel(message.getMouseWheelMessage());
19:   }
20:     if (message.hasDataMessage()) {
21:       reply = false;
22:      onData(message.getDataMessage());
23:     }
24:     if (message.hasConnectMessage()) {
25:       reply = false;
26:       onConnect(message.getConnectMessage());
27:     }
28:     if (message.hasFlingMessage()) {
29:       reply = true;
30:       builder.setFlingResultMessage(
31:           onFling(message.getFlingMessage(), sequenceNumber));
32:     }
33:     if (reply) {
34:      sendResponse(builder, sequenceNumber);
35:     }
36:   }
```

The definitions, proto files, and Java code from the Anymote protocol may all seem like a different way of saying that the protocol consists of a series of request messages and possible responses. From an application development perspective, that is true. As app developers, we can use the Anymote protocol, but we might need to implement on a new device or in another language. One goal of this hour is to provide a roadmap for accomplishing that. We will look at pairing protocol in a similar level of detail.

Pairing Protocol

Pairing is the act of making a connection between the Google TV and the remote device. For Pairing to occur, the remote device (a phone for example) and the Google TV must establish a trusted communication channel. The Pairing protocol is the set of messages and interactions required between the TV and the phone to establish that trusted channel.

The protocol consists of the client (phone) contacting the server (TV) and the server issuing a challenge or request for verification. The challenge from the TV, as we have seen, can consist of scanning a QR code or entering a numeric code.

The protocol must account for different types of devices. For example, for a remote device that does not have a camera, it is impossible to scan a QR code. For that reason, the client tells the server what kinds of challenges it can handle, and the server responds appropriately.

In the protocol, each message from the client requires a specific response from the server. This is done via an SSL session. The requests and responses are the following:

▶ A `PairingRequest` is sent from the client. The response is a `PairingAck` from Server.

▶ A request from the client is sent to get options for challenge. The server responds with a challenge option.

▶ Configuration details are sent from the client. A `ConfigurationAck` is sent from Server.

▶ Server issues a challenge.

▶ The user responds via client.

▶ The client checks the user's response and creates a `secretMessage`.

▶ The client sends the secret message. The server checks the secret message and if it is correct, sends `secretAck`, completing the process.

This sequence is shown in Figure 24.1. Note that OOB stands for out-of-band channel.

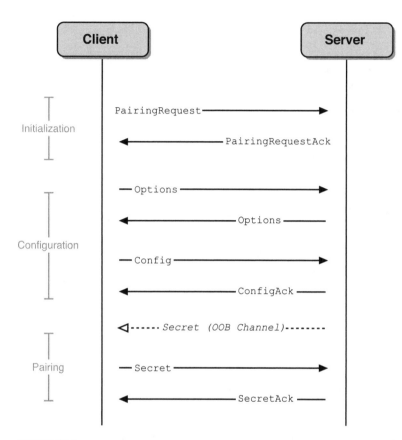

FIGURE 24.1
Pairing protocol message sequence.

As with the Anymote protocol, there are C++ and Java reference implementations of the Pairing protocol. The project and code can be found at http://code.google.com/p/ google-tv-pairing-protocol/.

The Pairing protocol also uses a `.proto` file to define message formats and options. The file `polo.proto` contains the message types shown in the message flow in Figure 24.1.

A `PairingRequest` and `PairingRequestAck` are shown in Listing 24.4.

LISTING 24.4   **PairingRequest and PairingRequestAck**

```
1: message PairingRequest {
2:     // String name of the service to pair with.  The name used should be an
3:     // established convention of the application protocol.
4:     required string service_name = 1;
5:     // Descriptive name of the client.
```

```
6:    optional string client_name = 2;
7: }
8: message PairingRequestAck {
9:    // Descriptive name of the server.
10:   optional string server_name = 1;
11:}
```

Looking at the message definition for Challenge options in Listing 24.5 provides information on the types of challenges currently supported. Challenges include a QR code type and input codes of numeric, alphanumeric, and hexadecimal.

LISTING 24.5 Challenge Option Message

```
1:    message Encoding {
2:        enum EncodingType {
3:          ENCODING_TYPE_UNKNOWN = 0;
4:          ENCODING_TYPE_ALPHANUMERIC = 1;
5:          ENCODING_TYPE_NUMERIC = 2;
6:          ENCODING_TYPE_HEXADECIMAL = 3;
7:          ENCODING_TYPE_QRCODE = 4;
8:        }
9:        required EncodingType type = 1;
10:       required uint32 symbol_length = 2;
11:   }
```

Using Anymote and Pairing in a Chrome Extension

Given Java and C++ implementations of the Anymote and Pairing protocols, we can consider using these protocols when the remote application is not an Android application. Any device or app that can implement these protocols can communicate with Google TV. That opens up the possibility of apps that can be used with an Android phone or an iPhone or iPad. For example, in a multiuser game, one user may use his Android phone and another user may use her iPod.

We'll examine a Google Chrome extension example that communicates with Google TV. For the Google Chrome extension, the Anymote and Pairing protocols are implemented as browser plug-ins. The plug-in is written in C++ and uses the Netscape Plug-in API (NPAPI).

The Chrome extension is written using HTML, CSS, and JavaScript. The JavaScript communicates with the NPAPI plug-in to send Anymote commands and to implement pairing.

Installing the Chrome Extension

You will first need to download the Chrome Extension project from https://code.google.com/p/google-tv-chrome-extensions/. To install the extension, choose the wrench icon on your Chrome browser and choose **Tools, Extensions**, as shown in Figure 24.2.

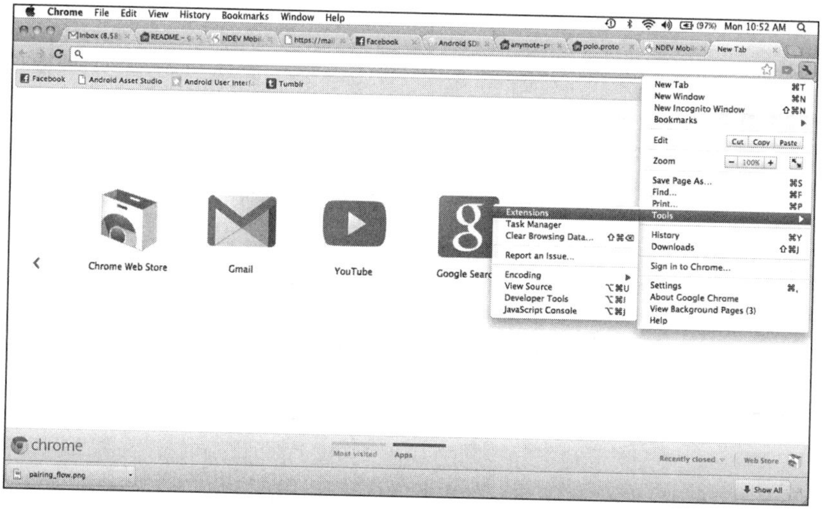

FIGURE 24.2
Installing a Chrome Extension.

On the Extensions page, choose the Developer Mode check box. Then choose **Load Unpacked Extension**. Select the folder where the Anymote example extension was downloaded. See Figure 24.3.

At this point, the extension is installed and can be used from the Chrome browser. A small icon appears in the top of the Chrome page. When you roll over it, it displays Anymote Example.

Using the Chrome Extension

When selected, a window pops up that steps through the process of discovery and pairing with a Google TV.

Choose Start Discovery, and the extension will find the IP address of the Google TV and populate it. Choose Begin Pairing Process, and a challenge will be presented on the TV. The extension will display the message in Figure 24.4.

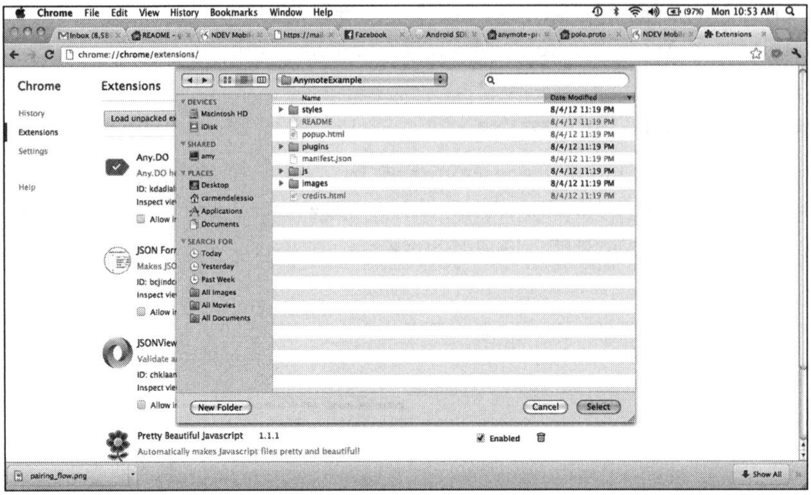

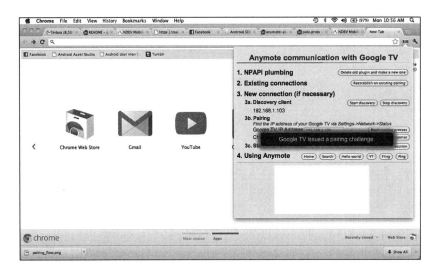

FIGURE 24.3
Folder where the extension is installed.

FIGURE 24.4
Using the Anymote Chrome Extension.

The response to the pairing challenge is to enter the code displayed on the TV. After the pairing is successful, the Anymote commands can be used.

If the user selects **YT**, a YouTube video will start on the TV, and the message Fling Result Successful will be displayed in the extension (see Figure 24.5).

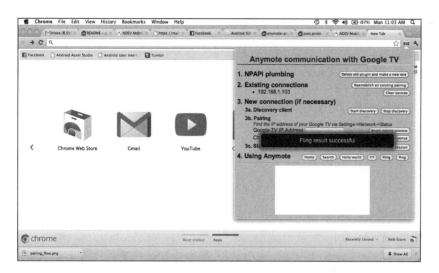

FIGURE 24.5
Extension showing Fling Result Successful.

Technology Used to Implement the Extension

The implementation of the NPAPI is done in C++. The NPAPI is called in JavaScript and used as the Anymote Library was in the Android code from Hours 22 and 23.

The JavaScript code for the Anymote example Chrome extension includes a file called popup. js. Popup.js makes the Anymote calls. These calls depend on the plug-in being installed. The following JavaScript calls are made to the Anymote protocol:

- sendAnymoteKeyEvent(googletvremote.anymote.KeyCode.HOME);

- sendAnymoteKeyEvent(googletvremote.anymote.KeyCode.SEARCH);

- sendAnymoteStringMessage('Hello, world');

- sendAnymoteFling('vnd.youtube://Nli4Vy2zGYA'); });

- sendAnymoteFling('http://code.google.com/p/google-tv-chrome-extensions/');

- sendAnymotePing();

Summary

In this hour, we examined the Anymote and Pairing protocols at a detailed level. The concept of `.proto` files for defining keys and messages was covered. We learned that there are C++ and Java reference implementations of these protocols and that they can be implemented on different devices and platforms. The implementation of the Anymote and Pairing protocols as a Chrome extension was covered from a user perspective, and the concept of implementing these protocols on an alternative platform was introduced.

Q&A

Q. What is a protocol buffer?

A. A protocol buffer is a message interchange format. It is used in the Anymote protocol.

Q. What two .proto files are included in the Anymote protocol, and what do they do?

A. They are the `keycode.proto` and `remote.proto` files. Keycodes lists all possible keys that can be used and the actions UP and DOWN. The `remote.proto` file includes request and response messages and the types of specific messages supported.

Q. What does fling mean in the Anymote protocol?

A. To fling means to start an Activity on the TV via an Intent.

Workshop

Quiz

1. What languages are used for reference versions of the Pairing protocol?

2. What types of messages are sent in the Anymote protocol?

3. When an options message is sent from a TV to a client for Pairing, what are the options for?

Answers

1. Java and C++.

2. KeyEvents, MouseEvents, MouseWheelEvents, Data, and Ping messages are supported.

3. Options in the pairing protocol refer to the options supported in a challenge. These may be a QR code or an alphanumeric code. For a client that does not have a camera, a QR code is not a good option, and the client could indicate that.

Exercises

1. Install the Chrome extension for the Anymote protocol based on the instructions in this hour.

2. Change the URL and YouTube video in the Anymote Example Chrome Extension and specify an alternative YouTube video to play. That requires installing the extension and modifying the JavaScript code in `popup.js`.

Index

How can we make this index more useful? Email us at indexes@samspublishing.com

Sams **Teach Yourself**

When you only have time
for the answers™

Whatever your need and whatever your time frame, there's a Sams **Teach Yourself** book for you. With a Sams **Teach Yourself** book as your guide, you can quickly get up to speed on just about any new product or technology—in the absolute shortest period of time possible. Guaranteed.

Learning how to do new things with your computer shouldn't be tedious or time-consuming. Sams **Teach Yourself** makes learning anything quick, easy, and even a little bit fun.

ASP.NET 4.0 in 24 Hours

Scott Mitchell
ISBN-10: 0672333058
ISBN-13: 9780672333057

Visual Basic 2010 in 24 Hours Complete Starter Kit

James Foxall

ISBN-10: 0672331136
ISBN-13: 9780672331138

Microsoft Dynamics CRM 4 in 24 Hours

Anne Stanton

ISBN-10: 0672330679
ISBN-13: 9780672330674

Microsoft Expression Web 3 in 24 Hours

Morten Rand-Hendriksen

ISBN-10: 0672330644
ISBN-13: 9780672330643

Visual C# 2010 in 24 Hours

Scott Dorman

ISBN-10: 0672331012
ISBN-13: 9780672331015

Sams **Teach Yourself**
Google TV™
App Development
in **24 Hours**

Carmen Delessio

SAMS

FREE
Online Edition

Your purchase of *Sams Teach Yourself Google TV App Development in 24 Hours* includes access to a free online edition for 45 days through the **Safari Books Online** subscription service. Nearly every Sams book is available online through **Safari Books Online**, along with thousands of books and videos from publishers such as Addison-Wesley Professional, Cisco Press, Exam Cram, IBM Press, O'Reilly Media, Prentice Hall, Que, and VMware Press.

Safari Books Online is a digital library providing searchable, on-demand access to thousands of technology, digital media, and professional development books and videos from leading publishers. With one monthly or yearly subscription price, you get unlimited access to learning tools and information on topics including mobile app and software development, tips and tricks on using your favorite gadgets, networking, project management, graphic design, and much more.

Activate your FREE Online Edition at
informit.com/safarifree

STEP 1: Enter the coupon code: PBHIDDB.

STEP 2: New Safari users, complete the brief registration form.
Safari subscribers, just log in.

If you have difficulty registering on Safari or accessing the online edition,
please e-mail customer-service@safaribooksonline.com